D1213756

A Dialogue of Comfort Against Tribulation

SAINT THOMAS MORE

A Dialogue of Comfort Against Tribulation

EDITED FOR MODERN READERS

WITH AN INTRODUCTION & NOTES

BY

Leland Miles

Indiana University Press

Bloomington AND *London*

for GINNY, CHRISTY, *and* GREG

"In good faith, uncle, I am not all thing afeard in this case only for myself, but well you wot I have cause to care also for many more, and that folk of sundry sorts, men and women both, and that not all of one age."

—Vincent to Anthony,
in the *Dialogue of Comfort* (III, 2)

Also available in a clothbound edition containing an augmented Introduction and enlarged Bibliography.

Library of Congress Catalog Card Number: 65-19701

Manufactured in the United States of America

ACKNOWLEDGMENTS

This book was produced during an ACLS fellowship at Harvard University, followed by a Fulbright research grant at King's College, London. For this aid, I am grateful to the American Council of Learned Societies and to the Board of Foreign Scholarships of the U.S. Department of State.

The resources of a number of libraries were brought to bear on this volume. Among the American libraries chiefly used were Harvard's Widener and Houghton; Boston's Athenaeum, General Theological, and Public libraries; St. John's Seminary in Brighton, Massachusetts; and Yale University's More Project collection. I am also grateful to Dean Samuel Miller for making available to me the resources of the Harvard Divinity School library.

In London, extensive aid was received from the British Museum and from the libraries at King's College, University College, and the University of London (Senate House). I am indebted to the many individuals on the staffs of these research centers for this support. Particular acknowledgment must be made to Joseph Scott, University College librarian, who permitted me to inspect the personal papers of More's first great biographer, R. W. Chambers; to A. H. Wesencraft, senior assistant librarian at the Senate House, who helped track down certain elusive quotations; to the cheerful supervisors of the Goldsmiths' Room, which became my London home; to Miss Doris Dormer, of the Senate House reference department; and especially to my assistant, Dorothy Hartnell-Beavis, who made valuable contributions to the editing of More's text.

Assistance of a special kind was provided by Professor Geoffrey Bullough, who generously allowed me to view his microfilm of the newly discovered Valencia holograph of More's *Passion* treatise. Mrs. T. W. South skillfully located and arranged visits to various historical sites associated with More, especially in London's Chelsea area. I am also indebted to Professor T. J. B. Spencer, Marjory Rigby, and their associates at the University of Birmingham, for stimulating me to give more thought than I had originally intended to More's literary artistry. To Professor Geoffrey Shepherd of Birmingham I am particularly grateful for data regarding More's nautical and medical metaphor.

Unusual aid came from His Grace, the Duke of Devonshire, and His Lordship, Baron Saint Oswald of Nostell, who made it possible for me to examine closely and at length the magnificent painting of the More family at Nostell Priory in Yorkshire. The painting is at the very least the only accurate copy of Holbein's group portrait; as such, it has supplied crucial evidence for More's great respect for both Boethius and Seneca.

Among others who lent help were Morton Bloomfield and Douglas Bush of Harvard's English Department; Beatrice White of Westfield College, London; Professor Raymond Albright, Reformation specialist at Episcopal Theological School, Cambridge, Massachusetts; Henry Collis, headmaster of Colet Court (St. Paul's Junior School); Hywel D. Lewis, chairman of the Department of the History and Philosophy of Religion at King's College; and David P. Edgell, executive secretary of the Fulbright Commission in London. Such aid was supplemented by Roy Battenhouse, who made many valuable suggestions for the improvement of the work; and by Joan Hermann, who painstakingly prepared the manuscript for the press.

King's College, London LELAND MILES

CONTENTS

Introduction

A Dialogue of Comfort Against Tribulation

PART I

PART II

PART III

Appendices

INTRODUCTION

I
The Revival of Interest in More

Robert Bolt's play, *A Man for All Seasons,* has in the last few years made Thomas More's name almost a household word in Europe and America. Yet it is only one of many signs of reawakened interest in Henry VIII's Lord Chancellor. Other manifestations of the "More Renaissance" are Yale University's project to publish all of More's works; the founding in Brussels in 1962 of the Amici Thomae Mori, an international society of More devotees; and the resurrection of the Elizabethan chronicle play, *The Book of Sir Thomas More,* which was given its first professional production in June, 1964, at the Nottingham Playhouse in England. More has even infiltrated popular fiction, one example being Josephine Tey's *The Daughter of Time* (1954). In this PMLA article disguised as a detective thriller, protagonist Alan Grant investigates the accuracy of More's *History of Richard III.*

The magnitude of this revival of interest, embracing both the popular and the scholarly worlds, has inspired many claims on More's behalf. G. K. Chesterton, for example, has suggested that More "may come to be counted . . . the greatest historical character in English history." And John Warrington, in his Introduction to the 1951 Everyman *Utopia,* proclaimed Sir Thomas "the supreme instance of nature perfected by grace." To determine whether such praise is justified, we must first look briefly at the historical circumstances which led to More's writing of the *Dialogue of Comfort.*

II
Historical Background

More's troubles with Henry VIII stemmed largely from the king's desire to divorce his wife, Catherine of Aragon, who was also his brother Arthur's widow. Henry's attitude was prompted by three considerations. First, Catherine had failed to produce a male heir—without which, in Henry's view, the kingdom would disintegrate. Second, the deaths of five of Catherine's six offspring (Mary alone surviving) nagged Henry's conscience. Was he being punished for violating the Scriptural injunction (Leviticus 20:21) against marrying a sister-in-law? Coinciding with these two factors was of course the king's infatuation with Anne Boleyn.

In 1527 Henry ordered Cardinal Wolsey to initiate divorce negotiations with Pope Clement VII. Unfortunately for Wolsey, the time was not propitious. Catherine's nephew, the Emperor Charles, had just sacked Rome and stood menacingly at the Pope's elbow. Also, Clement was understandably reluctant to reverse the decision of his predecessor, who had given papal sanction to the Henry-Catherine union despite the Leviticus injunction. After delaying action as long as possible, Clement abruptly advoked the case to Rome in August, 1529, and summoned Henry to appear there in forty days. The incensed monarch rejected the summons, dismissed Cardinal Wolsey for ineptness, and prevailed upon a reluctant More to accept the Lord Chancellorship (October, 1529).

Henry might have thought he could convert More into an ally; if so, he was badly mistaken. Sir Thomas almost immediately provoked the king by refusing (1530) to sign a new appeal to the Pope. In 1531 Henry, by way of strengthening his hand, compelled the clergy to proclaim him supreme head of the Church of England, "so far as the law of Christ allows." Disturbed by these developments, More resigned the Chancellorship in May, 1532. The king, exasperated by delay and opposition, finally married Anne in January, 1533, and assigned the divorce issue to his own compliant archbishop, Thomas Cranmer. The result surprised no one. Cranmer, acting on his own authority, annulled the marriage with Catherine and sanctioned the marriage with Anne. The new queen was immediately crowned at Westminster Abbey (June, 1533). More further irritated the king by refusing to attend the ceremony.

The inevitable confrontation between the two men now rushed inexorably toward its climax. In March, 1534, Parliament passed the Act of Succession fixing the royal inheritance on the off-spring of Henry's second marriage. All subjects were requested to swear an Oath of Allegiance to the Act. Refusal to swear would be misprision (i.e., concealment) of treason, with the attendant penalties of imprisonment and confiscation of property.

Actually, More had no major objection to the new Act. He realized that the question of royal succession was a political matter, and as such lay within the legitimate domain of king and Parliament. But the corollary oath (a separate document) was quite another matter, because it contained a statement affirming the king to be supreme head of the English Church. From More's point of view, such an affirmation was impossible. Nowhere could he find, in church councils or in the writings of his "old holy doctors," any authority for a layman as church head, or for the repudiation of the Pope's supremacy in ecclesiastical affairs. However, he carefully avoided condemning others who now took the oath. Nor did he utter any denial of the king's supremacy. On this crucial issue, he preferred to maintain a strict silence.

In April, 1534, More was summoned to Lambeth to take the oath. When he refused, he was immediately committed to the

Tower of London, where he spent the last fifteen months of his life. In November the noose tightened when Parliament passed the Act of Treasons, whereby any vocal denial of the king's supremacy was labeled high treason, punishable by death. There now followed four gruelling interrogations of More (April-June 1535). The purpose of these was to persuade him to take the oath; or alternatively, to trap him into a vocal denial of the king's ecclesiastical headship. Such a denial would now by law constitute treason, and would at once provide a legal justification for More's execution.

Sir Thomas was far too astute to be trapped. Yet at his formal trial (July 1, 1545) Solicitor-General Rich testified that, in a private conversation on June 12, More had uttered the necessary treasonous words. More hotly denied the charge, and it has been widely assumed that Rich committed perjury—probably on instructions from the king. The validity of this assumption has recently been enhanced by E. E. Reynolds, who discovered that Rich's official report of the June 12 conversation concedes that More remained silent on the issue of supremacy.

On the basis then of probably perjured evidence, More was sentenced to death and beheaded on July 6, 1535. Within days a *Paris News Letter* was reporting the execution all across Europe. The resulting uproar of protest resulted ultimately in More's beatification (1886) and then in his canonization (1935) as a Saint of the Roman Catholic Church. The canonization did not, however, meet with universal approval. Because of More's silence on the supremacy issue, some critics argued that he was at best "a negative martyr" and "an unsatisfactory saint."

III
Composition of the Dialogue of Comfort

There can be no question of the year in which the *Dialogue of Comfort* was composed. According to the title-pages of the 1557 and 1573 editions, the work was "made in the year of our Lord 1534 . . . while More was a prisoner in the Tower of London." The *Dialogue* (especially Part III) contains a series of meditations on the Passion, all of them building powerfully toward a final meditation in the last chapter. The logical sequel to such meditation would have been a work devoted entirely to Christ's pain on the Cross. It is not surprising to find, therefore, that in the 1557 Rastell edition of More's works, the *Comfort* treatise is followed by More's *History of the Passion.*

In the printer's preface (Rastell, p. 1350) to Mary Bassett's translation of the Second or Latin portion of the *History,* we are told that it also was written in 1534, but that composition was interrupted when More was "put from his books, pen, ink, and paper, and kept more straitly than before." The biographer Harpsfield's passage on More's being so "suddenly shut up" immediately precedes his comments on the new Acts of Supremacy and Treasons (November, 1534). The juxtaposition of Harpsfield's passages suggests that the *Passion* treatise must have been interrupted at about the time the king's agents secured these new legal devices for coercing More.

On the basis of such evidence, we can state with some precision that the *Dialogue of Comfort* was composed during the spring and summer following Sir Thomas's commitment to the Tower in April, 1534. The fragmentary *History of the Passion* must have been started sometime around September or October and interrupted before the turn of the year.

More significant, however, than the precise months of composition, is Cresacre More's assertion that the *Dialogue* was "for the most part written with no other pen than a coal." The prisoner More also had difficulties retaining and using books. There are at least three passages in the *Comfort* treatise which suggest that during the writing of that work his cell library was at best meager and at worst non-existent. For example, he appears to recollect faultily one of Aesop's fables (III, Intro.). More crucially, he wrongly cites Cassian's *Collations* where he should have cited the author's *Institutes* (II, 1). He would hardly have made this mistake had the two works been at hand. In another instance, More remarks that he has "half forgotten" a story in the *Collations,* because "it is so long since I read it." But he is willing to attempt the story anyway, "as far as my mind giveth me without new sight of the book" (II, 17). These passages might allude merely to the inadequacy of an improvised cell-library. But if this is so, why are even More's Biblical quotations from memory? If during this period More had been permitted even the most meager set of books, the Bible would surely have been among them.

Thus the evidence suggests that during the composition of the *Dialogue of Comfort,* More was not only without proper writing materials, but also without books for reference. It is doubtful if many literary works have been written under more adverse circumstances.

IV
More's Purposes in Writing

Two suggestions have been offered for More's motivation in writing the *Dialogue*. Great-grandson Cresacre More stressed Sir Thomas's wish to prepare the minds of Tudor Catholics for imminent persecution. Philip Hallett, on the other hand, in an Introduction to his 1937 edition, suggested that the work was written "chiefly for the comfort of More's own family." No one familiar with the circumstances under which the *Dialogue* was written can possibly quarrel with either of these suggestions. Yet transcending all other motivations, More wished—and desperately needed—to strengthen himself.

The Act of Treasons (November, 1534) stipulated the traditional penalty of disembowelment for all who openly denied the king's supremacy. The *Comfort* treatise was no doubt completed by the time the Act of Treasons was passed, and it certainly had been long completed by May, 1535, when More and his daughter Margaret watched Richard Reynolds and three Carthusians being dragged off on hurdles to Tyburn to be hanged, cut down while still alive, and disemboweled. But More's powers of anticipation were demonstrably keen. During happier days, when he and Henry had walked arm in arm at Chelsea, he had remarked prophetically to Roper: "If my head could win him a castle in France . . . , it should not fail to go." We are safe in assuming that More knew what lay in store for him when he was dispatched to the Tower in April of 1534.

It is therefore significant to note that Sir Thomas dreaded the prospect of painful death. At about the time the Act of Treasons was passed, he confessed to Margaret that he was "of a nature so shrinking from pain" that he looked on the future with a "heavy fearful heart." In the preceding letter to Margaret (Rogers, More's *Corres.,* No. 210), he similarly expressed disappointment that his flesh was "much more shrinking from pain and from death, than me thought it [proper for] a faithful Christian man." In the *Dialogue of Comfort* this fear permeates the last of the three Parts, which must have been written around August-September, 1534, when the passage of the Treasons Act was imminent. The pivotal chapter in this regard is No. 17 (Part III), which discusses the horror of bodily pain. More's anguish on this score runs the gamut of emotion in twelve separate chapters (III, 1-3, 17, 22-29). To no other type of persecution—or for that matter, to no other single theme—in the whole *Dialogue of Comfort* does More devote so much space.

When we consider Sir Thomas's forebodings as he sat in the Tower of London, it is obvious that the comforting arguments in Part III of the *Dialogue* are no mere academic exercise. Especially poignant and personal, in view of More's dread of pain, are Chapters 27 and 28: Bodily pain is terrible, More concedes; but the hellfire awaiting those who desert the faith is a thousand times worse. Yet Christ assures us that those who master pain with reason and grace will joyously behold God forever. The final chapter contains the most moving argument of all, and brings to a crescendo More's constant references to the Crucifixion. If we will meditate on the Passion, More declares, we will be caught up in the kind of ecstasy that characterizes the warrior who, in the frenzied excitement of combat, can lose a hand without even noticing it.

In short, the *Dialogue of Comfort* (especially Part III) speaks constantly of "violent death" and of "painful and shameful death." No one who knows the circumstances under which such passages were written can doubt for a moment that More's chief purpose in writing them was to steel and strengthen himself for execution. It is therefore fair to ask: Was this purpose achieved?

The answer lies largely in the accounts of More's execution by the early biographers Roper and Harpsfield, and by the anonymous writer of the *Paris News Letter,* which circulated through Europe immediately after More's death. These traditional accounts tell us that More comforted the tearful Thomas Pope, who came to tell him he must die by nine o'clock; that he sent money to his executioner, whom he embraced before the axe fell (the sentence had been commuted to beheading); that he kept his temper when, on the way to the scaffold, he was taunted by a woman who thought he had once wrongly judged against her; that he made the now immortal joke about the weakness of the scaffold stairs—"I pray, Master Lieutenant, see me safe up, and for my coming down let me shift for myself"; that he calmly acceded to the king's request that his speech be short; that he asked the executioner to strike accurately; and that he asserted he died the king's good servant, but God's first.

When we consider this remarkable composure on the scaffold, together with More's brave conduct along the way, we can only conclude that the *Dialogue of Comfort* succeeded in its chief purpose. The man who dreaded pain had *written* himself into facing it unflinchingly. Seldom if ever in literary history have we had such empirical proof that a writer achieved his goal.

V
Structure and Suspense

The *Dialogue of Comfort* is the only substantial literary work, written in English, which Thomas More ever completed. Any case for More's high stature in English literature must therefore be grounded primarily in this prison treatise, which has hitherto been largely ignored.

The two speakers in the *Dialogue* are Anthony and his nephew Vincent. The fact that their approximate ages are 78 and 26 immediately creates the youth versus age motif which the Renaissance so much relished, and which achieved such appealing and provocative forms in Castiglione's *The Courtier* and John Lyly's *Euphues*. Anthony crystallizes the motif in one of his many proverbs: "To the repressing of the bold courage of blind youth, there is a very true proverb, that as soon cometh a young sheep's skin to the market as an old" (II, 2).

The setting is Budapest, Hungary, in 1528. The Turks are about to invade the country, and Vincent has hastened to the sick Anthony to seek counsel on how to face the crisis. In the first of the three Parts which comprise the work, Anthony argues the thesis that tribulations are medicinal (Chap. 7): they inspire repentance, forestall potential sin, or test patience and thus increase heavenly merit. The argument is highly abstract, Scriptural, and dogmatic, lightened only by an occasional anecdote such as that of the "lusty lady" who vomited into her lover's face (Chap. 9).

The style and tone change radically in Part II, as Anthony descends from the cloud of theological dogma to the barnyard of everyday experience. Through the frequent illustrative use of the beast fable, he now analyses the tribulation of temptation as inspired by the devil. The four temptations are fear, pride, covetousness, and persecution. The latter is a temptation because through it the devil tempts us to desert Christ (Chap. 8). The theme is serious, but the merry tales are frequent. If Part I (to borrow some of More's phraseology) is for weeping, Part II is certainly for laughing.

Although persecution is announced as part of the formal structure of Part II, it is actually held off until Part III, with the result that tension and suspense are gradually built up within the work. Even when Sir Thomas can no longer delay the subject of persecution, he skillfully increases the tension by handling the lesser forms of persecution first. Thus we have discussions of the loss of outer goods like land, riches, fame, and high office. Then More moves on to the relatively minor harassment of the body itself, through forced labor (Part III, Chap. 18) or imprisonment (Chaps. 19-21). It is not until the very last chapters that More reaches the top of this scale or hierarchy of persecution, and finally comes to grips with the subject that has been increasingly on his, Vincent's, and the reader's mind—namely, painful death through physical torture. At the outset of Chapter 22, Vincent himself admits the torturous route by which the problem of painful death has been reached: "Now are we comen, uncle, with much work at the last, unto the last and uttermost point of . . . dread, . . . the terror of shameful and painful death."

What More does in effect, then, is to stalk the subject of persecution, and especially of painful death, much as a lion (one of his own favorite images) stalks its prey. The reader (not to mention Vincent) becomes increasingly impatient and eager to reach the discussion of fatal torture, yet simultaneously nervous that, once reached, the subject will prove unbearable to contemplate. In this sense, the *Dialogue of Comfort* is like a lengthy piece of adhesive tape pulled slowly off the skin.

VI
Adaptation of Historical Materials

In the construction of his dialogue format, More shows talent not only for creating suspense and climax, but also for adapting historical events to literary purposes. We are told that, at the time of the Anthony-Vincent conversations, Hungary was rent with internal dissension. Other allusions make it clear that More knew the source of this dissension, namely, the rival claims of John Zapolya of Transylvania and Archduke Ferdinand of Austria. Each of these men had managed to get himself crowned king of Hungary, whereupon Ferdinand in 1527 had temporarily defeated Zapolya. The latter appealed to his patron Suleiman the Magnificent for aid. The Grand Turk invaded Hungary on his protégé's behalf in 1529. The fact that the *Dialogue of Comfort* takes place *before* Suleiman's invasion, and only a "little while" *after* the crown was disputed, clearly pinpoints the time-setting as 1528.

Actually, Suleiman had made an earlier invasion of Hungary in 1526. Using blitzkrieg tactics, he had penetrated all the way to Budapest, carried off more than 100,000 captives, and withdrawn his entire army back across the Danube in less than six months. Why does More fail to mention this earlier invasion? We know that he was not ignorant of it, because he alludes vaguely to the major tragedy of that campaign, namely, the death of the courageous Hungarian boy-king Louis II at the battle of Mohacs (August, 1526). Quite apart from such allusions, it can be proved that More, as a member of the Privy Council, was fully informed on all aspects of the 1526 invasion. Wolsey, the king, and the Council received over a dozen dispatches on this subject, including reports (dated Feb.-Oct. 1526) on the assembling Turkish army, the death of Louis II, the entry of the Turks into Budapest, and the Turkish withdrawal.

When we consider such evidence, we are led inevitably to the conclusion that More deliberately suppressed any concrete mention of the earlier invasion, for obvious dramatic purposes. After all, the emotional power of the *Dialogue of Comfort* derives its intensity from the fact that invasion has not yet taken place. In terms of *imminent* invasion, Anthony's instructions on how to face confiscation of property, imprisonment, and painful death have a grim and practical sense of urgency. Such instructions would cease to be compelling if the invasion had already been completed.

VII
More's Allegory: Henry VIII and the Grand Turk

Of course the question might well be raised: Why did More go to such lengths to create a historical framework based on the 1529 Turkish invasion of Hungary? And why all the mystery on the title page, where we are told (not very convincingly) that the *Dialogue* was written first by a Hungarian in Latin, then translated into French, and finally translated into English?

The answer is that More needed an allegorical smokescreen behind which to attack Henry VIII, and behind which to offer comfort to English Catholics, who at that time stood in great danger of persecution by Henry. In Sir Thomas's situation, an open attack on the king would have been unthinkable. More was now a prisoner in the Tower. He had incurred the king's wrath by refusing to take the oath of supremacy. His life hung on his ability to keep silent—on his ability to keep from being trapped into a vocal denial of the king's right to be head of the church. Further, the manuscript of the *Dialogue of Comfort* might at any time have fallen into Henry's hands. Under such circumstances, More needed the same kind of allegorical protection that was to become standard equipment in English poetry of the 16th and 17th centuries.

The key to the allegory is supplied by the biographer Harpsfield, who tells us that More's purpose was to treat the persecution of English Catholics: "Albeit full wittily and wisely, that the books might the more safely go abroad, he doth not expressly meddle with these matters, and coloreth the matter under the name of an Hungarian, and of the persecution [by] the Turk in Hungary."

On this excellent authority, then, we can safely pronounce the Grand Turk Suleiman to be a symbol for Henry VIII. It is to More's credit as a literary artist that he should have selected, as the key figure in his allegory, a historical personage whose personality and methods would immediately invoke images of Henry in any Tudor Catholic's mind. Suleiman, for example, was a lover of culture; his interest in legal reform gained him the title of "Lawgiver." Yet, like Henry, he was highly susceptible to harem intrigue, on one occasion murdering two of his own sons and on another, his own grand vizier. Few Tudors who read Anthony's descriptions of the Turk's penchant for murder, imprisonment of enemies, and property-confiscation, would have failed to perceive the obvious parallels with certain of Henry's more reprehensible activities.

This is not to say that More had in mind any elaborate and carefully thought out allegorical scheme for the *Dialogue of Comfort*. Indeed, any attempt to interpret the work as a detailed and interlocked allegory of the *Faerie Queene* type would probably be unwarranted. But if (on Harpsfield's authority) we accept the Turk as representing Henry VIII, and the Hungarians as representing English Catholics, then certain subsidiary symbols necessarily follow. For example, the Turkish army then represents those allied with Henry, such as Cromwell and others who were increasingly to be known as Protestants. Also, the Hungarian deserters—i.e., those who forsake Christ and go over to Islam and the Turk—then represent those English Catholics who, for whatever motives, decided to take the oath of supremacy.

VIII
Autobiographical Revelation

There can be no question that Uncle Anthony is a thin allegorical disguise for More himself. For one thing, Anthony's conversations contain many allusions to More's family, friends, and colleagues. According to Harpsfield, for example, at least four anecdotes in the *Dialogue* refer to More's second wife, Dame Alice. Thus we hear Alice joke that, having been to confession, she can now sin afresh (II, 14); we see her "strait bracing in her body to make her middle small" (II, 21); we note her disgust at More's lack of ambition (III, 11); and we laugh at her fear of suffocation when locked in from the outside (III, 21). Alice is probably also the wife who is glad to let her husband have "all the words," provided she supplies them.

Far more important than allusions to family and colleagues are the innumerable references in Anthony's conversations to what we know, from other sources, were More's own habits, traits, attitudes, and activities. Thus Anthony speaks (III, 21) of the Carthusians, with whom More lived for four years; and of the Bridgettines, whose house of Sion he visited to talk with his friend Richard Reynolds. He alludes (II, 20) to the erection of a new building at Chelsea, and to a crucifix prayer which More often said there. We also find reflected in Anthony's remarks More's well-known reverence for the authority of the Church fathers (e.g., I, 12 and II, 7); his kindness toward children and parents (II, 23); his championing of the active life (II, 20); and especially his famous habit of "of looking sadly when he meant merrily" (II, 18).

Indeed, some of the views which the fictional Anthony expresses were repeated by the real More in the Tower. Thus Anthony's touching insistence that we love our enemies (III, 29) is echoed in one of More's final prayers. And to Dame Alice, More said the same thing about property that Anthony later argues in the *Dialogue,* namely, that the owners of real estate change with bewildering rapidity, thus proving the vanity of ownership. Even the delightful fable of the ass and wolf who went to confession to the fox (II, 14-15) is intimately connected with More's family—it had been recounted in a letter from his step-daughter Alice Alington, sent to More in August, 1534, as he was at work on the *Comfort* treatise.

If Anthony is unquestionably More, then who is Vincent? Highly tantalizing is Father Hallett's suggestion that he might be a screen for Margaret Roper. For one thing, Vincent at 26 is near Margaret's age (30) at the time the *Dialogue* was written. Further, a number of his family observations appear to be allusions to More's own household. Thus Vincent admits at one point (III, 2) that he is worried not so much for himself as for his large and diverse family of many ages—this undoubtedly a reference to the unusually cosmopolitan character of More's own family group. At another point (Part I, Intro.) Vincent refers to certain troubles that have afflicted the family even before news of the impending Turkish invasion. It does not strain credulity to see in this passage an allusion to More's resignation as Chancellor, his fall to relative poverty, and other difficulties preceding his imprisonment.

IX
Dramatic Elements

Through use of the "Turkish" framework, More manifests a flair not only for political allegory and autobiographical allusion, but also for characterization.

Character change is most noticeable in the case of Vincent. At the outset he is meek, silent, deferential. His objections are largely token, and are quickly withdrawn in the face of Anthony's verbal onslaughts. However, in Chapter 15 of Part I, Vincent spots a hole in Anthony's armor and ventures into it. The uncle has been arguing that tribulations are a sign of God's favor, and are sent only to those God hopes to have with him in heaven. But if this is so, Vincent counters, then all the church prayers are wrong. We ought instead to pray that everybody get sick and have as much disease and misfortune as possible!

From here on, Vincent emerges gradually from the doldrums. In Chapter 16 of Part I, Anthony concedes that his nephew is aiming a disconcerting number of arrows at the target of his arguments. By Part II, Chapter 4, Vincent has gotten mischievous. He is not only trading puns with Anthony, but is beginning to challenge the other's evidence; the testimony of an unlearned girl, he says, is hardly enough basis for believing Anthony's strange story of a fever which was allegedly hot and cold simultaneously. As we enter Part III, Vincent is arguing heatedly, even to the point of accusing Anthony (Chap. 19) of employing "sophistical fantasies."

Vincent's increasing boldness underscores a further dramatic quality of the *Dialogue of Comfort,* namely conflict. Indeed, the work increasingly takes on the tenor of a debate, in which Anthony's purpose is to change Vincent's attitude. More's chief argumentative devices are reserved for the last three chapters (III, 27-29). The first device is the lure of heavenly joys (III, 28). The second is the threat of hell (Chaps. 27-28); through this device, Anthony tries literally to frighten Vincent into preferring death by torture to an apostasy which will bring hellfire. The third and supreme device is the shame technique (e.g., III, 24, 28): How can we disdain suffering for Christ, when he suffered so much for us?

This last argument is brilliantly executed in the gripping final chapter (III, 29). Pagan soldiers die for nothing but renown, weak women and children have gone unflinchingly to martyrdom, even heretics cheerfully die for their beliefs. How can we do less? Romantic lovers die for sweethearts, even though their ladies have shown them no kindness, and even though in death they can get no reward. Are we to love Christ less than men love women? It is a powerful climactic argument. Vincent is shamed, strengthened, and convinced by it. No doubt other men were too.

X
Poetic Qualities

If More shows a dramatic flair in his creation of conflict through argumentation, it must also be added that in the *Dialogue of Comfort* his poetic gifts, denied any substantial outlet elsewhere, reach fruition. His favorite and omnipresent poetic device is alliteration. He can scarcely write a sentence, or even a clause, without using it. In his combining of alliteration with balancing, More anticipates certain features of what was later caller Euphuism.

One of the two most prominent types of metaphor in the *Comfort* treatise is that drawn from sea lore. Thus More suggests that tribulation is a kind of ballast, a wooden beam set on the ship of the heart, so that the ship will not be blown under water by the "boisterous blast of pride" (I, 9). Again, comfort is said to be like mounds of earth packed against the walls of our heart, to hold back the tempestuous sea of tribulation (I, Intro.). This image of a stormy sea, usually linked with that of a storm-tossed ship, became one of More's favorite metaphors for earthly existence, recurring in the Tower letters.

Even more dominant than nautical metaphor is More's use of figures drawn from the field of medicine. Not only are tribulations like ill-tasting but wholesome medicine (I, 7), but philosophers are mere pharmacists in relation to the great physician God. It is God alone who can drive away "the deadly disease of damnation," because His grace is the only medicine that can cure the sickness of sin (I, 1). In the same vein, painful death is like unpleasant medicine—both are ultimately beneficial (III, 25).

The notion of philosophers as druggists was probably a poetic extension of Ecclesiasticus 38:1, where the Holy Spirit is described as a Physician, and which More quotes in the relevant chapter (I, 1). Much of the remaining medical metaphor is no doubt derived from Jerome and other patristic writers with whom More was thoroughly familiar. The notion of God-Christ as a Physician, for example, is prominent in the works of Augustine, on whose *City of God* More had lectured as a young lawyer.

Closely related to More's metaphorical gift is his use of extended analogy. The most striking example, and probably the most provocative passage in the whole work, is More's concept of the world as a prison. He elaborates it extravagantly over three chapters (III, 19-21). As these chapters evolve, men become prisoners assigned to a single jail (earth) from which they cannot escape. They all await execution (death) for a common crime (original sin). This speculation drives on to the startling conclusion (Chap. 21) that God is Himself the Chief Jailer of this universal prison. Just as any competent jailer punishes rowdy convicts by placing them in the stocks, so God punishes His unruly prisoners by placing them in the stocks of gout, palsy, or fever.

Though the germ of this startling analogy lies in More's Epigram 101, that particular poem is not (as are most of More's Epigrams) a translation from the Greek Anthology. The likeliest source is Plato, who remarked that "man is a prisoner" of the Gods (*Phaedo* 62), and who accordingly, in his *Republic* VII, 514-16, pictured men as prisoners in a cave, so severely chained that they could see on the wall only shadows of the real objects which exist outside.

XI

Change of Pace: "Merry Tales" and Beast Fables

In addition to exhibiting poetic qualities, More shows skill at change of pace, especially in the form of comic relief. By way of conceding the value of wit and humor in discussion, More had placed in Anthony's mouth, in the first chapter of Part II, an acknowledgment that merriment is suitable sauce for the meat of theological dialogue. To supply this sauce for the meat, More employs a surprising variety of techniques.

Prominent among them is the witty aphorism. Thus: If a great man's finger aches, many men's mouths blowing out praise won't help as much as one little boy blowing upon his finger (III, 10). Allied with the aphorism in More's bag of tricks is ludicrous imagery, playful banter, humorous symbol, and the self-directed barb. Even More's verbosity comes in for some spoofing, as Anthony wistfully confesses his own garrulity.

Most effective as change of pace devices, however, are the many stories which, interlaced amongst the theology, give the *Dialogue of Comfort* its unique flavor. First there are the adventure narratives, especially the thrilling account of the Turkish night-alarm (II, 12). The second group comprise the "jests" or "merry tales," hundreds of which were in circulation in Tudor England. Almost all of More's jests treat the perennial battle of the sexes. Those which are autobiographically oriented are dependably funny. Like an experienced speaker who knows that he has one sure-fire joke, More is well aware that his wife Dame

Alice is always good for a chuckle. The non-autobiographical jests, however, tend to be grim and macabre, a sample being the weird account of the carver who was almost crucified (II, 18). We can accept only with qualification Chambers' insistence that the merry tales give the *Dialogue* a happy, "carefree" atmosphere.

Like the merry tales, More's beast fables (drawn chiefly from Aesop or the Aesopian cycle) are used to lighten or alter an otherwise somber discussion. In More's hands these fables frequently achieve literary distinction. Mother Maud's Tale, for example, provides some colorful character contrast between the worried ass and the carefree wolf (II, 14-15). The whole fable has a delightful Uncle Remus flavor, witness such sentences as "Father Reynard . . . shook his great pair of beads upon him, almost as big as bowls, and asked him [the ass] wherefore he came so late."

Such fables, like the adventure thrillers and the merry tales, rarely hamper or delay the main line of argument. On the contrary, they almost always carry it forward, vivify it, and often clinch the point at hand. The fable of how the snail got its shell is told not merely for its fun value, but because it supplies a symbol of those possession-bound mortals who worship their houses rather than God (III, 23). In this clever interlocking of abstract discussion and colorful anecdote, More shows himself to be an artist of the first rank.

XII
A Masterpiece?

Shall we then proclaim the *Dialogue of Comfort* a masterpiece? Unfortunately, no. As it has come down to us through the traditional texts, the work is marred by tedious repetition, eccentric chapter division, intermittent disintegration of the dialogue format, and structural false starts. It is, in fact, nothing more than a first draft, possibly smuggled out of the Tower a few pages at a time by More's servant, John Wood. Indeed, when we consider how Vincent (representing Margaret) constantly stresses his intention to write down everything that Anthony says, we must consider seriously the possibility that the work was dictated to Margaret, and then recorded by her piecemeal outside the Tower.

In any event, the *Dialogue* has all the faults of a work written hurriedly and left largely unrevised. It is a classic that might have been. Therein lies the real tragedy for English literature of More's imprisonment. Yet with all its faults, it deserves a far greater readership than it has ever received.

XIII
The Nature of this Edition

This modern spelling edition is based on the 1557 Rastell text, collated with the Tottell (1553) and Fowler (1573) printed versions. The manuscript of the *Dialogue* in the British Museum (Royal 17-D-XIV) was also consulted. The Rastell readings have been followed except where the other versions are, in the editor's judgment, clearly preferable.

A one-page glossary of frequently recurring archaisms has been placed at the beginning of the text. Other archaic terms and usages, if and as they might cause difficulty, are glossed on their first appearance in any Part. The valuable notes in Hallett's 1937 edition have been expanded to include (among other things) the sources of previously unidentified allusions. Other apparatus includes a comparison of chapter divisions between this and earlier editions, a Thomas More Chronology, a Selected *Dialogue of Comfort* Bibliography, and a Synopsis of the main line of argument.

In one respect the present edition extends an approach begun in the 1951 Sheed and Ward version, namely in the attempt to reduce More's long and involved sentences to something resembling modern sentence structure. When the deletion of a single connective word, or the addition of a single verb or noun, has offered the possibility of bringing grammatical order out of chaos, the editor has not hesitated to make the deletion or addition, indicating the former by a single ellipsis (. . .), and the latter by brackets. Two ellipses (. . .   . . .) indicate the occasional deletion of more than one sentence. This editorial policy has involved, as corollaries, a radical modernization of More's punctuation, capitalization, paragraphing, and chapter division. Such a procedure is imperative if we hope to bring the *Dialogue of Comfort* to a larger audience than has hitherto existed. It would indeed be a tragedy if the structural and other difficulties of the *Dialogue of Comfort* should continue to make it less known than the Latin *Utopia,* which is widely read chiefly because it has been translated into the modern idiom.

To the same end, this edition is frankly abridged, though not so severely as Henry Bowden's *Crumbs of Comfort* in 1915. The aim here is not "crumbs," but the *Dialogue* in its best possible dress, stripped of the wearying repetition which has alienated so many readers for so long. In addition to deleting inartistically repetitious material, the Latin Biblical quotations and some of the minor abstract argument have been excised, together with some of the less significant or relevant chapters. Where whole chapters have (infrequently) been eliminated, they have been summarized at the appropriate points in the text. This is especially true of certain "structure" chapters which, while important, can be conveniently summarized. The result is an abridgement of about twenty per cent.

The purpose of this volume, then, is to bring a significant and unjustly neglected literary work to the attention of students and the general public, and at the same time to supply urgently needed material for scholarly investigation. A corollary purpose has been to supply a *balanced* approach to More as a man, historical personage, and writer. Early Protestant treatments of More were incorrigibly biased; but they were no worse than recent sentimental panegyrics, which likewise have no place in responsible scholarship.

The ecumenical spirit of our time demands a more objective approach. This volume is perhaps a modest start in that direction.

A DIALOGUE OF COMFORT AGAINST TRIBULATION

Made
in the Year of Our Lord 1534
by Sir Thomas More, Knight,
While He Was Prisoner
in the
Tower of London

M · D · XXVII

PLATE 1. Portrait of Sir Thomas More (1527), by Hans Holbein the Younger. Of several extant versions by Holbein, this is the earliest. Copyright, The Frick Collection, New York.

GLOSSARY

This list includes only the meanings of archaic words and the archaic meanings of contemporary words which recur frequently in the text. Words requiring glosses which appear only once or twice in the text are footnoted at the end of the chapter in which they first appear.

an: if
assay: trial, test
aught: anything
but if: unless
commodity: advantage, convenience
convenient: appropriate, proper
despite: injury
device: scheme
devise: think
fain: gladly, preferably, willingly
fantasy: foolish delusion, worrisome thought
fond: foolish
ghostly: spiritual
grudge: bother, complain
guise: habit, manner
haply: by chance, perhaps
jeopard: jeopardize, risk
let: hesitate, hinder, stop
lewd: ignorant, wicked (non-carnally)
list, lust: choose, desire (not necessarily carnal), like
lusty: eager, joyful
marry!: Mary!
meet: moderate, suitable
mind: attitude, opinion
naught: wicked
pardie!: by God!
passion: agony, suffering
pavis: shield
peevish: foolish, trifling
peradventure, percase: perhaps
privy: private, secret
require: request
room: high office, position
silly: helpless, miserable, pitiful
sith: since
sleight: stratagem, trick
strait: rigid, severe
train: trick
trow: believe, swear, trust
wanton: carefree, undisciplined (not necessarily sexually)
weal: welfare
ween: imagine, suppose, think
wherefore: why
wist: knew
wit: knowledge; (to) wit: know
wont: accustomed
wot: know

[PART I]

[*Setting*: Budapest, Hungary, in 1528. The Turks are about to invade the country. In a preliminary battle, they have already killed the Hungarian King, Louis II. Terrified, Vincent rushes to his ailing uncle, Anthony, to seek counsel on how to face the crisis.]

Introduction

[Anthony Reviews the Turk's Victories]

VINCENT: Who would have weened, O my good uncle, afore a few years passed, that such as in this country would visit their friends lying in disease and sickness should come, as I do now, to seek and fetch comfort of them? Or in giving comfort to them, use the way that I may well use to you? For albeit that the priests and friars be wont to call upon sick men to remember death, yet we worldly friends, for fear of discomforting them, have ever had a guise in Hungary to lift up their hearts, and put them in good hope of life. But now, good uncle, the world is here waxen such, and so great perils appear to fall at hand, that methinketh the greatest comfort that a man can have is when he may see that he shall soon be gone.

[Yet] we that are likely long to live here in wretchedness have need of some comfortable counsel against tribulation, to be given by such as you be, good uncle, that have so long lived virtuously and are so learned in the law of God [that] very few be better in this country here. [You] have had of such things as we do now fear good experience and assay in yourself, as he that hath been taken prisoner in Turkey two times in your days, and now likely to depart hence ere long. But that may be your great comfort, good uncle, sith you depart to God. But us here shall you leave of your kindred a sort of sorry comfortless orphans, to all whom your good help, comfort, and counsel hath long been a great stay—not as an uncle unto some and to some as one farther of kin, but as though unto us all you had been a natural father.

ANTHONY: Mine own good cousin, I cannot much say nay but that there is indeed, not here in Hungary only but almost also in all places of Christendom, such a customable[1] manner of unchristian comforting . . . that in any sick man it doth more harm than good, [by] drawing him in time of sickness with looking and longing for life from the meditation of death, judgment, heaven, and hell[2] . . . . Yet is that manner in my mind more than mad, where such kind of comfort is used to a man of mine age. For as we well wot that a young man may die soon, so be we very sure that an old man cannot live long. And yet . . . there is (as Tully saith) no man for all that so old but that he hopeth yet that he may live one year more, and of a frail folly delighteth to think thereon.[3] And comforting himself therewith (other men's words of like manner comfort adding more sticks to that fire), [he] shall in a manner burn up quite the pleasant moisture that most should refresh him —the wholesome dew, I mean, of God's grace, by which he should wish with God's will to be hence, and long to be with him in heaven.

Now where you take my departing from you so heavily, as of him whom you recognize of your goodness to have had here before help and comfort, would God I had to you and to other more done half so much as myself reckoneth had been my duty to do. But whensoever God take me hence, to reckon yourselves comfortless, as though your chief comfort stood in me—therein make you, methinketh, a reckoning very much like as though you would cast away a strong staff and lean upon a rotten reed. For God is and must be your comfort, and not I. And He is a sure comforter that, as He said unto His disciples, never leaveth His servants in [the] case of[4] comfortless orphans; not even when He departed from His disciples by death. But both, as He promised, sent them a comforter, the Holy Spirit of His Father and Himself, and made them also sure that to the world's end He would ever dwell with them Himself.[5] And therefore if you be part of His flock and believe His promise, how can you be comfortless in any tribulation, when Christ and His Holy Spirit, and with them their inseparable Father (if you put full trust and confidence in them), be never neither one finger breadth of space nor one minute of time from you?

VINCENT: O my good uncle, even these selfsame words, wherewith you well prove that because of God's own gracious presence we cannot be left comfortless, make me now feel and perceive what a miss of much comfort we shall have when you be gone. For albeit, good uncle, that while you do tell me this I cannot but grant it for true, yet if I now had not heard it of you I had not remembered it, nor it had not fallen in my mind. And over that, like as our tribulations shall in weight and number increase, so shall we need not only such good word or twain, but a great heap thereof, to stable[6] and strength the walls of our hearts against the great surges of this tempestuous sea.

ANTHONY: Good cousin, trust well in God and He shall provide you teachers abroad[7] convenient in every time, or else shall Himself sufficiently teach you within.

VINCENT: Very well, good uncle. But yet if we would leave the seeking of outward learning where we may have it, and look to be inwardly taught only by God, then should we thereby tempt God, and displease Him. . . . I now see the likelihood that when you be gone we shall be sore destitute of any such other like [you]. Therefore thinketh me that God of duty bindeth me to sue to you now, good uncle, in this short time that we have you, that . . . against these great storms of tribulation with which both I and all mine are sore beaten already (and now upon the coming of this cruel Turk fear to fall in far more), I may learn of you [m]uch plenty of good counsel and comfort. Th[en] I may, with the same laid up in remembrance, govern and stay the ship of our kindred and keep it afloat from peril of spiritual drowning.

You be not ignorant, good uncle, what heaps of heaviness hath of late fallen among us already, with which some of our poor family be fallen into such dumps, that scantily can any such comfort as my poor wit can give them anything assuage their sorrow.[8] And now sith these tidings have come hither so brim[9] of the great Turk's enterprise into these parts here, we can almost neither talk nor think of any other thing else than of his might and our mischief.[10] There falleth so continually before the eyes of our heart a fearful imagination of this terrible thing. [We fear] his mighty strength and power; his high malice and hatred; and his incomparable cruelty—with robbing, spoiling, burning, and laying waste all the way that his army cometh. Then, [he is known for] killing or carrying away the people far thence from home, and there sever[ing] the couples and the kindred asunder, every one far from other. Some [are] kept in thraldom, and some kept in prison, and some for a triumph[11] tormented and killed in his presence.

Then send[s he] his people hither, and his false faith therewith, so that such as are here and remain still shall either both lose all and be lost too,[12] or forced to forsake the faith of our Saviour Christ, and fall to the false sect of Mahomet.[13] And yet (which we more fear than all the remnant), no small part of our own folk that dwell even here about us are, as we fear, falling to him or already confedered[14] with him. . . . If it so be, [it] shall haply keep [t]his quarter from the Turk's incursion. But then shall they that turn to his law leave all their neighbors nothing, but shall have our good[s] given them, and our bodies both, but if we turn as they do, and forsake our Savior too. And then—for there is no born Turk so cruel to Christian folk as is the false Christian that falleth from the faith[15]—we shall stand in peril (if we persevere in the truth) to be more hardly handled and die more cruel death by our own countrymen at home, than if we were taken hence and carried into Turkey.

These fearful heaps of peril lie so heavy at our hearts while we wot not into which we shall fortune to fall (and therefore fear all the worst), that as our Savior prophesied of the people of Jerusalem, many wish among us already, before the peril come, that the mountains would overwhelm them or the valleys open and swallow them up and cover them.[16] Therefore, good uncle, against these horrible fears of these terrible tribulations, of which some, ye wot well, our house already hath and the remnant stand in dread of, give us (while God lendeth you us) such plenty of your comfortable counsel as I may write and keep with us, to stay us when God shall call you hence.

ANTHONY: Ah, my good cousin, this is an heavy hearing, and likewise as we that dwell here in this part fear that thing sore now which, [a] few years past, feared it not at all. So doubt I not that ere it long be, they shall fear it as much that think themself now very sure because they dwell farther off. Greece feared not the Turk when that I was born; and within a while after, that whole empire was his.[17] The great sultan of Syria thought himself more than his match; and long since you were born hath he that empire too.[18] Then hath he taken Belgrade,[19] the fortress of this realm, and since hath he destroyed our noble young goodly king.[20] And now strive there twain[21] for us. Our Lord send the grace that the third dog[22] carry not away the bone from them both.

What should I speak of the noble strong city of the Rhodes,[23] the winning whereof he counted as a victory against the whole corps of Christendom, sith all Christendom was not able to defend that strong town against him? Howbeit, if the princes of Christendom everywhere about would, whereas need was, have set to their hands in time, the Turk had never taken any one place of all those places. But partly [because] dissensions [have] fallen among ourself, partly [because] no man careth what harm other folk feel (but each part suffereth other to shift for itself), the Turk is in few years wonderfully increased, and Christendom on the other side very sore decayed. And all this worketh our wickedness, with which God is not content.

But now, . . . you desire of me some plenty of comfortable things, which ye may put in remembrance and comfort therewith your company. Verily, in the rehearsing and heaping of your manifold fears, myself began to feel that the[y] should much need (against so many troubles) many comfortable counsels! For surely a little before your coming, as I devised with myself upon the Turk's coming, it happed my mind to fall suddenly from that into the devising upon my own departing. . . . I fully put my trust and hope to be a saved soul by the great mercy of God. Yet sith no man is here so sure that without revelation [he] may clean stand out of dread, I bethought me also upon the pain of hell. And after, I bethought me then upon the Turk again. And first methought his terror nothing when I compared with it the joyful hope of heaven. Then compared I it on the other side with the fearful dread of hell; and therein casting in my mind those terrible devilish tormentors with the deep consideration of that furious endless fire, methought that if the Turk with his whole host and all trumpets and his timbrels too, were (to kill me in my bed) come to my chamber door, in respect of the other reckoning I [would] regard him not a rush.[24]

And yet when I now heard your lamentable words, laying forth as it were present before my face that heap of heavy sorrowful tribulations that, beside those that are already fallen, are in short space like to follow, I waxed therewith myself suddenly somewhat afflight.[25] And therefore I will allow your request in this behalf, [so] that [you sh]ould have store of comfort aforehand ready by you, to resort to and to lay up in your heart as a triacle[26] against the poison of all desperate dread that might rise of occasion of sore tribulation. And herein shall I be glad, as my poor wit will serve me, to call to mind with you such things as I before have read, heard, or thought upon, that may conveniently serve us to this purpose.

1 customary.
2 These are the "four last things" about which More wrote in his unfinished treatise, *De quatuor novissimus,* composed around 1522, shortly after he was knighted and appointed Under-Treasurer. Rastell included the piece in his 1557 edition of More's *English Works,* pp. 72-101. Later editions include two by D. O'Connor (1903 & 1935). Also, W. E. Campbell, in *The English Works of Sir Thomas More* (1931), I, 457-99.
3 From *De senectute* (*On Old Age*), Chap. 7, sec. 24, by Marcus Tullius Cicero (106-43 B.C.), Roman statesman, orator, and author. See the Loeb trans. by W. A. Falconer (1923), and note George Twigg-Porter, "Cicero, Classic Gerontologist," *Classical Bulletin,* XXXIX (Nov. 1962), 1-4.
4 in the position of.
5 John 14:18-28—"I will not leave you orphans: I will come to you. . . ." Cf. Matt. 28:20.
6 stabilize, steady.
7 from without (as distinguished from God, who teaches from within).
8 Apparently an allusion to the series of disasters which struck More and his family, beginning with his resignation as Lord Chancellor (May 1532) and preceding his commitment to the Tower (April 1534), e.g., his fall from affluence to relative poverty, his increasing illness, his being charged with misprision of treason in the case of the nun Elizabeth Barton. Consult R. W. Chambers, *Thomas More,* pp. 252-304. The invasion of the Turk into Hungary, which has not yet occurred within the narrative context of the *Dialogue of Comfort,* would then symbolize Henry's persecution of More via imprisonment, property confiscation, and execution.
9 public; i.e., much discussed.
10 injury; i.e., the potential injury to be inflicted by the Turk.
11 victory celebration.
12 I.e., lose their property and also their lives.
13 More here intimates that deserting Christ for the false religion of Islam is equivalent to taking the oath of supremacy recognizing Henry as head of the Church.
14 confederated, in league with.
15 Another strike at Henry, former "Defender of the Faith." However, for a different view of Henry as a ruler much loved by his troops because, though riddled with disease, he was always present and knew what to do in a crisis, see Hester W. Chapman, *Two Tudor Portraits* (Boston: Little Brown, 1960), pp. 88-89.
16 Luke 23:28-30—"Then shall they begin to say to the mountains: Fall upon us. And to the hills: Cover us."
17 The Byzantine Empire under Palaeologus fell in 1453 when Muhammad II captured Constantinople. Since the Greek empire fell "a little while after" Anthony's birth, he must have been born around 1450 and must now be about 78 years old (assuming the time-setting to be 1528).
18 The Sultan of Syria (Ashraf Tuman Bey) lost Syria, Egypt, and Arabia to Selim I in 1517. Note that Syria fell "long" after Vincent's birth. If we take this to mean roughly 15 years after, then Vincent must now be around 26.
19 Suleiman I captured this Hungarian southern border fortress in 1521, then diverted his attention to assaulting Rhodes.
20 Louis II of Hungary perished, age 20, at the battle of Mohacs in August, 1526. Philip E. Hallett, in his 1937 edition of the *Dialogue of Comfort,* p. viii, suggests that the Turks' destruction of the "noble young king" allegorically represents Henry VIII's fall into heresy in renouncing the Pope's authority (?).
21 The two contenders for the Hungarian throne were John Zapolya, voivode of Transylvania, appointed vassal king by the Turks upon the death of Louis II; and Ferdinand, archduke of

Austria, who had himself crowned in 1527.

22 Suleiman I, to whom Zapolya appealed for help. It is this appeal which has precipitated the impending invasion. The "bone" is of course the throne.

23 This island (near Crete) fell to the Turks in late 1522. For details of the Turkish conquest, consult such works as Edward S. Creasy, *History of the Ottoman Turks* (1961); and William R. Shepherd, "The Ottoman Empire, 1481-1683," *Historical Atlas,* 8th ed. (New York: Barnes & Noble, 1956), p. 128A.

24 I.e., as less than a candle (in comparison with hellfire). A "rushlight" was a lowgrade candle made from the pith of various rush stems and dipped in grease. See James O. Halliwell, *Dictionary of Archaic and Provincial Words,* 9th ed. (1878), I, 699.

25 worried.

26 antidote.

Chapter 1

[The Inadequacy of Pagan Philosophers]

First shall you, good cousin, understand this, that the natural wise men of this world, the old moral philosophers,[1] labored much in this matter, and many natural reasons have they written, whereby they might encourage men to set little by such goods or such hurts either, the going or the coming whereof are the matter and the cause of tribulation. [Such] are the goods of fortune:[2] riches, favor, friends, fame, worldly worship, and such other things; or of the body, as beauty, strength, agility, quickness, and health. These things (ye wot well) coming to us, are matter of worldly wealth, and taken from us by fortune or by force or the fear of the losing, be matter of adversity and tribulation. For tribulation seemeth generally to signify nothing else but some kind of grief, either pain of the body or heaviness of the mind.

Now the body not to feel that it feeleth, all the wit in the world cannot bring about. But that the mind should not be grieved neither with the pain that the body feeleth, nor with occasions of heaviness offered and given unto the soul itself, this thing labored the philosophers very much about. And many goodly sayings have they toward the strength and comfort against tribulation, exciting men to the full contempt of all worldly loss and despising of sickness, and all bodily grief, painful death, and all.

Howbeit, in very deed, for anything that ever I read in them, I never could yet find that ever those natural reasons were able to give sufficient comfort of themself. For they never stretch so far but that they leave untouched, for lack of necessary knowledge, that special point which is not only the chief comfort of all, but without which also all other comforts are nothing. That [point] is to wit, the referring the final end of their comfort unto God, and to repute and take for the special cause of comfort, that by the patient sufferance of their tribulation they shall attain His favor, and for their pain receiveth reward at His hand in heaven. And for lack of knowledge of this end they did (as they needs must) leave untouched also the very special mean, without which we can never attain to this comfort, that is to wit, the gracious aid and help of God to move, stir, and guide us forward, in the referring all our ghostly comfort, yea, and our worldly comfort too, all unto that heavenly end. And therefore, as I say, for the lack of these things, all their comfortable counsels are very far insufficient.

Howbeit, though they be far unable to cure our disease of themself, and therefore are not sufficient to be taken for our physicians, some good drugs have they yet in their shops for which they may be suffered to dwell among our poticaries[3]—if their medicines be made not of their own brains, but after the bills made by the great physician God, prescribing the medicines Himself, and correcting the faults of their erroneous receipts.[4] For without this way taken with them, they shall not fail to do as many bold blind poticaries do which, either for lucre or of a foolish pride, give sick folk medicines of their own devising, and therewith kill up in corners[5] many such simple folk as they find so foolish [as] to put their lives in such lewd and unlearned blind Bayards' hands.[6]

We shall therefore neither fully receive these philosophers' reasons in this matter, nor yet utterly refuse them. But, using them in such order as shall beseem them, the principal and the effectual medicines against these diseases of tribulation shall we fetch from that high, great, and excellent physician without whom we could never be healed of our very deadly disease of damnation. For our necessity wherein, the Spirit of God spiritually speaketh of Himself to us, and biddeth us of all our health give Him the honor, and therein this saith unto us: "Honor thou the physician, for him hath the high God ordained for thy necessity."[7]

Therefore let us require that high physician, our Blessed Savior Christ, whose holy manhood God ordained for our necessity,[8] to cure our deadly wounds[9] with the medicine made of the most wholesome blood of His own blessed body. . . . Likewise as He cured by the incomparable medicine our mortal malady, it may like Him to send us and put in our minds such medicines at this time, as against the sickness and sorrows of tribulations may . . . comfort and strength us in His grace. So our deadly enemy the devil may never have the power by his poisoned dart of murmur,[10] grudge, and impatience to turn our short sickness of worldly tribulation into the endless everlasting death of infernal damnation.

1 More no doubt has in mind such thinkers as Plato (427?-347 B.C.), the Stoic Marcus Aurelius (121-180), and Seneca (4 B.C.?-65 A.D.). More calls them "natural wise men" (cf. the term "natural theology") because their views are derived from rational argument and observation of nature, rather than from Scriptural revelation.

2 I.e., the blessings of Lady Fortune, a personified device by which medieval and Renaissance writers signified the vicissitudes of life. She turned a wheel on which the ambitious were capriciously spun from high to low estate, or vice versa. The standard reference is Howard Patch, *The Goddess Fortuna in Medieval Literature* (1927).

3 apothecaries, pharmacists.

4 prescriptions.

5 The expression could mean street intersections or gutters (Halliwell II, 271), but probably refers to the private corner a man may seek in which to suffer or die.

6 bayhorse. An old proverb, "as bold as blind bayard," was applied to those who failed to look before they leaped. It is so used in *Piers Plowman*, Chaucer, and Skelton (see Halliwell, I, 153). Thus More's metaphor suggests that pharmacists, left to themselves, are foolishly and dangerously self-confident.

7 Ecclesiasticus 38:1. In the Tower More's Bible seems intermittently to have been taken from him. In any event, many of the Biblical quotations appear to be from memory, and do not therefore (even in their Latin form, omitted from this edition) correspond precisely to the Vulgate text. See Hallett's ed. of the *Dialogue*, p. x.

8 need.

9 I.e., the wounds of sin, which are "deadly" in that they deprive man of eternal life. Such wounds are "cured" by the sanctifying "medicine" of divine grace. This metaphor recurs frequently.

10 cursing or protesting beneath one's breath.

Chapter 2

[The Need for a Foundation of Faith][1]

[ANTHONY (continuing):] Sith all our principal comfort must come of God, we must first presuppose in [any person] to whom we shall with any ghostly counsel give any effectual comfort, one ground to begin withal, whereupon all that we shall build must be supported and stand. That is to wit, the ground and foundation of faith, without which had ready before,[2] all the spiritual comfort that any man may speak of can never avail a fly. For likewise as it were utterly vain to lay natural reasons[3] of comfort to him that hath no wit, so were it undoubtedly frustrate to lay spiritual causes of comfort to him that hath no faith. For except a man first believe that Holy Scripture is the word of God, and that the word of God is true, how can a man take any comfort of that [which] the Scripture telleth him therein? Needs must the man take little fruit of the Scripture, if he either believe not that it were the word of God, or else ween that though it were, it might yet be for all that untrue.

This faith as it is more faint or more strong, so shall the comfortable words of Holy Scripture stand the man in more stead or less. This virtue of faith can neither any man give himself nor yet any one man another. . . . Though men may with preaching be ministers unto God therein, and the man with his own free will obeying freely the inward inspiration of God be a weak worker with Almighty God therein, yet is the faith indeed the gracious gift of God himself. For as Saint James saith: "Every good gift and every perfect gift is given from above, descending from the Father of Lights."[4] Therefore, feeling our faith by many tokens very faint, let us pray to Him that giveth it that it may please Him to help and increase it. And let us first say with him in the Gospel: "I believe, good Lord, but help Thou the lack of my belief."[5] And after let us pray with the apostles: "Lord, increase our faith."[6]

And finally, let us . . . not suffer the strength and fervor of our faith to wax lukewarm (or rather key-cold), and in manner loose [its] vigor by scattering our minds abroad about so many trifling things that of the matters of our faith we very seldom think. . . . We [sh]ould withdraw our thought from the respect and regard of all worldly fantasies, and so gather our faith together into a little narrow room.[7] And like the little grain of mustard seed, which is of nature hot,[8] set it in the garden of our soul, all weeds pulled out for the better feeding of our faith. Then shall it grow, and so spread up in height, that the birds (that is to wit the holy angels of heaven) shall breed in our soul, and bring forth virtues in the branches of our faith.[9] And then with the faithful trust, that through the true belief of God's word we shall put in His promise, we shall be well able to command a great mountain of tribulation to void[10] from the place where he[11] stood in our heart. Whereas with a very feeble faith and a faint we shall be scant able to remove a little hillock. . . .

VINCENT: Forsooth, good uncle, methinketh that this foundation of faith, which, as you say, must be laid first, is so necessarily requisite, that without it all spiritual comfort were utterly given in vain. And therefore now shall we pray God for a full and a fast faith. And I pray you, good uncle, proceed you farther in the process of your matter of spiritual comfort against tribulation.

ANTHONY: That shall I, cousin, with goodwill.

1 This chapter, emphasizing faith, is missing from the Corpus Christi manuscript, which is one of two extant manuscripts of the *Dialogue of Comfort*. For the background of the faith vs. works issue, see David B. Knox, *The Doctrine of Faith in the Reign of Henry VIII* (1961).

2 existing in advance.

3 logical arguments.

4 James 1: 17.

5 Mark 9:23. The "him in the Gospel" is the father who asked Christ to heal his afflicted son.

6 Luke 17:5.

7 Cf. Matt. 7:13-14 (Sermon on the Mount): "Wide is the gate . . . that leadeth to destruction. . . . How narrow is the gate that leadeth to life." More is here reflecting a standard doctrine of medieval and early Renaissance mysticism, namely, that the first step in approaching God is for the soul to "collect" or contract itself away from all distracting things.

8 capable of swift germination.

9 Cf. Luke 13:18-19: "The kingdom of God . . . is like a grain of mustard

seed, which a man took and cast into his garden: and it grew and became a great tree, and the birds of the air lodged in the branches thereof." Though More's bird-tree imagery is merely a Scriptural paraphrase, his implied notion of the soul rising through faith or love to union with the angels is paralled in Pico della Mirandola's *De hominis dignitate* (*On the Dignity of Man*). See Elizabeth Forbes' translation of Pico's "Oration on Man" in *The Renaissance Philosophy of Man*, ed. Ernest Cassirer and others (1948), pp. 227-8.

10 disappear. See Matt. 17:19—"I say to you, . . . if you have faith as a grain of mustard seed, you shall say to this mountain, Remove from hence hither, and it shall remove." Cf. Mark 11:23.

11 it—i.e., the tribulation.

Chapter 3

[Man's First Comfort His Desire to be Comforted]

[ANTHONY:] I will in my poor mind assign for the first comfort the desire and longing to be by God comforted, and not without some reason call I this the first cause of comfort. For like as the cure of that person is in a manner desperate that hath no will to be cured, so is the discomfort of that person desperate that desireth not his own comfort.

And here shall I note you two kinds of folk that are in tribulation and heaviness: one sort that will seek for no comfort, another sort that will. And yet of those that will not are there also two sorts. For first, one sort there are that are so drowned in sorrow that they fall into a careless deadly dullness, regarding nothing, thinking almost of nothing, no more than if they lay in a lethargy. With [them] it may so fall that wit and remembrance will wear away, and fall even fair from them. And this comfortless kind of heaviness in tribulation is the highest kind of the deadly sin of sloth.

Another sort are there that will seek for no comfort, nor yet none receive, but are in their tribulation (be it loss or sickness) so testy, so fumish,[1] and so far out of all patience, that it booteth[2] no man to speak to them. And these are in a manner with impatience as furious as though they were in half a frenzy, and may with a custom of such fashioned behavior fall in thereto full and whole. And this kind of heaviness in tribulation is even a mischievous high branch of the mortal sin of ire.

Then is there, as I told you, another kind of folk which fain would be comforted, and yet are they of two sorts too. One sort are those that in their sorrow seek for worldly comfort; and of them shall we now speak the less, for the divers occasions that we shall after have to touch them in more places than one. But this will I here say, that I learned of Saint Bernard:[3] he that in tribulation turneth himself into worldly vanities, to get help and comfort by them, fareth like a man that in peril of drowning catcheth whatsoever cometh next to hand, and that holdeth he fast be it never so simple a stick. But then that helpeth him not. For that stick he draweth down under the water with him, and there lie they drowned both together. So surely if we custom ourself to put our trust of comfort in the delight of these peevish worldly things, God shall for that foul fault suffer our tribulation to grow so great, that all the pleasures of this world shall never bear us up, but all our peevish pleasure shall in the depth of tribulation drown with us.

The other sort [of people who seek comfort] is, I say, . . . those that long and desire to be comforted of God. And as I told you before, they have an undoubted great cause of comfort even in that point alone. . . . This mind of theirs may well be cause of great comfort unto them for two great considerations. The token[4] is that they see themself seek for their comfort where they cannot fail to find it; for God both can give them comfort, and will. He can, for He is almighty. He will, for He is all good, and hath Himself promised: "Ask and ye shall have."[5] He that hath faith (as he must needs have that shall take comfort) cannot doubt but that God will surely keep His promise. And therefore hath he a great cause to be of good comfort, as I say, in that he considereth that he longeth to be comforted by Him, which his faith maketh him sure will not fail to comfort him.

But here consider this, that I speak here of him that in tribulation longeth to be comforted by God. And it is he that referreth the manner of his comforting to God, holding himself content whether it be by the taking away or the minishment of the tribulation itself, or by the giving him patience and spiritual consolation therein. For of him that only longeth to have God take his trouble from him, we cannot so well warrant that mind[6] for a cause of so great comfort. For both may he desire that [which] never mindeth to be the better, and may miss also the effect of his desire because his request is haply not good for himself.[7] And of this kind of longing and requiring we shall have occasion farther to speak hereafter. But he which, referring the manner of his comfort unto God, desireth of God to be comforted, asketh a thing so lawful and so pleasant unto God, that he cannot fail to speed.[8] And therefore hath he, as I say, great cause to take comfort in the very desire itself.

Another cause hath he to take of that desire a very great occasion of comfort. For sith his desire is good and declareth unto himself that he hath in God a good faith, it is a good token unto him that he is not an abject, cast out of God's gracious favor, while he perceiveth that God hath put such a virtuous well-ordered appetite in his mind. For as every evil mind cometh of the world and ourself and the devil, so is every such good mind, either immediately or by the mean of our good angel or other gracious occasion, inspired into man's heart by the goodness of God Himself. And what a comfort, then, may this be unto us, when we by that desire perceive a sure undoubted token that toward our final salvation our Saviour is Himself so graciously busy about us!

1 angry.
2 profits, avails.
3 St. Bernard of Clairvaux (1090-1153), the French mystic abbot, whose poem, "De contemptu mundi," is typical of his distaste for "worldly vanities." The passage on the man drowning is similar to Bernard's sermon, *De conversione,* Chap. VIII, secs. 15-16. This data was supplied by Bruno S. James of the Collegio Universitario "John Henry Newman," Napoli.
4 sign (of reassurance).
5 Matt. 7:7.
6 guarantee that attitude.
7 I.e., such a person might either desire (and get) the removal of his tribulation, even though this is not the best solution for him; or he might not get his request at all because in God's eyes such a request is not to his benefit.
8 succeed.

Chapter 4

[Tribulation Prompts Men to Desire God's Comfort]

VINCENT: Forsooth, good uncle, this good mind of longing for God's comfort is a good cause of great comfort indeed. Our Lord in tribulation send it us. But by this I see well that woe may they be which in tribulation lack that mind and that desire . . . to be comforted by God, but are either of sloth or impatience discomfortless, or of folly seek for their chief ease and comfort anywhere else.

ANTHONY: That is, good cousin, very true, as long as they stand in that state. But then must you consider that tribulation is yet a mean to drive him from that state. And that is one of the causes for which God sendeth it unto man. For albeit that pain was ordained of God for the punishment of sins (for which they that never can now but sin can never be but ever punished in hell), yet in this world, in which His high mercy giveth men space to be better, the punishment by tribulation that He sendeth serveth ordinarily for a mean of amendment. Saint Paul was himself sore against Christ, till Christ gave him a great fall and threw him to the ground, and strake him stark blind. And with that tribulation he turned to him at the first word, and God was his physician, and healed him soon after both in body and soul by His minister Ananias, and made him His blessed apostle.[1]

Some are in the beginning of tribulation very stubborn and stiff against God, and yet at length tribulation bringeth them home. The proud king Pharaoh did abide and endure two or three of the first plagues, and would not once stoop at[2] them. But then God laid on a sorer lash that made him cry to Him for help. And then sent he for Moses and Aaron, and confessed himself a sinner and God for good and righteous, and prayed them to pray for him, and to withdraw that plague, and he would let them go. But when his tribulation was withdrawn, then was he naught again.[3] So was his tribulation occasion of his profit, and his help again cause of his harm. For his tribulation made him call to God, and his help made hard his heart again. Many a man that in an easy tribulation falleth to seek his ease in the pastime of worldly fantasies, findeth in a greater pain all those comforts so feeble, that he is fain to fall to the seeking of God's help. . . .

1 Acts 9:1-18.
2 yield because of.
3 See Exodus 7-8.

Chapter 5

[The Man Who Refuses God's Help]

[However, sometimes we find a man who, even in deep trouble, refuses to seek comfort from God. In such cases this man's friends should (a) emphasize to him that God is the chief source of comfort; (b) urge him to pray to God for a desire to seek divine comfort; (c) pray for him themselves; (d) encourage the troubled man to ask other people to pray for him.]

Chapter 6

[Impropriety of Desiring Only that Tribulation Be Removed]

VINCENT: Verily methinketh, good uncle, that this counsel is very good. . . . Howbeit, what if the man have *this* desire of God's comfort, that is to wit, that it may please God to comfort him in his tribulation by taking that tribulation from him? Is not this a good desire of God's comfort and a desire sufficient for him that is in tribulation?

ANTHONY: No, cousin, that is it not. . . . . . . A man may many times well and without sin desire of God the tribulation to be taken from him. But neither may we desire that in every case, nor yet very well in no case (except very few), but under a certain condition, either expressed or implied. For tribulations are, ye wot well, of many sundry kinds. Some [occur] by loss of goods or possessions, some by the sickness of ourself, and some by the loss of friends or by some other pain put unto our bodies, some [too] by the dread of the losing these things that we fain would save—under which fear fall all the same things that we have spoken before. For we may fear loss of goods or possessions or the loss of our friends—their grief and trouble or our own—by sickness, imprisonment, or other bodily pain. We may be troubled with the dread of death. And many a good man is troubled most of all with the fear of that thing which he that most need hath, feareth least of all, that is to wit, the fear of losing through deadly sin the life of his silly soul. . . .

But now, as I said, where the kinds of tribulation are so divers, some of these tribulations a man may pray God take from him, and take some comfort in the trust that God will so do. And therefore against hunger, sickness, and bodily hurt, and against the loss of either body or soul, men may lawfully many times pray to the goodness of God either for themself or their friend. And toward this purpose are expressly prayed many devout orisons in the common service of our Mother Holy Church. And toward our help in some of these things serve some of the petitions in the *Pater noster,* wherein we pray daily for our daily food and to be preserved from the fall in temptation and to be delivered from evil.

But yet may we not alway pray for the taking away from us of every kind of temptation. For if a man should in every sickness pray for his health again, when should he shew himself content to die and to depart from God? And that mind must a man have, ye wot well, or else it will not be well [with him]. One tribulation is it to good men to feel in themself the conflict of the flesh against the soul, the rebellion of sensuality against the rule and governance of reason, the relics that remain in mankind of old original sin, of which Saint Paul so sore complaineth in his Epistle to the Romans.[1] And yet may we not pray, while we stand in this life, to have this kind of tribulation utterly taken from us. For it is left us by God's ordinance to strive against it, and fight withal, and by reason and grace to master it, and use it for the matter of our merit.[2]

For the salvation of our soul may we boldly pray. For grace may we boldly pray, for faith, for hope and for charity, and for every such virtue as shall serve us to heavenward. But as for all other things before remembered,[3] in which is contained the matter of every kind of tribulation, we may never well make prayers so precisely but that we must express or imply a condition therein. That is to wit, that if God see the contrary better for us, we refer it whole to His will, and instead of our grief taking away, pray that God may send us of His goodness either spiritual comfort to take it gladly, or strength at the least wise to bear it patiently. For if we determine with ourself that we will take no comfort in nothing but in the taking of our tribulation from us, then either prescribe we to God that we will He shall no better turn do us, though He would, than we will ourself appoint him. Or else do we declare that what thing is best for us, ourself can better tell than He.

And therefore, I say, let us in tribulation desire His help and comfort, and let us remit the manner of that comfort unto His own high pleasure. Which when we do, let us nothing doubt but that like as His high wisdom better seeth what is best for us than we can see ourself, so shall His high sovereign goodness give us that thing that shall indeed be best. For else, if we will presume to stand to our own choice (except it so be that God offer us the choice Himself, as He did to David in the choice of his own punishment after his high pride conceived in the numbering of his people),[4] we may foolishly choose the worst.

[Then] by the prescribing unto God ourself so precisely what we will that He shall do for us—except that of His gracious favor He reject our folly—He shall for indignation grant us our own request. And after shall we well find that it shall turn us to harm. How many men attain health of body that [it] were better for their soul's health their bodies were sick still? How many get out of prison that hap on such harm abroad as the prison should have kept them from? How many that have been loath to lose their worldly goods have in keeping of their goods soon after lost their life?

So blind is our mortality and so unware what will fall, so unsure also what manner mind we will ourself have tomorrow, that God could not lightly[5] do man a more vengeance than in this world to grant him his own foolish wishes. What wit have we poor fools to wit [w]hat will serve us, when the blessed apostle himself, in his sore tribulation praying thrice unto God to take it away from him, was answered again by God, in a manner that he was but a fool in asking that request. [For] the help of God's grace in that tribulation to strength[en] him was far better for him than to take that tribulation from him.[6]

And therefore, by experience perceiving well the truth of the lesson, he giveth us good warning not to be too bold of our minds when we require aught of God, nor to be precise in our asking, but refer the choice to God at His own pleasure. For His own Holy Spirit so sore desireth our weal, that as men might say, He groaneth for us in such wise as no tongue can tell. Saith Saint Paul: "What we may pray . . . that were behovable[7] for us, cannot ourself tell; but the Spirit Himself desireth for us with unspeakable groanings."[8] . . .   . . . Be we very sure that as [this Spirit] beginneth to work with us, so (but if ourself flit from Him) He will not fail to tarry with us. And then, He dwelling with us, what trouble can do us harm? "If God be with us," saith Saint Paul, "who can stand against us?"[9]

1 Rom. 7:23—"But I see another law in my members, fighting against the law of my mind and captivating me in the law of sin that is in my members." Cf. Rom. 5:12-16, 1 Cor. 9:27, Eph. 3:16. The Renaissance was keenly aware of the conflict between soul and body, not only because of

St. Paul's teachings but also because the much admired Plato had treated that "immortal conflict" (*Laws* X, 906) in such then-popular dialogues as *Phaedo* 81, 94; the *Republic* IV, 440, IX, 588-90; and *Timaeus* 44, 90. See Miles, *Colet,* pp. 81-83.

2 Here and elsewhere (e.g., in Chapters 7 and 10, Part I), More alludes to merits needed to cancel out the demerits which have accrued to one's record as a result of misdeeds. In Catholic theology, even repentant souls must, through confession and assigned penances, work off demerits for "mortal" or deadly sins. An "indulgence," the abuse of which spurred the Reformation, was simply a partial or full exemption from the assigned penance. Demerits not cancelled through penance or indulgence in this life must be worked off in purgatory. As More notes, souls unrepentant of deadly or major sins go to hell. However, one who commits "venial" or minor sins need not confess or perform penance; release from purgatorial punishment in these cases is gained simply by genuine repentance. Souls unrepentant of venial sins go to purgatory rather than hell, because the sinner probably committed them without full reflection, knowledge, or consent. See under the appropriate headings in Donald Attwater, *A Catholic Dictionary* (1949).

3 previously mentioned.

4 2 Kings 24. In his vanity, David insisted on a census to determine how many people he ruled.

5 easily.

6 See 2 Cor. 2:9.

7 advantageous.

8 Rom. 8:26.

9 Rom. 8:31.

Chapter 7

[Tribulations Are Medicinal]

[Anthony proposes that every tribulation is a medicine or blessing in disguise, provided men accept and use it in the right spirit. This is so because God sends tribulation either to inspire us to repentance for past sin; or to prevent us from falling into potential sin; or to test our patience.]

Chapter 8

[On Those Who Suffer through Their Own Fault]

VINCENT: This seemeth me very good, good uncle, saving that it seemeth somewhat brief and short, and thereby, methinketh, somewhat obscure and dark.

ANTHONY: We shall, therefore, to give it light withal, touch every member[1] somewhat more at large. One member is, you wot well, of them that fall in tribulation through their own certain well-deserving deed open and known unto themself—as where we fall in a sickness following upon our own gluttonous feasting, or a man that is punished for his own open fault. These tribulations, lo, and such other like, albeit that they may seem discomfortable in that a man may be sorry to think himself the cause of his own harm, yet hath he good cause of comfort in them if he consider that he may make them medicinable for himself, if he himself will.

For . . . there was due to that sin, except it were purged here, a far greater punishment after this world in another place. [Yet] this worldly tribulation of pain and punishment, by God's good provision for him put upon him here in this world before [death], shall by the mean of Christ's passion (if the man will in true faith and good hope, by meek and patient sufferance of his tribulation so make it) serve him for a sure medicine to cure him. And [it will] clearly discharge him of all the sickness and disease of those pains that else he should suffer after. For such is the great goodness of Almighty God, that He punisheth not one thing twice. . . .

This punishment is put unto the man, not of his own election and free choice, but so by force as he would fain avoid it, and falleth in it against his will. And therefore seemeth [it] worthy no thank.[2] Yet so far passeth the great goodness of Almighty God the poor unperfect goodness of man, that though men make their reckoning one here with another such, God yet of His high bounty in man's account toward Him alloweth it far otherwise. . . .

A man fall[s] in his pain by his own fault, and also first against his will. Yet as soon as he confesseth his fault and applieth his will to be content to suffer that pain and punishment for the same and waxeth sorry (not . . . only [because] he shall sustain such punishment, but . . . also [because] he hath offended God and thereby deserved much more), our Lord from that time counteth it not for pain taken against his will. But it shall [then] be a marvellous good medicine and work, as a willingly taken pain, the purgation and cleansing of his soul with gracious remission of his sin, and of the far greater pain that else had been prepared therefore peradventure forever in hell. For many there are undoubtedly that would else drive forth and die in their deadly sin. Yet [they] in such tribulation, feeling their own frailty so effectually, and the false flattering world failing them so fully, turn goodly to God and call for mercy, and by grace make virtue of necessity and make a medicine of their malady, taking their trouble meekly, and make a right godly end.

Consider well the story of Achan that committed sacrilege at the great city of Jericho—whereupon God took a great vengeance upon the children of Israel, and after told them the cause and bade them to seek the fault and try it out by lots.[3] When the lot fell upon the very man that did it (being tried by the falling first upon his tribe, and then upon his family, and then upon his house, and finally upon his person), he might well see that he was deprehended[4] and taken against his will. But yet at the good exhortation of Joshua saying unto him, "Mine own son, give glory to the God of Israel, and confess and shew me what thou hast done, and hide it not," he confessed humbly the theft, and meekly took his death therefore. And [he] had, I doubt not, both strength and comfort in his pain, and died a very good man—which, if he had never come in tribulation, had been in peril never haply to have had just remorse[5] thereof in all his whole life, but might have died wretchedly and gone to the devil eternally. Thus made this thief a good medicine of his well-deserved pain and tribulation.

Consider the well-converted thief that hung on Christ's right hand.[6] Did not he, by his meek sufferance and humble knowledge of his fault, asking forgiveness of God and yet content to suffer for his sin, make of his just punishment and well-deserved tribulation a very good special medicine to cure him of all pain in the other world and win him eternal salvation? And thus I say that this kind of tribulation, though it seem the most base[7] and the least comfortable, is yet if the man will so make it a very marvel-

lous wholesome medicine, and may therefore be to the man tha
will so consider it a great cause of comfort and spiritual conso
lation.

1 every part of the argument.
2 reward (from God).
3 Joshua (Josue) 7.
4 apprehended, discovered.
5 I.e., justifying remorse: the repent ance necessary for salvation.
6 Luke 23:39-43.
7 the lowest type.

Chapter 9

[Tribulation Sent to Prevent Rather Than Punish Sin]

VINCENT: Verily, mine uncle, this first kind of tribulation hav you to my mind opened sufficiently, and therefore I pray yo resort now to the second.

ANTHONY: The second kind was, you wot well, of such tribu lation as is so sent us by God, that we know no certain cause de serving that present trouble—as we certainly know that upo such a surfeit we fell in such a sickness; or as the thief knowet that for such a certain theft he is fallen into such a certain punish ment. But yet, sith we seldom lack faults against God worthy an well deserving great punishment, indeed we may well think (an wisdom it is so to do), that with sin we have deserved it, and tha God for some sin sent it, though we certainly know not ourself fo which. . . . . . .

But yet may, then, this kind of tribulation be to some men o more sober living and thereby of the more clear conscience, some what a little more comfortable. . . . They may none otherwis reckon themself than sinners—for, as Saint Paul saith: "My con science grudgeth me not of anything, but yet am I not thereb justified."[1] And as Saint John saith: "If we say that we have no sin in us, we beguile ourself and truth is there not in us."[2] Yet . . . the cause is to them not so certain as it is to the other afore-remembered in the first kind.[3] And . . . it is also certain that God sometime sendeth tribulation for keeping and preserving a man from such sin as he should else fall in, and sometimes also for exercise of their patience and increase of merit. [Hence] great cause of increase in comfort have those folk of the clearer conscience in the fervor of their tribulation, in that they may take the comfort of a double medicine, and of that thing also that is of the kind which we shall finally speak of, that I call better than medicinable.

So let us somewhat consider how this [second type of] tribulation sent us by God is medicinable, in that it preserveth us from the sins into which we were else like to fall. If that thing be a good medicine that restoreth us our health when we lose it, as good a medicine must this needs be that preserveth our health while we have it, and suffereth us not to fall into that painful sickness that must after drive us to a painful plaster.[4] Now seeth God sometime that worldly wealth is with one that is yet good. . . . [God] foresee[s] how much weight of worldly wealth the man may bear, and how much will overcharge him and enhance his heart so high that grace should fall from him low. God of his goodness (I say) preventeth his fall, and sendeth him tribulation betime while he is yet good, to gar him ken[5] his Maker and, by less liking the false flattering world, [to] set a cross upon the ship of his heart and bear a low sail thereon, that the boisterous blast of pride blow him not under the water.[6]

Some young lovely lady, lo, that is yet good enough, God seeth a storm come toward her that would, if her wealth and her fat feeding should a little longer last, strike her into some lecherous love, and instead of her old-acquainted knight, lay her abed with a new-acquainted knave. But God, loving her more tenderly than to suffer her fall into such shameful beastly sin, sendeth her in season a goodly fair fervent fever that maketh her bones to rattle. [It] wasteth away her wanton flesh, and beautifieth her fair fell[7] with the color of a kite's claw, and maketh her look so lovely that her lover would have little lust to look upon her. And maketh her also so lusty[8] that if her lover lay in her lap, she should so sore long to break unto him the very bottom of her stomach, that she should not be able to restrain it from him, but suddenly lay it all in his neck!

Did not, as I before shewed you, the blessed apostle himself confess that the high revelations that God had given him might have enhanced him into so high pride that he might have caught a foul fall, had not the provident goodness of God provided for his remedy? And what was his remedy, but a painful tribulation, so sore that he was fain[9] thrice to call to God to take the tribulation from him?[10] And yet would not God grant his request, but let him lie therein, till Himself that saw more in Saint Paul than Saint Paul saw in himself, wist well the time was come in which He might well without his harm take it from him.

And thus you see, good cousin, that tribulation is double medicine, both a cure of the sin passed, and a preservative from the sin that is to come. . . . Howbeit, I will advise no man to be so bold as to think that their tribulation is sent them to keep them from the pride of their holiness! Let men leave that kind of comfort hardly[11] to Saint Paul till their living be like [his]; but of the remnant may men well take great comfort and good beside.

1 1 Cor. 4:4.
2 1 John 1:8.
3 I.e., to the previously mentioned kind of people who suffer tribulation as punishment because of some known sin.
4 remedy.
5 make him recognize.
6 A heavy wooden cross as ballast, combined with the use of lower sails only, would keep a ship from overturning in high wind. Through his favorite nautical metaphor, More therefore is suggesting that Christianity, with its teaching of humility, is a good antidote to unbalancing pride.
7 skin.
8 joyful. More is here being humorously ironic.
9 prompted.
10 2 Cor. 12:7-9. God afflicted Paul with severe bodily pain.
11 wholly.

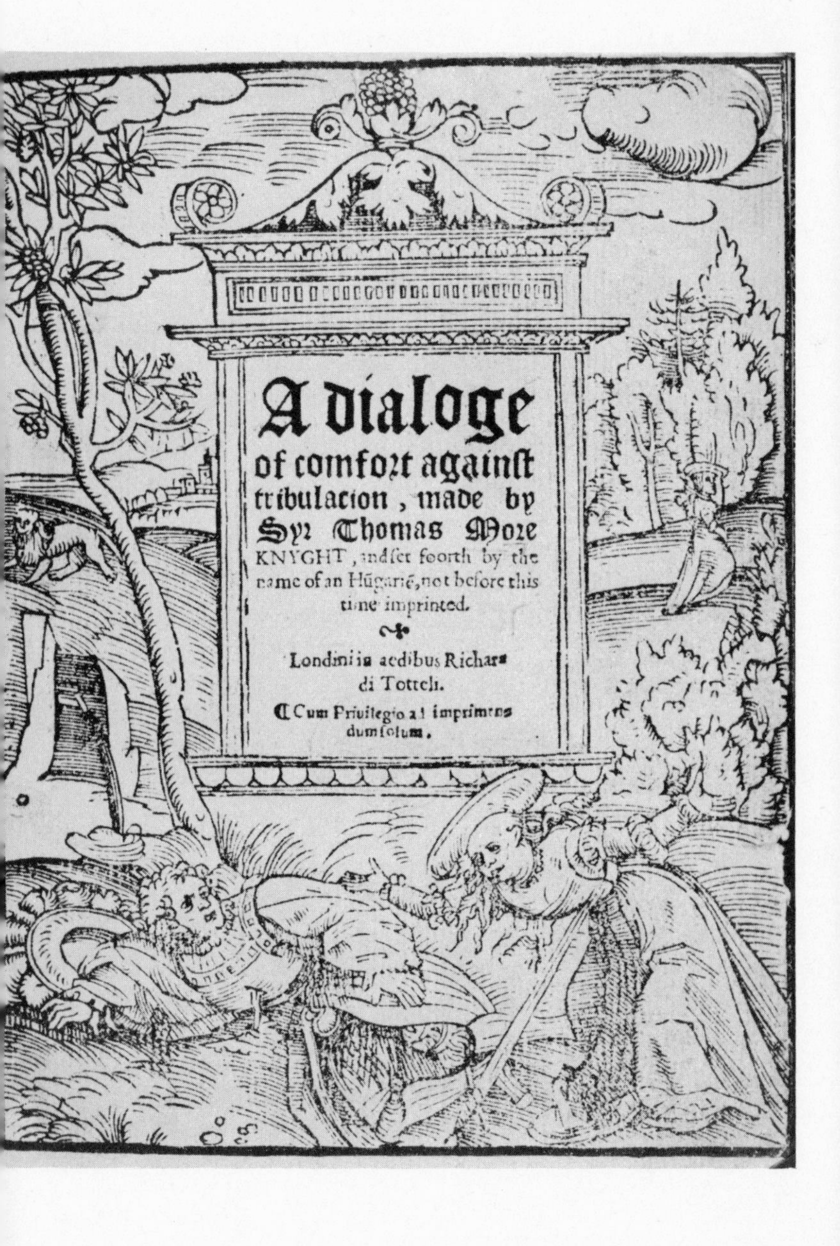

A dialoge
of comfort against
tribulacion, made by
Syr Thomas More
KNYGHT, and set foorth by the
name of an Hũgariẽ, not before this
time imprinted.

Londini in aedibus Richardi Totteli.

Cum Priuilegio ad imprimendum solum.

PLATE 2. Title page of the 1553 edition by Tottell. Reproduced, with permission, from the collection of The British Museum.

Chapter 10

[Tribulation to Test Patience and Increase Merit]

VINCENT: The third kind [of tribulation], uncle, yet remaineth now behind, that . . . is sent a man by God . . . not for his sin, neither committed nor which would else come, and therefore [is] not medicinable, but [is] sent for exercise of our patience and increase of our merit and therefore [is] better than medicinable. . . .

Yet can I not see by what reason a man may in this world, where the tribulation is suffered, take any more comfort therein than in any of the other twain that are sent a man for his sin, sith he cannot here know whether it be sent him for sin before committed, or sin that else should fall, or for increase of merit and reward after to come—namely[1] sith every man hath cause enough to fear and think that his sin already passed hath deserved it, and that it is not without peril a man to think otherwise.

ANTHONY: This that you say, cousin, hath place of truth in far the most part of men. And therefore must they not envy nor disdain (sith they may take in their tribulation consolation for their part sufficient) that some other, that more be worthy, take yet a great deal more. For as I told you, cousin, though the best must confess himself a sinner, yet be there many men—though to the multitude few—that for the kind of their living, and thereby the clearness of their conscience, may well and without sin have a good hope that God sendeth them some great grief for exercise of their patience and for increase of their merit.

[This] appeareth not only by Saint Paul, in the place before remembered,[2] but also by the holy man Job, which in sundry places of his dispicions[3] with his burdenous comforters letted not to say that the clearness of his own conscience declared and shewed to himself that he deserved not that sore tribulation that he then had.[4] Howbeit, as I told you before, I will not advise every man at adventure[5] to be bold upon this manner of comfort. But yet some men know I such, as I durst (for their more ease and comfort in their great and grievous pains) put them in right good hope that God sendeth it unto them not so much for their punishment as for exercise of their patience. And some tribulations are there also that grow upon such causes, that in those cases I would never let but alway would without any doubt give that counsel and comfort to any man.

VINCENT: What causes, good uncle, be those?

ANTHONY: Marry, cousin, wheresoever a man falleth in tribulation for the maintenance of justice, or for the defense of God's cause. For [suppose] I should hap to find a man that had long lived a very virtuous life, and had at last happed to fall into the Turk's hands, and there did abide by the truth of his faith, and with the suffering of all kind of torments taken upon his body, still did teach and testify the truth. If I should in his passion give him spiritual comfort, might I be bold to tell him no farther but that he should take patience in his pain, and that God sendeth it him for his sin, and that he is well worthy to have it although it were yet much more? He might then well answer me, and such other comforters, as Job answered his: "Burdenous and heavy comforters be you."[6] Nay, I would not fail to bid him boldly, while I should see him in his passion, cast sin and hell and purgatory and all upon the devil's pate and doubt not but, [just] as if he gave over his hold all his merit were lost, and he turned to misery; so if he stand and persevere still in the confession of his faith, all his whole pain shall turn all into glory.

Yea, more shall I yet say than this: [Suppose] there were a Christian man that had among those infidels committed a very deadly crime, such as were worthy death not by their laws only, but by Christ's too, as manslaughter or adultery or such other thing like? If when he were taken he were offered pardon of his life upon condition that he should forsake the faith of Christ,

[and] if this man would now rather suffer death than so do, should I comfort him in his pain but as I would a malefactor?

Nay, this man, though he should have died for his sin, dieth now for Christ's sake, while he might live still if he would forsake Him. The bare patient taking of his death should have served for the satisfaction of his sin—through the merit of Christ's Passion I mean, without help of which no pain of our own could be satisfactory. But now shall Christ for his forsaking of his own life in the honor of his faith forgive the pain of all his sins, [out] of His mere liberality, and accept all the pain of his death for merit of reward in heaven. [God] shall assign no part thereof to the payment of his debt in purgatory, but shall take it all as an offering, and requite it all with glory. And this man among Christian men, all[7] had he been before a devil, nothing after would I doubt to take him for a martyr.

VINCENT: Verily, good uncle, methinketh this is said marvellous well, and it specially delighteth and comforteth me to hear it, because of our principal fear that I first spake of, the Turk's cruel incursion into this country of ours.

ANTHONY: Cousin, as for the matter of that fear, I purpose to touch [that] last of all; nor I meant not here to speak thereof, had it not been that the vehemency of your objection brought it in my way. But rather would I else have put some example for this place[8] of such as suffer tribulation for maintenance of right and justice, and that rather choose to take harm than do wrong in any manner of matter. For surely . . . a man may . . . have great comfort in the clearness of his conscience, that hath a false crime put upon him and by false witness proved upon him, and he falsely punished and put to worldly shame and pain therefore. An hundred times more comfort may he have in his heart that, where white is called black and right is called wrong, abideth by the truth and is persecuted for justice.[9]

VINCENT: Then if a man sue me wrongfully for my own land in which myself have good right, it is a comfort yet to defend it well, sith God shall give me thank therefore.

ANTHONY: Nay, nay, cousin, nay, there walk you somewhat wide.[10] For there you defend your own right for your temporal avail. . . . Saint Paul counselleth: "Defend not yourself, my most dear friend.[11] And our Saviour counselleth: "If a man will strive with thee at the law and take away thy coat, leave him thy gown too."[12] The defense, therefore, of our own right asketh no reward. Say you speed well if you get leave, look hardly for no thank.[13] But on the other side, [suppose] you do as Saint Paul biddeth: "Seek not for your own profit but for other folk's."[14] [You] defend, therefore, of pity a poor widow or a poor fatherless child, and rather suffer sorrow by some strong extortioner than suffer them take wrong.

Or [suppose] you be a judge and will have such zeal to justice that you will rather abide tribulation by the malice of some mighty man than judge wrong for his favor. Such tribulations, lo, be those that are better than only medicinable. And every man upon whom they fall may be bold so to reckon them, and in his deep trouble may well say to himself the words that Christ hath taught him for his comfort: "Blessed be the merciful men, for they shall have mercy given them. Blessed be they that suffer persecution for justice, for theirs is the kingdom of heaven."[15]

Here is an high comfort, lo, for them that are in the case. And in this case their own conscience can shew it them, and so may fulfil their hearts with spiritual joy that the pleasure may far surmount the heaviness and the grief of all their temporal trouble. . . . . . .

1 especially.
2 2 Cor. 12:7?
3 disputations.
4 See Job 6, 23, 31.
5 at random.
6 Job 16:2.
7 although.
8 for this part of the discussion.
9 More must surely have been thinking here (in 1534) of his own unjust imprisonment. In the preceding sentence, the false crime attested to by "a false witness" possibly alludes to the charges that (a) More took bribes; (b) wrote against the Book of the Nine Articles; and (c) was party to treason with the Nun of Kent. See Chambers, pp. 269-71, 294-300; and Reynolds, pp. 229-30 ff. In any event, the allusion is a curious anticipation of More's own trial (July 1535), in which Solicitor-General Richard Rich apparently perjured himself by claiming that More had denied to him the

king's right to be head of the English Church (Chambers, pp. 337-9).
10 I.e., you are way off the mark; you have badly missed the point.
11 Rom. 12:19.
12 Matt. 5:40.
13 Say you succeed in the lawsuit; God will hardly reward you for that.
14 Phil. 2:3-4; cf. 1 Cor. 10:24.
15 Matt. 5:7, 10.

Chapter 11

[Another Comfort in Tribulation Sent to Punish]

[Anthony notes belatedly that the first or lowest type of tribulation (that sent to punish sin) involves a comfort he forgot to mention. If this life exists for the purpose of earning merit toward salvation, then tribulation sent to punish sin—if accepted humbly—not only compensates for punishment which would otherwise need to be suffered in purgatory, but also counts toward the merits required for entrance to heaven.]

Chapter 12

[Certain Protestant Arguments Refuted]

VINCENT: Verily, good uncle, this liketh me very well; but yet is there, ye wot well, some of these things now brought in question. For as for any pain due for our sin to be minished in purgatory by the patient sufferance of our tribulation here, there are, ye wot well, many that utterly deny that, and affirm for a sure truth that there is no purgatory at all. And then is, if they say true, the cause of the comfort gone, if the comfort that we should take be but in vain and need[ed] not. They say, ye wot well also, that men merit nothing at all, but God giveth all for faith alone, and that it were sin and sacrilege to look for reward in heaven either for our patience and glad suffering for God's sake, or for any other good deed. And then is there gone, if this be thus, the other cause of our farther comfort too.[1]

ANTHONY: Cousin, if some things were as they be not, then should some things be as they shall not. I cannot indeed say nay, but that some men have of late brought up some such opinions and many more than these besides, and have spread them abroad. . . . That is a right heavy thing, to see such variances in our belief rise and grow among ourself to the great encouraging of the common enemies of us all, whereby they have our faith in derision and catch hope to overwhelm us all. Yet do there three things not a little comfort my mind.

The first is, that in some communications had of late together, hath appeared good likelihood of some good agreement to grow together in one accord of our faith. The second, that in the meanwhile, till this may come to pass, contentions, dispicions, with uncharitable behavior, is prohibited and forbidden in effect upon all parts: all such parts, I mean, as fell before to fight for it.[2] The third is, that all Germany,[3] for all divers opinions,[4] yet as they agree together in profession of Christ's name, so agree they now together in preparation of a common power in defense of Christendom against our common enemy the Turk. And I trust in God that this shall not only help us here to strength us in this war, but also that as God hath caused them to agree together in the defense of His name, so shall He graciously bring them to agree together in the truth of His faith. Therefore will I let God work and leave off contention. And nothing shall I now say, but that with which they that are themself of the contrary mind shall in reason have no cause to be discontented.[5]

For first, as for purgatory, though they think there be none, yet . . . they deny not that all the corps of Christendom by so many hundred years have believed the contrary—and among them[6] [are] all the old interpreters of Scripture from the apostles' days down to our time, of whom they [the Protestants] deny not many for holy saints . . . . I dare not now believe these men[7] against all those. These men must of their courtesy hold my poor fear excused. And I beseech our Lord heartily for them, that when they depart out of this wretched world they find no purgatory at all, so[8] God keep them from hell!

As for the merit of man in his good works, neither are they that deny it full agreed among themself, nor any man is there almost of them all that sith they began to write hath not somewhat changed and varied from himself. And far the more part are thus far agreed with us, that . . . no good work is aught worth to heavenward without faith; and that no good work of man is rewardable in heaven of its own nature, but through the mere[9] goodness of God that lust to set so high a price upon so poor a thing. And [they agree] that this price God setteth through Christ's Passion, and [because] also that they be His own works with us—for good works to Godward worketh no man without God work with him.

And . . . we grant them also that no man may be proud of his works for his own unperfect working, [because] in all that man may do he can do God no good, but is a servant unprofitable and doth but his bare duty. As we, I say, grant unto them these things, so this one thing or twain do they grant us again: that men are bound to work good works if they have time and power, and that whoso worketh in true faith most, shall be most rewarded. But then set they thereto, that all his reward shall be given him for his faith alone, and nothing for his works at all, because his faith is the thing, they say, that forceth him to work well.

Strive will I not with them for this matter now. But yet this I trust to the great goodness of God: that if the question hang on that narrow point (while Christ saith in the Scripture in so many places that men shall in heaven be rewarded for their works),[10] He shall never suffer our souls that are but mean-witted men, and can understand His words but as Himself hath set them, and as old holy saints have construed them before, and as all Christian people this thousand year have believed, to be damned for lack of perceiving such a sharp subtle thing. Specially sith some men that have right good wits and are, beside that, right well learned too, can in no wise perceive for what cause or why these folk that from good works take away the reward and give that reward all whole to faith alone, give the reward to faith rather than to charity. For this grant they themself, that faith serveth of nothing but if she be companied with her sister charity. And then saith the Scripture too: "Of these three virtues, faith, hope, and charity, of all these three, the greatest is charity."[11] And therefore [it is] as worthy to have the thank[12] as faith.

Howbeit, as I said, I will not strive therefore; nor, indeed, as our matter standeth, I shall not greatly need. For if they say that he which suffereth tribulation or martyrdom for the faith shall have high reward, not for his work but for his well working faith, yet sith that they grant that have it[13] he shall, the cause of high comfort in the third kind of tribulation standeth. And that is, you wot well, the effect of all my purpose.

VINCENT: Verily, good uncle, this is truly driven and tried unto the uttermost, as it seemeth me. And therefore I pray you proceed at your pleasure.

1 Through Vincent, More here enumerates a number of Protestant arguments. The technique is similar to the device of the Messenger in the *Dialogue concerning Tyndale,* ed. W. E. Campbell in More's *English Works,* II, 16-18.

2 as were previously fighting over it—i.e., over the issue of purgatory and related matters.

3 the source of the heretical Lutheranism.

4 despite their various opinions (i.e., differing views).

5 The mild, tolerant tone here stands in great contrast to the virulence of More's controversial writings. In the *Dialogue concerning Tyndale,* for example, More had called Luther "a fond incestuous lecher" and "a very limb of the devil." See the Campbell ed., pp. 6-8, 220-25, 256-9, 265-72, 294-6, 319-24, and *passim.* Chambers himself has observed (p. 313) that "from the time he enters the Tower, those harsh words [against heretics] cease."

6 I.e., among those who believe in purgatory.

7 the Protestants.

8 provided. (A typical burst of More humor.)

9 simple, pure.

10 E.g., Matt. 21:28, Mark 9:40, John 9:4. Cf. James 1:14-26—"Do you see that by works a man is justified, and not by faith only?"

11 1 Cor. 13:13.

12 God's thanks or reward. In his controversial writings, More had been very sensitive on this issue. He even attacked Tyndale's New Testament for substituting "love" for "charity," arguing that in so doing Tyndale sought maliciously to disguise Catholic truth. See Campbell, More's *English Works,* I, 208-11.

13 the "high reward" of salvation.

Chapter 13

[Those Spared Tribulation Are Destined for Hell]

ANTHONY: Cousin, it were a long work to peruse every comfort that a man may well take of tribulation. . . . But meseemeth we cannot lightly better perceive what profit and commodity (and therefore what comfort) they may take of it that have it, than if we well consider what . . . discomfort the lack thereof should be to them that never have it.

So is it now that all holy men agree, and all the Scripture is full, and our own experience proveth at our eye, that we be not come into this wretched world to dwell here, nor have not, as Saint Paul saith, our dwelling city here; but we be seeking for the city that is to come.[1] And therefore Saint Paul sheweth us that we do seek for it, *because he would put us in mind that we should seek for it*[2] as they that are good folk and fain would come thither too. For surely whoso setteth so little thereby that he listeth not to seek therefore—it will, I fear me, be long ere he come thereat, and marvellous great grace if ever he come thither. Saith Saint Paul: "Run so that you may get it."[3] If it must then be gotten with running, when shall he come at it that lift not one step towards it?

Now because that this world is, as I tell you, not our eternal dwelling but our little-while wandering, God would that we should in such wise use it as folk that were weary of it, and that we should in this vale of labor, toil, tears, and misery not look for rest and ease, game, pleasure, wealth, and felicity.[4] For they that do so, fare like a fond fellow that, going towards his own house where he should be wealthy, would for a tapster's pleasure[5] become an hostler by the way, and die in a stable, and never come at home. And would God that those that drown themself in the desire of this world's wretched wealth were not yet more fools than so. But alas! their folly as far passeth the foolishness of that other fond fellow as there is difference between the height of heaven and the very depth of hell. For our Savior saith: "Woe may you be that laugh now, for you shall wail and weep."[6] Saith the Scripture: "There is time of weeping and there is time of laughing."[7] But, as you see, he setteth the weeping time before, for that is the time of this wretched world. And the laughing time shall come after in heaven.

There is also a time of sowing and a time of reaping too. Now must we in this world sow that we may in the other world reap. And in this short sowing time of this weeping world must we water our seed with the showers of our tears, and then shall we have in heaven a merry laughing harvest for ever. Saith the prophet: "They went forth and sowed their seeds weeping." But what saith he shall follow thereof? "They shall come again more than laughing, with great joy and exultation, with their handfuls of corn in their hands."[8] Lo, they that in their going home towards heaven sow their seeds with weeping shall at the day of judgment come to their bodies again with everlasting plentiful laughing.

And for to prove that this life is no laughing time, but rather the time of weeping, we find that our Savior Himself wept twice or thrice, but never find we that He laughed so much as once. I will not swear that He never did, but at the least wise He left us no ensample of it. But on the other side He left us ensample of weeping. Of weeping have we matter enough, both for our own sins and for other folks' too. For surely [this] should we do: bewail their wretched sins and not be glad to detract[9] them nor envy them neither.

Alas, silly souls, what cause is there to envy them that are ever wealthy in this world and ever out of tribulation—which, as Job saith, "lead all their days in wealth, and in a moment of an hour descend into their graves and be painfully buried in hell?"[10] Saint Paul saith unto the Hebrews that those that [God] loveth He chastiseth: "And He scourgeth every son of His that He receiveth."[11] Saint Paul saith also: "By many tribulations must we go into the kingdom of God."[12] And no marvel, for our Saviour Christ said of Himself unto His two disciples that were going into the castle of Emmaus: "Know you not that Christ must suffer and so go into His kingdom?"[13]

And would we, that are servants, look for more privilege in our Master's house than our Master Himself? Would we get into His kingdom with ease when He Himself got not into His own but by pain? His kingdom hath He ordained for His disciples, and He saith unto us all: "If any man will be my disciple, let him learn at me to do as I have done, take his cross of tribulation upon his back and follow me."[14] He saith not here, "Lo, let him laugh and make merry."

Now if heaven serve but for Christ's disciples, and they be those that take their cross of tribulation, when shall these folk come there that never have tribulation? And if it be true that Saint Paul saith that God chastiseth all them that He loveth, and scourgeth every child whom He receiveth, and to heaven shall none come but such as He loveth and receiveth—when shall they then come thither whom he never chastiseth nor never doth vouchsafe to file[15] His hands upon . . . ? And if we cannot (as Saint Paul saith we cannot) come to heaven but by many tribulations, how shall they come thither then that never have none at all?

Thus see we well by the very Scripture itself how true the words are of old holy saints, that with one voice in a manner say all one thing, that is to wit, that we shall not have both continual wealth in this world and in the other too. And therefore, . . . they that in this world without any tribulation enjoy their long continual course of never interrupted prosperity have a great cause of fear and of discomfort. . . . They [might] be far fallen out of God's favor and stand deep in His indignation and displeasure while He never sendeth them tribulation—which He is ever wont to send them whom He loveth. They therefore, I say, that are in tribulation have on the other side a great cause to take in their grief great inward comfort and spiritual consolation.

1 Heb. 13:14. More's attention was early drawn to this passage by St. Augustine, on whose *De civitate dei* (*The City of God*) More had lectured as a young man. The lectures have been lost. See the biographies of More by William Roper (p. 6) and Nicholas Harpsfield (p. 13) in the Hitchcock editions. Also Reynolds, pp. 24-25.
2 The italicized words are not found in the 1553 edition. This fact, together with similar evidence elsewhere, suggests that when Rastell set up the 1557 text, he consulted some manuscript source in addition to the 1553 printed version.
3 1 Cor. 9:24.
4 Apart from Scriptural sources which More cites in the chapter, this paragraph in particular no doubt owes something to the *De miseria humanae conditionis* (*On the Misery of the Human Condition*), otherwise called *De contemptu mundi*, by Pope Innocent III (1161-1216). It is also significant that about the time More's passage was being composed, he is recorded as linking Boethius with the *De contemptu mundi* theme. See the Letter of Margaret Roper to Alice Alington, dated August, 1534, in Rogers, *More's Letters*, p. 519.
5 as a result of drunkenness.
6 Luke 6:25.
7 Ecclesiastes 3:4.
8 Psalms 125:6-7.
9 speak ill of.
10 Job 21:13.
11 Heb. 12:6.
12 Acts 14:21.
13 Luke 24:26.
14 Matt. 16:24.
15 defile.

Chapter 14

[Priests Who Falsely Counsel Rich Men]

VINCENT: Verily, good uncle, this seemeth so indeed. Howbeit yet, methink that you say very sore[1] in something concerning such persons as are in continual prosperity. And they be, you wot well, not a few, [but] those are they also that have the rule and authority of this world in their hand. And I wot well that when they talk with such great cunning[2] men as can I trow tell the truth, and when they [the rich men] ask them [the chaplains] whether, while they make merry here on earth all their life, they may not yet for all that have heaven after too, they [the chaplains] do tell them "yes, yes, well enough." For I have heard them tell them so myself.

ANTHONY: I suppose, good cousin, that no very wise man, and specially none that very good is therewith, will tell any man fully of that fashion; but surely such as so say to them, I fear me that they flatter them either for lucre or fear. Some of them think peradventure thus: "This man maketh much of me now, and giveth me money also to fast and watch and pray for him. But so, I fear me, would he do no more if I should go tell him now that all that I do for him will not serve him, but if he go fast and watch and pray for himself too. For [suppose] I should set thereto and say farther that my diligent intercession for him should, I trust, be the mean that God should the sooner give him grace to amend and fast and watch and pray and take affliction in his own body for the bettering of his sinful soul. He would be wondrous wroth with that. For he would be loath to have any such grace at all as should make him go leave of any of his mirth, and so sit and mourn for his sin." Such mind as this, lo, have there some of those [priests] that are not unlearned and have worldly wit at will.[3] [They] tell great men such tales as perilously beguile them, rather than the flatterer that so telleth them would with a true tale jeopard to lose his lucre.

Some [chaplains] are there also that such tales tell them [rich men] for consideration of another fear. For seeing the man so sore set on his pleasure, . . . they despair any amendment of him whatsoever they should shew him. And then seeing also beside that the man doth no great harm, but of a gentle nature doth some good men some good, they pray God themself to send him grace. And so they let him lie lame still in his fleshly lusts at the pool that the Gospel speaketh of, beside the temple wherein they washed the sheep for the sacrifice.[4]

And they tarry to see the water stirred. And when his good angel coming from God shall once begin to stir the water of his heart and move him to the lowly meekness of a simple sheep, then if he call them to him they will tell him another tale, and help to bear him and plunge him into the pool of penance over head and ears. But in the meanwhile [they] fear lest when he would wax never the better, he would wax much the worse, and from gentle, smooth, sweet, and courteous wax angry, rough, froward, and sour—and thereupon be troublous and tedious to the world. [So] to make fair weather withal[5] they give him fair words for the while, and put him in good comfort, and let him for the remnant stand at his own adventure.[6]

And in such wise deal they with him as the mother doth sometime with her child . . . when the little boy will not rise in time for her but lie still abed and slug.[7] And when he is up, [he] weepeth because he hath lien so long, fearing to be beaten at school for his late coming thither. She telleth him then that it is but early days,[8] and he shall come time enough, and biddeth him: "Go, good son, I warrant thee, I have sent to thy master myself; take thy bread and butter with thee, thou shalt not be beaten at all." And thus, so she may send him merry forth at the door that he weep not in her sight at home, she studieth not much upon the matter though he be taken truly and beaten when he cometh to school.

Surely thus, I fear me, fare there many friars and state's chaplains too, in comfort giving to great men when they be loath to displease them. I cannot commend their thus doing, but surely I fear me thus they do.

1 speak very harshly.
2 knowledgeable—i.e., the chaplains and friars to whom More refers in the last paragraph of the chapter.
3 worldly knowledge at their disposal.
4 See John 5:2.
5 I.e., to keep him (the rich man) in a good mood.
6 and for the rest, let him take his chances.
7 snore, sleep.
8 still early in the morning.

Chapter 15

[Should We Pray Then for Trouble?]

VINCENT: But yet, good uncle, though that some [priests] do thus, this answereth not the full matter. For we see that the whole Church in the common service use divers collects[1] in which all men pray specially for the princes and the prelates, and generally every man for other and for himself too, that God would vouchsafe to send them all perpetual health and prosperity. And I can see no good man pray God send another [man] sorrow, nor no such prayers are there put in the priest's portas,[2] as far as I can hear.

And yet if it were as you say, good uncle, that perpetual prosperity were to the soul so perilous and tribulation thereto so fruitful, then were (as meseemeth) every man bounden of charity not only to pray God send their neighbor sorrow, but also to help thereto themself! And when folk are sick, not pray God send them health, but when they come to comfort them they should say: "I am glad, good gossip,[3] that you be so sick, I pray God keep you long therein." And neither should any man give any medicine to another, nor take any medicine himself neither, for by the minishing of the tribulation he taketh away part of the profit from his soul, which can with no bodily profit be sufficiently recompensed.

And also this, wot you well, good uncle, that we read in Holy Scripture of men that were wealthy and rich, and yet were good withal. Solomon was, you wot well, the richest and the most wealthy king that any man could in his time tell of, and yet was he well beloved with God. Job was also no beggar, pardie, nor no wretch otherwise, nor lost his riches and his wealth. . . . For proof that prosperity may stand with God's favor, "God restored him double of all that ever he lost,"[4] and gave him after long life to take his pleasure long. Abraham was eke,[5] you wot well, a man of great substance, and so continued all his life in honor and in wealth.[6] Yea, and when he died too, he went unto such wealth that Lazarus, [who] died in tribulation and poverty, the best place that he came to was that rich man's bosom.[7]

Finally, good uncle, this we find at our eye, and every day we prove it by plain experience, that many a man is right wealthy and yet therewith right good, and many a miserable wretch as evil as he is wretched. And therefore it seemeth hard, good uncle, that between prosperity and tribulation the matter should go thus:

that tribulation should be given alway by God to those that He loveth, for a sign of salvation; and prosperity sent for displeasure, as a token of eternal damnation.

1 various prayers.
2 portable breviaries.
3 friend, crony.
4 Job 42:10.
5 also.
6 See Gen. 13:2.
7 Luke 16:22.

Chapter 16

[Tribulation Can Be Spiritual As Well As Physical]

ANTHONY: Either I said not, cousin, or else meant I not to say, that for an undoubted rule worldly prosperity were always displeasant to God. . . .   . . . But this is the point, lo, that standeth here in question between you and me: not whether every prosperity be a perilous token, but whether continual wealth in this world without any tribulation be a fearful sign of God's indignation. And therefore, [with] this mark that we must shoot at set up well in our sight, we shall now mete for the shoot[1] and consider how near toward, or how far off, your arrows are from the prick.[2]

VINCENT: Some of my bolts,[3] uncle, will I now take up myself, and prettily[4] put them under my belt again. For some of them, I see well, be not worth the meting[5]—and no great marvel th[at] I shoot wide while I somewhat mistake the mark . . .   . . .

ANTHONY: First must you, cousin, be sure that you look well to the mark, and that can you not but if you know what thing tribulation is. For sith that is one of the things that we principally speak of, but if you consider well what that is, you may miss the mark again. I suppose now that you will agree that tribulation is every such thing as troubleth and grieveth a man either in body or mind, and is as it were the prick of a thorn, a bramble, or a briar thrust into his flesh or into his mind. And surely, cousin, the prick that very sore pricketh the mind as far almost passeth in pain the grief that paineth the body, as doth a thorn sticking in the heart pass and exceed in pain the thorn that is thrust in the heel.

Now, cousin, if tribulation be this that I call it, then shall you soon consider this, that there be more kinds of tribulation than peradventure you thought on before. And thereupon it followeth also that . . . every kind of tribulation is an interruption of wealth and prosperity, which . . . may be discontinued by more ways than you would before have weened. Then say I this unto you, cousin, that sith tribulation is not only such pangs as pain the body, but every trouble also that grieveth the mind, many good men have many tribulations that every man marketh not, and consequently their wealth interrupted therewith when other men are not [a]ware. For trow you, cousin, that the temptations of the devil, the world, and the flesh, soliciting the mind of a good man unto sin, is not a great inward trouble and secret grief to his heart? To such wretches as care not for their conscience, but like unreasonable beasts follow their foul affections, many of these temptations be no trouble at all, but matter of their pleasure. But unto him, cousin, that standeth in dread of God, the tribulation of temptation is so painful, that to be rid thereof or sure of the victory therein—be his substance never so great—he would gladly give more than half.

Now, if he that careth not for God think this trouble but a trifle, and [that] with such tribulation prosperity [is] not interrupted, let him cast in his mind if himself hap upon a fervent longing for the thing which get he cannot . . . , as percase his pleasure of some certain good woman that will not be caught. And then let him tell me whether the ruffle of his desire shall so torment his mind as all the pleasures that he can take beside shall for lack of that one, not please him of a pin. And I dare be bold to warrant him that the pain in resisting, and the great fear of falling that many a good man hath in his temptation, is an anguish and a grief every deal as great as his.

Now say I farther, cousin, that if this be true (as in very deed true it is) that such trouble is tribulation and thereby consequently an interruption of prosperous wealth, no man precisely meaneth to pray for [God] to keep him in continual prosperity without any manner of discontinuance or change in this world. For that prayer, without other condition added or employed, were inordinate and were very childish. For it were to pray that either they should never have temptation, or else that (if they had) they might follow it and fulfil their affection. Who dare, good cousin, for shame or for sin, [f]or himself or any man else, make this manner kind of prayer? Besides this, cousin, the Church, ye wot well, adviseth every man to fast, to watch, and pray, both for taming of his fleshly lusts, and also to mourn and lament his sin before committed, and to bewail his offense done against God. And as they did at the city of Nineveh, and as the prophet David did for their sin, [to] put affliction to their flesh.[6]

And when a man so doth, cousin, is this no tribulation to him because he doth it himself? For I wot well you would agree that it were, if another man did it against his [the victim's] will. Then is tribulation, you wot well, tribulation still, though it be taken well in worth.[7] Yea, and though it be taken too with very right goodwill, yet is pain, you wot well, pain. And therefore so it is, though a man do it himself. Then sith the Church adviseth every man to take tribulation for his sin, whatsoever words you find in any prayer, they never mean (you may be fast and sure) to pray God to keep every good man nor every bad man neither from every manner kind of tribulation. . . . . . .

Now before I meddle with your second [point], your third will I join to this. For upon this answer will the solution of your ensamples conveniently depend. As for Solomon, [he] was (as you say) all his days a marvellous wealthy king and much was he beloved with God, I wot well, in the beginning of his reign. But that the favor of God persevered[8] him, as his prosperity did, that can I not tell. And therefore will I not warrant it. But surely we see that his continual wealth made him fall first into [m]uch wanton folly in multiplying wives to an horrible number, contrary to the commandment of God given in the law of Moses; and secondly taking to wife among other such as were infidels, contrary to another commandment of God's written law also. . . .

Finally, by the mean of his miscreant wife, he fell into maintenance of idolatry himself. And of this find we no amendment or repentance, as we find of his father. And therefore, though he were buried where his father was, yet whether he went to the rest that his father did through some secret sorrow for his sin at last—that is to say, by some kind of tribulation—I cannot tell. And [I] am content, therefore, to trust well and pray God he did so. But surely we be not sure. And therefore the ensample of Solomon can very little serve you, for you might as well lay it for a proof that God favoreth idolatry as that He favoreth prosperity—for Solomon was, you wot well, [involved] in both.

As for Job, sith our question hangeth upon prosperity perpetual, the wealth of Job that was with so great adversity so sore interrupted can, as yourself seeth, serve you for no ensample. And that God gave him here in this world all thing double that he lost little toucheth my matter, which denieth not prosperity to be God's gift and given to some good men too, namely[9] such as have tribulation too.

But in Abraham, cousin, I suppose is all your chief hold,[10] because that you not only shew riches and prosperity perpetual in him, through the course of all his whole life in this world, but that after his death also. Lazarus, that poor man that lived in tribulation and died for pure hunger and thirst, had after his death his place of comfort and rest in Abraham that wealthy rich man's bosom.

But here must you consider that Abraham had not such continual prosperity, but that it was discontinued with divers tribulations: 1. Was it nothing to him, trow you, to leave his own country, and at God's sending to go into a strange land which God promised him and his seed for ever? But in all his [Abraham's] whole life He gave him . . . never a foot. 2. Was it no trouble, that his cousin Lot and himself were fain to part company because their servants could not agree together? 3. Though he recovered Lot again from the three kings, was his taking[11] no trouble to him, trow you, in the meanwhile? 4. Was the destruction of the five cities no heaviness to his heart? A man would ween "yes" that readeth in the story what labor he made to save them. 5. His heart was, I dare say, in no little sorrow when he was fain to let Abimelech the king have his wife, whom though God provided to keep undefiled and turned all to wealth, yet was it no little woe to him in the meantime.

6. What continual grief was it to his heart many a long day that he had no child of his own body begotten? He that doubteth thereof shall find it in Genesis of his own moan made to God. 7. No man doubteth but Ishmael was great comfort unto him at his birth. And was it no grief then, when he must cast out the mother and the child both?[12] 8. Isaac, that was the child of promission:[13] Although God kept his life (*that* was unlooked for), yet while the loving father bound him and went about to behead him and offer him up in sacrifice—who but himself can conceive what heaviness his heart had then?[14] I would ween in my mind (because you speak of Lazarus) that Lazarus's own death panged him not so sore. . . . . . .

But now, good cousin, let us look a little longer here upon the rich Abraham and Lazarus the poor. And as we shall see Lazarus set in wealth somewhat under the rich Abraham, so shall we see another rich man lie full low beneath Lazarus, crying and calling out of his fiery couch that Lazarus might with a drop of water falling from his finger's end, a little cool and refresh the tip of his burning tongue. Consider well now what Abraham answered to the rich wretch. "Son, remember that thou hast in thy life received wealth and Lazarus in likewise pain; but now receiveth he comfort and thou sorrow, pain, and torment."[15] . . . . . . Here was laid expressly to Lazarus no very great virtue by name, nor to this rich glutton no great heinous crime but the taking of his continual ease and pleasure without any tribulation or grief—whereof grew sloth and negligence to think upon the poor man's pain. For that [he] ever himself saw Lazarus and wist him die for hunger at his door—that laid neither Christ nor Abraham to his charge.

And therefore, cousin, this story, lo, of which by occasion of Abraham and Lazarus you put me in remembrance, well declareth what peril is in continual worldly wealth, and contrariwise what comfort cometh of tribulation. And thus as your other ensamples of Solomon and Job nothing for the matter further you, so your ensample of rich Abraham and poor Lazarus have not a little hindered you!

1 measure the (accuracy of Vincent's) shooting—i.e., ascertain how closely the arrows of Vincent's arguments have approached the target of Anthony's propositions.
2 target.
3 arrows.
4 cunningly, sneakily.
5 measure—i.e., not worth considering.
6 Jonas 3:6-8; 2 Kings 12:16.
7 self-inflicted, because deserved.
8 remained with.
9 especially.
10 strongest argument.
11 (initial) capture.
12 The foregoing episodes are treated respectively in Gen. 12:1, 13:7, 14:16, 18:17, 20:2, 15:3, and 21:10.
13 I.e., the son promised to Abraham. See Gen. 15:2-4, and 21:1-2.
14 Gen. 22:10.
15 Luke 16:25.

Chapter 17

[God Wants Us to Vanquish the Tribulation He Sends]

[Vincent admits that his arguments have been demolished, with one exception: If tribulation—whether spiritual or physical—be beneficial, he still cannot see why any man would want to pray for relief therefrom. Anthony's paradoxical answer: God sends us tribulation in the forms of famine and pestilence and storms; yet he certainly hopes we will overcome these obstacles. God sends tribulation to prompt us to pray to him for relief. When we do call on God for help, he often intervenes miraculously, as when Peter was in prison or the disciples were about to drown.]

Chapter 18

[The Perils of Witchcraft]

VINCENT: Verily, good uncle, with this good answer I am well content.

ANTHONY: Yea, cousin, but many men are there with whom God is not content, which abuse this great high goodness of His, whom neither fair treating nor hard handling can cause to remember their Maker. But in wealth they be wanton and forget God and follow their lust. And when God with tribulation draweth them toward Him, then wa[x] they wood[1] and draw back all that ever they may, and rather run and seek help at any other hand than to go set it at his. Some for comfort seek to the flesh, some to the world, and some to the devil himself.

[Take] some man that in worldly prosperity is very dull,[2] and hath deep stepped into many a dire sin—which sins, when he did them, he counted for part of his pleasure. God, willing of His goodness to call the man to grace, casteth a remorse into his mind among . . . his first sleep, and maketh him lie a little while and bethink him. Then beginneth he to remember his life, and from that he falleth to think upon his death, and how he must leave all this worldly wealth within a while behind here in this world and walk hence alone. He wotteth not whither, nor how soon, he shall take his journey thither, nor can tell what company he shall meet there. And then beginneth he to think that it were good to make sure and to be merry,[3] so that he be wise therewith lest there hap to be such black bugs indeed as folk call devils, whose torments he was wont to take for poets' tales.

Those thoughts, if they sink deep, are a sore tribulation. And surely if he take hold of the grace that God therein offereth him, his tribulation is wholesome and shall be full comfortable to remember. [For] God by this tribulation calleth him and biddeth him come home out of the country of sin that he was bred and brought up so long in, and come into the land of behest[4] that floweth milk and honey. . . .

But some men now, when this calling of God causeth them to be sad, they be loath to leave their sinful lusts that hang in their hearts, and specially if they have any such kind of living as they must needs leave off or fall deeper in sin. Or if they have done so many great wrongs that they have many mends[5] to make that must (if they follow God) minish much their money. Then are these folks, alas, woefully bewrapped;[6] for God pricketh upon them of His great goodness still. And the grief of this great pang pincheth them at the heart, and of wickedness they wry[7] away, and from this tribulation they turn to their flesh[8] for help and labor to shake off this thought. And then they mend[9] their pillow and lay their head softer, and assay to sleep. And when that will not be, then they find a talk a while with them [their wives] that lie by them. If that cannot be neither, then they lie and long for day, and then get them forth about their worldly wretchedness, the matter of their prosperity, [performing] the selfsame sinful things with which they displease God most.

And at length, with many times using this manner, God utterly casteth them off. And then they set nought neither by God nor devil: "When the sinner cometh even into the depth, then he contemneth[10] and setteth nought by nothing,"[11] saving worldly fear[12] that may fall by chance or that needs must (they wot well) fall once by death. But, alas, when death cometh, then cometh again their sorrow. Then will no soft bed serve, nor no company make him merry. Then must he leave his outward worship and comfort of his glory, and lie panting in his bed as it were on a pine bank.[13] Then cometh his fear of his evil life and of his dreadful death. Then cometh the torment, his cumbered[14] conscience and fear of his heavy judgment. Then the devil draweth him to despair with imagination of hell, and suffereth him not then to take it for a fable. And yet if he do, then findeth it the wretch no fable. Ah, woe worth the while that folk think not of this in time! . . . . . .

Some have I seen even in their last sickness, set up in their death-bed underpropped with pillows, take their playfellows to them and comfort themself with cards. And this, they said, did ease them well to put fantasies out of their heads. And what fantasies, trow you? Such as I told you right now: of their own lewd life and peril of their soul, of heaven and of hell that irked them to think of. And therefore [they] cast it out with cards-play as long as ever they might, till the pure pangs of death pulled their heart from their play and put them in the case[15] they could not reckon their game. And then left them their gameners[16] and slyly slunk away, and long was it not ere they galped[17] up the ghost. And what game they came then to, that God knoweth and not I. I pray God it were good, but I fear it very sore.

Some men are there also that do (as did King Saul) in their tribulation go seek unto the devil. This king had commanded all such to be destroyed as use the false abominable superstition of this ungracious[18] witchcraft and necromancy. And yet fell he to such folly afterward himself that ere he went to battle he sought unto a witch, and besought her to raise up a dead man to tell him how he should speed.[19] Now had God shewed him by Samuel before that he should come to naught. And he went about none amendment, but waxed worse and worse, so that God lust not to look to him. And when he sought by the prophet to have answer of God, there came none answer to him. Which thing he thought strange, and because he was not with God heard at his pleasure, he made suit to the devil, desiring a woman by witchcraft to raise up dead Samuel.

But speed had he such thereof as commonly they have all that in their business meddle with such matters. For an evil answer had he, and an evil speed thereafter: his army discomfited,[20] and himself slain. And, as it is rehearsed in Paralipomenon [First Chronicles], the tenth chapter of the first book, one cause of his fall was [that] for lack of trust in God . . . he left to take counsel of God, and fell to seek counsel of the witch against God's prohibition in the law—and against his own good deed, by which he punished and put out all witches so late afore.

Such speed let them look for that play the same part as I see many do, that in a great loss send to seek a conjuror to get their gear[21] again. . . . Marvellous things there they see sometime, but never great of their good. And many fond fools are there that when they lie sick will meddle with no physic[22] in no manner wise, nor send his water[23] to no cunning man,[24] but [instead] send his cap or his hose to a wise woman, otherwise called a witch. Then sendeth she word again that she hath spied in his hose where, when he took no heed, he was taken with a sprite[25] between two doors as he went in the twilight. But the sprite would not let him feel it in five days after, and it hath all the while festered in his body, and it is the grief[26] that paineth him so sore.

But [says the witch] let him go to no leechcraft,[27] nor any manner physic, other than good meat and strong drink, for syrups[28] should souse him up.[29] But he shall have five leaves of vallerian[30] that she enchanted with a charm, and gathered with her left hand. Let him lay those five leaves to his right thumb—not bind it fast to, but let it hang loose thereat by a green thread. He shall never need to change it. Look it fall not away, but let it hang till he be whole and he shall need no more. In such wise [perform] witches, and in such mad medicines have there many fools more faith a great deal than in God.

And thus, cousin, as I tell you, all these kind of folk that in their tribulation call not upon God, but seek for their ease and help otherwhere, to the flesh and the world and to the flinging[31] fiend—the tribulation that God's goodness sendeth [to them] for good, themself by their folly turn into their harm. And they that on the other side seek unto God therein, both comfort and profit they greatly take thereby.

1 they became furious.
2 jaded.
3 I.e., to make sure of salvation, and thus have peace of mind.

4 promise.
5 amends, penances.
6 bewildered, anxious.
7 turn, swerve.
8 family.
9 rearrange.
10 despises, scorns (everything).
11 Proverbs 18:3.
12 disaster.
13 an instrument of torture.
14 encumbered, guilty.
15 in such a (sick) condition.
16 gamesters, playfellows.
17 vomited (gave up . . . ; i.e., died).
18 lacking God's grace or favor.
19 succeed (in battle). See 1 Paralipomenon (First Chronicles).
20 defeated.
21 to recover their goods or possessions. More here begins a satiric attack on the Tudor belief in witchcraft. Readers interested in this subject should examine K. M. Briggs, *"Pale Hecate's Team." An Examination of the Beliefs on Witchcraft and Magic among Shakespeare's Contemporaries . . .* (1962).
22 laxative.
23 urine.
24 I.e., the doctor.
25 (evil) spirit.
26 infection (of the evil spirit).
27 let him not resort to draining the blood (by use of leeches).
28 medicines.
29 do him injury.
30 an herb, supposedly possessing medicinal properties.
31 raging.

Chapter 19

[Hidden Advantages of Tribulation over Wealth]

VINCENT: I like well, good uncle, all your answers herein; but one doubt yet remaineth there in my mind which riseth upon this answer that you make. And that doubt solved, I will as for this time, mine own good uncle, encumber you no further. For methink I do you very much wrong to give you occasion to labor yourself so much, in matter of some study,[1] with long talking at once. I will therefore at this time move you but one thing, and seek some other time at your more ease for the remnant.

My doubt, good uncle, is this: I perceive well by your answers gathered and considered together that you will well agree that a man may both have worldly wealth and yet well go to God. And that on the other side a man may be miserable and live in tribulation and yet go to the devil. . . . . . . If this be thus, I can perceive no cause why you should give the preeminence unto tribulation, or wherefore you should reckon more cause of comfort therein than you should reckon to stand in prosperity, but rather a great deal less, by in a manner half. Sith that in prosperity the man is well at ease and may also, by giving thank to God, get good unto his soul. Whereas in tribulation, though he may merit by patience (as in abundance of worldly wealth the other may by thank), yet lacketh he much comfort that the wealthy man hath, in that he sore is grieved with heaviness and pain. Besides this also, that a wealthy man well at ease may pray to God quietly and merrily with alacrity and great quietness of mind. Whereas he that lieth groaning in his grief cannot endure to pray nor think almost upon nothing but upon his pain.

ANTHONY: To begin, cousin, where you leave,[2] the prayers of him that is in wealth and him that is in woe, if the men be both naught, their prayers be both like. For neither hath the one lust to pray nor the other neither. And as that one is let with his pain, so is the other with his pleasure—saving that the pain stirreth him sometime to call upon God in his grief, though that man be right bad; where[as] the pleasure pulleth his [the rich man's] mind another way, though the man be meetly good.

And this point I think there are few that can (if they say true) say that they find it otherwise. For in tribulation (which cometh, you wot well, in many sundry kinds), any man that is not a dull beast or a desperate wretch calleth upon God, not hoverly[3] but right heartily, and setteth his heart full whole upon his request, so sore he longeth for ease and help of his heaviness. But when men are wealthy and well at their ease, while our tongue pattereth upon our prayers apace, good God, how many mad ways our mind wandereth the while.

Yet wot I well that in some tribulation such sore sickness there is or other grievous bodily pain, that hard it were for a man to say a long pair of Matins. And yet some that lie a-dying say full devoutly the Seven Psalms and other prayers with the priest at their aneling.[4] But those that for the grief of their pain cannot endure to do it, or that be more tender and lack that strong heart and stomach that some other have, God requireth no such long prayers of them. But the lifting up of their heart alone without any word at all is more acceptable to

Him of one in such case than long service so said as folk use to say it in health. The martyrs in their agony made no long prayers aloud, but one inch of such a prayer so prayed in that pain was worth a whole ell[5] and more, even of their own prayers prayed at some other time.

Great learned men say that Christ, albeit He was very God and as God was in eternal equal bliss with His Father, yet as man merited not for us only, but for Himself too. . . . . . . And then if it thus be, of all His holy prayers the chief seemeth me those that He made in His great agony and pain of His bitter Passion. The first [was] when He thrice fell prostrate in His agony—when the heaviness of His heart with fear of death at hand, so painful and so cruel as He well beheld it, made such a fervent commotion in His blessed body, that the bloody sweat of His holy flesh dropped down on the ground. The other were the painful prayers that He made upon the cross where, [because of] the torment that He hanged in ([from] beating, nailing, and stretching out all His limbs, with the wresting of His sinews and breaking of His tender veins, and the sharp crown of thorn so pricking Him into the head), . . . His blessed blood streamed down all His face.[6]

In all these hideous pains, in all their cruel despites, yet two very devout and fervent prayers He made: the one for their pardon that so dispiteously put Him to His pain; and the other about His own deliverance, commending His own soul unto His Holy Father in heaven. These prayers of His, among all that ever He made, made in His most pain, reckon I for the chief. And these prayers of our Saviour at His bitter Passion, and of His holy martyrs in the fervor of their torment, shall serve us to see that there is no prayer made at pleasure so strong and effectual as in tribulation.

Now come I to the touching of the reason[7] you make, where you tell me that I grant you that both in wealth and in woe some man may be naught and offend God. . . . . . . Therefore you cannot see for what cause I should give any preeminence in comfort unto tribulation. But rather [do you] allow prosperity for the thing more comfortable, and that not a little, but in manner by double, sith therein hath the soul comfort and the body both—the soul by thank given unto God for His gift, and then the body by being well at ease. . . . . . . [But] a man in prosperity, though he be bound to thank God of His gift wherein he feeleth ease, and may be glad also that he giveth thank to God, yet for that he taketh his ease here hath he little cause of comfort—except . . . the sensual feeling of bodily pleasure you lust for to call by the name of comfort. Nor I say not nay, but that sometime men use so to take it when they say: "This good drink comforteth well mine heart." But comfort, cousin, is properly taken by them that take it right rather for the consolation of good hope, that men take in their heart of some good growing toward them, than for a present pleasure with which the body is delighted and tickled for the while.

Now, though a man without patience can have no reward for his pain, yet when his pain is patiently taken for God's sake and his will conformed to God's pleasure therein, God rewardeth the sufferer after the rate of his pain. And this thing appeareth by many a place in Scripture, of which some have I shewed you and yet shall I shew you more. But never found I any place in Scripture that I remember in which, though the wealthy man thank God for His gift, our Lord promised any reward in heaven because the man took his ease and his pleasure here. . . . I speak but of such comfort as is very comfort indeed, by which a man hath hope of God's favor and remission of his sins, with minishing of his pain in purgatory or reward else in heaven. And such comfort cometh of tribulation, and for tribulation well taken; but not for pleasure, though it be well taken. Therefore of your comfort that you double by prosperity you may (as I told you) cut very well away the half.

Now why I give prerogative in comfort unto tribulation far above prosperity (though a man may do well in both), of this thing will I shew you causes two or three. First, as I before have at length shewed you out of all question, continual wealth interrupted with no tribulation is a very discomfortable token of everlasting damnation. . . . Another [point] is that the Scripture much commendeth tribulation as occasion of more profit than wealth and prosperity, not to them only that are therein, but to them too that resort unto[8] them, and therefore saith Ecclesiastes: "Better is it to go to the house of weeping and wailing for some man's death than to the house of a feast; for in that house of heaviness is a man put in remembrance of the end of every man and while he yet liveth he thinketh what shall come after."[9]

And after yet he farther saith: "[In] the heart of wise men . . . heaviness is, and [in] the heart of fools is there . . . mirth and gladness."[10] And verily, there as you shall hear worldly mirth seem to be commended in Scripture, it is either commonly[11] spoken, as in the person of some worldly disposed people; or understanden of rejoicing spiritual; or meant of some small moderate refreshing of the mind against an heavy discomfortable dullness.[12] . . . . . .

1 in a matter which requires so much reflection.
2 where you leave off—i.e., with the last point Vincent has made.
3 hesitatingly.
4 anointing—i.e., the sacrament of Extreme Unction, given at death.
5 An old English unit of length, chiefly for cloth, equal to forty-five inches.
6 Understandably, the Crucifixion was much on More's mind, and resulted in a final (unfinished) Tower work, *The History of the Passion,* published in the 1557 Rastell edition of More's *English Works,* pp. 1270-1404. The Second or Latin portion of the work, translated for Rastell by Mary Bassett, was edited by Philip E. Hallett (1941).
7 argument.
8 associate with.
9 Ecclesiastes 7:3.
10 Ecclesiastes 7:5.
11 vulgarly.
12 melancholy.

Chapter 20

[Prosperity and Tribulation: Further Comparisons]

[Anthony's arguments continue: The man in tribulation can easily wish to do the good deeds of the rich man, and thus gain merit simply for the wish. But the rich man will not easily wish for tribulation in order to earn the merit of patience. Any merit the rich man earns is by his good deeds, independent of his wealth. Many good deeds, such as living with a contrite heart, require no wealth. When a rich man gives money he is reducing his wealth and, in proportion as he gives, is moving toward poverty. It is therefore not the wealth, but the "tribulation" of giving away wealth, that earns merit. Any wicked man can thank God for riches, but it takes a good man to thank God for trouble. Therefore, more merit is attached to thanking God for tribulation than to thanking him for good fortune.This is what "the philosophers" (i.e., Aristotle, in *Nichomachean Ethics,* Book II, Sec. 3) mean when they say that "virtue standeth in things of hardness and difficulty."]

Chapter 21

[Vincent Apologizes for Arguing]

[ANTHONY (continuing):] And therefore, good cousin, to finish our talking for this time lest I should be too long a let unto your other business, if we lay first for a sure ground a very fast faith whereby we believe to be true all that the Scripture saith, understanden truly as the old holy doctors declare it and as the Spirit of God instructeth . . . , then shall we consider tribulation as a gracious gift of God, a gift that He specially gave His special friends; the thing that in Scripture is highly commended and praised; a thing whereof the contrary long continued is perilous; a thing which, but if God send it, men have need by penance to put upon themself and seek it; a thing that helpeth to purge our sins passed; a thing that preserveth us from sins that else would come; a thing that causeth us to set less by the world; a thing that exciteth us to draw more toward God; a thing that much minisheth our pains in purgatory; a thing that much increaseth our final reward in heaven; the thing by which our Saviour entered His own kingdom; the thing with which all His apostles followed Him thither; the thing which our Saviour exhorteth all men to; the thing without which He saith we be not His disciples; the thing without which no man can get to heaven. . . . . . .

Now, if God will we shall hence,[1] then doth He much more for us. For he that [cheerfully] this way taketh cannot go but well. For of him that is loath to leave this wretched world mine heart is much in fear lest he die not well. Hard it is for him to be welcome that cometh against his will, that saith unto God when He cometh to fetch him: "Welcome, my Maker, maugre my teeth."[2] But he that so loveth Him, that he longeth to go to Him, my heart cannot give me but he shall be welcome. . . .

VINCENT: Mine own good uncle, I pray God reward you, and at this time will I no longer trouble you. I trow I have this day done you much tribulation with my importune objections of very little substance. And you have even shewed me an ensample of sufferance, in bearing my folly so long and so patiently. And yet shall I be so bold upon you farther as to seek sometime to talk forth of the remnant the most profitable point of tribulation, which you said you reserved to treat of last of all.[3]

ANTHONY: Let that be hardly[4] very shortly, cousin, while this is fresh in mind.

VINCENT: I trust, good uncle, so to put this in remembrance that it shall never be forgotten with me.[5] Our Lord send you such comfort as He knoweth to be best.

ANTHONY: That is well said, good cousin, and I pray the same for you and for all our other friends that have need of comfort—for whom, I think, more than for yourself you needed of some counsel.[6]

VINCENT: I shall with this good counsel that I have heard of you do them some comfort, I trust in God, to whose keeping I commit you.

ANTHONY: And I you also. Farewell, mine own good cousin.

1 to heaven. I.e., if God decides we must die (rather than recover from sickness or escape some disaster).
2 despite my (clenched) teeth—i.e., in spite of my resistance.
3 Vincent alludes here to persecution by the Turk—a subject Anthony is reserving as a climax to the whole discussion. See Part III.
4 assuredly, definitely.
5 I.e., Vincent intends to write down what he has learned.
6 Hallett sugests, in his 1937 ed. of the *Dialogue,* p. v, that More is here alluding to his own family and friends, and that he might therefore have written the *Dialogue* more to comfort others than himself.

PLATE 3. Sketch for "The Family of Thomas More," by Hans Holbein (1527). Shown are, from the left: daughter, Elizabeth Dauncey; friend, Margaret Giggs Clement; father, Sir John More; daughter-in-law, Anne Cresacre; Sir Thomas More; son, John More; fool, Henry Patenson; daughter, Cecily Heron; daughter, Margaret Roper; and second wife, Dame Alice. Reproduced, with permission, from the Kupferstichkabinett, Kunstmuseum, Basel, Switzerland.

FAMILIA THOMÆ MORI ANGL: CANCELL:

Thomas Morus A°.50. Alicia Thomæ Mori uxor A°.57. Iohannes Morus pater A°.76. Iohannes Morus Thomæ filius A°.19. Anna Grisacria Iohannis Mori Sponsa A°.15. Margareta Ropera Thomæ Mori filia A°.22.

PLATE 4. "The Family of Thomas More," described by the critic, Stanley Morison, as "an oil copy of the Holbein watercolor" (*The Likeness of Thomas More,* London: Burns & Oates, 1963). Whether or not it is the original by Holbein, it is, at the very least, the most accurate of any known copy. Shown are, from the left: friend, Margaret Giggs Clement; daughter, Elizabeth Dauncey; father, Sir John More; daughter-in-law, Anne Cresacre; Sir Thomas More; son, John More; fool, Henry Patenson; daughter, Cecily Heron; daughter, Margaret Roper; secretary, John Harris; and second wife, Dame Alice. Ages given on the painting itself correspond to 1527. Reproduced, by permission, from the collection of The Right Honorable Lord Saint Oswald, Baron of Nostell, Yorkshire, England.

[PART II]

[*Setting*: Anthony's home, a few days later.]

Introduction

[One Good Joke Deserves Another]

VINCENT: It is to me, good uncle, no little comfort that as I came in here I heard of your folk that you have had since my last being here (God be thanked) meetly good rest and your stomach somewhat more come to you. . . . I had heard before that in respect of the great grief[1] that for a month space had holden you, you were a little before my last coming to you somewhat eased and relieved. For else would I not for no good [purpose] have put you to the pain to talk so much as you then did.

Yet after my departing from you, remembering how long we tarried together and that we were all that while in talking . . . of disease and sickness and other pain and tribulation, I was in good faith very sorry and not a little wroth with myself for mine own oversight, that I had so little considered your pain. And very feard I was till I heard other word, lest you should have waxed weaker and more sick thereafter. But now I thank our Lord that hath sent the contrary, for else a little casting back[2] were in this great age of yours no little danger and peril.

ANTHONY: Nay, nay, good cousin, to talk much (except some other pain let me) is to me little grief. A fond old man is often as full of words as a woman. It is, you wot well, as some poets paint us, all the lust of an old fool's life to sit well and warm with a cup and a roasted crab, and drivel and drink and talk. But in earnest, cousin, our talking was to me great comfort and nothing displeasant at all. For though we communed of sorrow and heaviness, yet was the thing that we chiefly thought upon not the tribulation itself but the comfort that may grow thereon. And therefore am I now very glad that you be come to finish up the remnant.

VINCENT: Of truth, my good uncle, it was comfortable to me, and hath been since to some other of your friends to whom, as my poor wit and remembrance would serve me, I did, and not needless[ly], report and rehearse your most comfortable counsel. And now come I for the remnant, and am very joyful that I find you so well refreshed and so ready thereto. But this one thing, good uncle, I beseech you heartily: that if I, for delight to hear you speak in the matter, forget myself and you both, and put you to too much pain, remember you your own ease, and when you lust to leave, command me to go my way and seek some other time.

ANTHONY: Forsooth, cousin, many words, if a man were very weak, spoken (as you said right now) without interpausing, would peradventure at length somewhat weary him. And therefore wished I the last time after you were gone, when I felt myself (to say the truth) even a little weary, that I had not so told you still a long tale alone, but that we had more often interchanged words and parted the talking between us, with ofter interparling[3] upon your part in such manner as learned men use between the persons whom they devise, disputing in their feigned dialogues.[4] But yet in that point I soon excused you, and laid the lack even where I found it, and that was even upon mine own neck. For I remembered that between you and me it fared as it did once between a nun and her brother.

Very virtuous was this lady, and of a very virtuous place and close religion,[5] and therein had been long. In all which time, she had never seen her brother. [He] was in like wise very virtuous too, and had been far off at an university, and had there taken the degree of doctor in divinity. When he was come home he went to see his sister as he that highly rejoiced in her virtue. So came she to the grate that they call (I trow) the locutory. And after their holy watchword spoken on both the sides after the manner used in that place, the one took the other by the tip of the finger—for hand would there none be wrungen through the grate. And forthwith began my lady to give her brother a sermon of the wretchedness of this world and the frailty of the flesh and the subtle sleights of the wicked fiend, and gave him surely good counsel (saving somewhat too long) how he should be well ware[6] in his living and master well his body for saving of his soul.

And yet, ere her own tale came all at an end, she began to find a little fault with him, and said: "In good faith, brother, I do somewhat marvel that you, that have been at learning so long and are doctor and so learned in the law of God, do not now at our meeting (while we meet so seldom) to me that am your sister and a simple unlearned soul, give of your charity some fruitful exhortation. . . . I doubt not but you can say some good thing yourself." "By my troth, good sister," quoth her brother, "I cannot for you, for your tongue hath never ceased, but said enough for us both!" And so, cousin, I remember that when I was once fallen in,[7] I left you little space to say aught between. But now will I therefore take another way with you, for I shall of our talking drive you to the one-half.

VINCENT: Now forsooth, uncle, this was a merry tale. But now if you make me talk the one-half, then shall you be contented far otherwise than there was of late a kinswoman of your own[8]—but which will I not tell you, guess her an you can. Her husband had much pleasure in the manner and behavior of another honest man, and kept him therefore much company, by the reason whereof he was at his meal time the more oft from home.

So happed it on a time that his wife and he together dined or supped with that neighbor of theirs, and then she made a merry quarrel to him for making her husband so good cheer out a door that she could not have him at home. "Forsooth mistress," quoth he (as he was a dry, merry man), "in my company nothing keepeth him but one [thing]. Serve you him with the same, and he will never be from you." "What gay thing may that be?" quoth our cousin then. "Forsooth, mistress," quoth he, "your husband loveth well to talk, and when he sitteth with me I let him have all the words." "All the words!" quoth she. "Marry, that am I content he shall have all the words with goodwill, as he hath ever had. But I speak them all myself and give them all to him, and for aught that I care for them so shall he have them still. But otherwise to say that he shall have them all, you shall keep him still rather than he get the half!"[9]

ANTHONY: Forsooth, cousin, I can soon guess which of our kin she was. I would we had none therein, for all her merry words, that less would let their husbands to talk.

VINCENT: Forsooth, she is not so merry but she is as good. But where you find fault, uncle, that I speak not enough: I was in good faith ashamed that I spake so much, and moved you such questions as I found (upon your answer) might better have been spared, they were so little worth. But now sith I see you be so well content that I shall not forbear boldly to shew my folly, I will be no more so shamefast, but ask you what me lust.

1 illness.
2 relapse.
3 interruptions.
4 As e.g., in Plato and especially in the Greek satirist Lucian (c. 125-c. 190 A.D.), three of whose dialogues More had translated into Latin as a young man. See Reynolds pp. 37-38. The first edition of More's efforts, together with Erasmus's translation of Lucian's *Tyrannicida,* was published in Paris in 1506 under the title *Luciani dialogo compluria opuscula ab Erasmo et Thoma Moro in latinorum linguam traductio.* In his allusion to "feigned dialogues," More might also have had in mind various Tudor works. Note Arnold C. Hills, "Some Early Tudor Dialogues Referred to by Sir Thomas More in His Controversial Works," University of London M.A. Thesis, 1938.
5 enclosed nunnery.
6 wary, alert (to temptation).
7 when I had once gotten started (talking).
8 Probably More's second wife, Dame Alice, who was a vigorous talker. See Hallett, ed., *Dialogue,* p. viii.
9 The wife's final statement is a pun. She will be glad to let her husband have all the words, but she will supply them—i.e., she will do all the talking. Rather than share even half the conversation with him, she would rather he continue to go off with his friends.

Rastell's version of this difficult passage differs from the 1553 and 1573 versions. See P. S. and H. M. Allen, *Sir Thomas More: Selections from His English Works* (Oxford: Clarendon, 1924), Notes, pp. 181-2.

Chapter 1

[A Justification for Merry Tales]

[VINCENT (continuing):] And first, good uncle, ere we proceed farther, I will be bold to move you one thing more of that we talked when I was here before. For when I revolved in my mind again the things that were concluded here by you, methought ye would in no wise that in any tribulation men should seek for comfort either in worldly thing or fleshly. Which mind, uncle, of yours seemeth somewhat hard.

For a merry tale with a friend refresheth a man much, and without any harm lighteth his mind and amendeth his courage and his stomach, so that it seemeth but well done to take such recreation. And Solomon saith, I trow, that men should in heaviness give the sorry man wine to make him forget his sorrow.[1] And Saint Thomas saith that proper pleasant talking, which is called wittiness, is a good virtue serving to refresh the mind and make it quick and lusty to labor and study again; where[as] continual fatigation would make it dull and deadly.[2]

ANTHONY: Cousin, I forgot not that point, but I longed not much to touch it. For neither might I well utterly forbear it where the cause might hap to fall that it should not hurt; and on the other side, if the case so should fall, methought yet it should little need to give any man counsel to it.[3] Folk are prone enough to such fantasies[4] of their own mind. You may see this by ourself which, coming now together to talk of as earnest sad matter as men can devise, were fallen yet even at the first into wanton idle tales. And of truth, cousin, as you know very well, myself am of nature even half a giglot[5] and more. I would I could as easily mend my fault as I well know it; but scant can I refrain it, as old a fool as I am. Howbeit, so partial will I not be to my fault as to praise it.

But [now] you require my mind in the matter, whether men in tribulation may not lawfully seek recreation and comfort themself with some honest mirth. First agree that our chief comfort must be in God, and that with Him we must begin, and with Him continue, and with Him end also. [But] a man to take now and then some honest worldly mirth, I dare not be so sore as utterly to forbid it, sith good men and well learned have in some case allowed it, specially for the diversity[6] of divers men's minds. . . .

If we were all such as would God we were and such as natural wisdom would we should be, . . . I would then put no doubt but that unto any man the most comfortable talking that could be were to hear of heaven. [But] now, God help us, our wretchedness is such that in talking a while thereof men wax almost weary and (as though to hear of heaven were an heavy burden!) they must refresh themself after with a foolish tale. Our affection toward heavenly joy waxeth wonderful cold. If dread of hell were as far gone, very few would fear God. But that[7] yet a little sticketh in our stomachs, mark me, cousin, [when] at the sermon, and commonly towards the end, somewhat the preacher speaketh of hell and heaven. Now, while he preacheth of the pains of hell, still they stand and yet give him the hearing. But as soon as he cometh to the joys of heaven, they be busking them backward[8] and flock-meal fall away.[9]

It is in the soul somewhat as it is in the body. Some are there of nature or of evil custom come to that point that a worse thing sometime more steadeth[10] them than a better. Some man if he be sick can away with no wholesome meat nor no medicine can go down with him, but if it be tempered with some such thing for his fantasy[11] as maketh the meat or the medicine less wholesome than it should be. And yet while it will be no better, we must let him have it so.

Cassianus, the very virtuous man, rehearseth in a certain collation of his that a certain holy father in making of a sermon spake of heaven and heavenly things so celestially, that much of his audience with the sweet sound thereof began to forget all the world and fall asleep.[12] Which when the father beheld, he dissembled[13] their sleeping, and suddenly said unto them, "I shall tell you a merry tale." At which word they lift[ed] up their heads and hearkened unto that; and after the sleep therewith broken, heard him tell on of heaven again. In what wise that good father rebuked then their untoward minds so dull unto the thing that all our life we labor for (and so quick and lusty toward other trifles!), I neither bear in mind nor shall here need to rehearse.

But . . . you demand me whether in tribulation men may not sometime refresh themself with worldly mirth and recreation. I can no more say but [this]: He that cannot long endure to hold up his head and hear talking of heaven, except he be now and then between (as though heaven were heaviness) refreshed with a merry foolish tale, there is none other remedy but you must let him have it. Better would I wish it, but I cannot help it.

Howbeit, let us by mine advice at the least wise make those kinds of recreation as short and as seld[om] as we can. Let them serve us but for sauce and make them not our meat. And let us pray unto God, and all our good friends for us, that we may feel such a savor in the delight of heaven, that in respect of the talking of the joys thereof all worldly recreation [will] be but a grief to think on. And be sure, cousin, that if we might once purchase the grace to come to that point, we never found of worldly recreation so much comfort in a year as we should find in the bethinking us of heaven in less than half an hour.

VINCENT: In faith, uncle, I can well agree to this, and I pray God bring us once to take such a savor in it. And surely as you began the other day, by faith must we come to it, and to faith by prayer. But now I pray you, good uncle, vouchsafe to proceed in our principal matter.

1 Proverbs 31:6.
2 See St. Thomas Aquinas (1225-1274), *Summa theologia,* II:ii:168:2, entitled "Whether There Can Be a Vir-

tue about Games?" Herein, despite contrary views noted from Ambrose and Chrysostom, Aquinas (citing support from Aristotle and Augustine) argues that "just as a man needs bodily rest for the body's refreshment, because he cannot always be at work . . . , so too is it with the soul. . . . The remedy for weariness of soul must needs consist in the application of some pleasure, by slackening the tension of the reason's study."

3 I.e., Anthony had not been enthusiastic to handle the subject: on the one hand he could hardly oppose pleasant recreation where it would do a man good; yet on the other hand there is no need to counsel men to have fun—they will do that on their own.

4 The reference is to merry tales, which are unreal fantasies in relation to heavenly truth.

5 a merry person—one addicted to excessive mirth.

6 diversion, recreation.

7 I.e., "dread of hell."

8 I.e., moving toward the rear entrance.

9 and piecemeal (i.e., in two's and three's) disappear (out the door!).

10 stands (them) in good stead.

11 fancy.

12 The story is actually told in Book V, Chap. 31 of John Cassian's (360-432?) *Institutes of the Coenobia,* rather than in the *Collations* (i.e., Conversations, Conferences).

13 ignored.

Chapter 2

[An Old Man Is Like a Candlewick]

[Anthony compares his life to a candlewick that has burned so low, people think it has gone out. But when they peer down to look at it closely, it impishly flares up and burns them on the nose. Since Anthony cannot tell what day will be his last, he must concentrate on a few important points of counsel.]

Chapter 3

[Voluntary and Involuntary Tribulation]

[There are, says Anthony, three chief kinds of tribulations: (a) those sought willingly; (b) those suffered willingly but not sought; (c) those which can't be avoided (e.g., sickness, loss of friends). In Part I he discussed the third kind, so he will now concentrate on the first and second kinds.]

Chapter 4

[Anthony's Strange Fever: A Digression]

[ANTHONY (continuing):] The first kind also will I shortly pass over too. For the tribulation that a man willingly taketh himself, which no man putteth upon him against his own will, is you wot well, as I somewhat touched the last day, such affliction of the flesh or expense of his goods as a man taketh himself or willingly bestoweth, in punishment of his own sin and for devotion to God.

Now, in this tribulation needeth he no man to comfort him. For while no man troubleth him but himself, which feeleth how farforth he may conveniently bear, [he] of reason and good discretion shall not pass that.[1] Wherein if any doubt arise, counsel [he] needeth and not comfort. The courage that for God's sake and his soul's health kindleth his heart and enflameth it thereto shall, by the same grace that put it in his mind, give him such comfort and joy therein, that the pleasure of his soul shall pass the pain of his body. Yea, and while he hath in heart also some great heaviness for his sin, yet when he considereth the joy that shall come of it, his soul shall not fail to feel then that strange case which my body felt once in great a fever.

VINCENT: What strange case was that, uncle?

ANTHONY: Forsooth, cousin, even in this same bed, it is now more than fifteen year ago, I lay in a tertian[2] and had passed,[3] I trow, three or four fits. But after fell there on me one fit out of course,[4] so strange and so marvellous, that I would in good faith have thought it impossible. For I suddenly felt myself verily both hot and cold throughout all my body. Not in some part the one and some part the other, for that had been, you wot well, no very strange thing to feel the head hot while the hands were cold. But the selfsame parts, I say, so God save my soul, I sensibly felt and right painfully too, all in one instant both hot and cold at once.

VINCENT: By my faith, uncle, this was a wonderful thing, and such as I never heard happen any man else in my day, and few men are there of whose mouths I could have believed it.

ANTHONY: Courtesy, cousin, peradventure letteth you to say that you believe it not yet of my mouth neither; and surely for fear of that, you should not have heard it of me neither, had there not another thing happed me soon after.

VINCENT: I pray you what was that, good uncle?

ANTHONY: Forsooth, cousin, this: I asked a physician or twain that then looked unto me, how this should be possible. And they twain told me both that it could not be so but that I was fallen into some slumber and dreamed that I felt it so.

VINCENT: This hap hold I little cause [for] you to tell that tale more boldly.[5]

ANTHONY: No, cousin, that is true, lo. But then happed there another [incident, namely] that a young girl in this town, whom a kinsman of hers had begun to teach physic,[6] told me that there was such a kind of fever indeed.

VINCENT: By our Lady, uncle, save for the credence of you, the tale would I not yet tell again upon that hap of the maid.[7] For though I know her now for such as I durst[8] well believe her, it might hap her very well at that time to lie because she would you should take her for cunning.[9]

ANTHONY: Yea, but then happed there yet another hap[10] thereof, cousin, that a work of Galen, *Of Different Fevers*, [wa]s ready to be sold in the booksellers' shops. In which work she shewed me then the chapter where Galen[11] saith the same.

VINCENT: Marry, uncle, as you say, that hap happed well;[12] and that maid had (as hap was)[13] in that one point more cunning than had both your physicians besides—and hath, I ween, at this day in many points more.

ANTHONY: In faith so ween I too; and that is well wared on her,[14] for she is very wise and well learned, and very virtuous too. But see now what age is. Lo, I have been so long in my tale that I have almost forgotten for what purpose I told it! Oh, now I remember me. Lo, likewise I say, as myself felt my body then both hot and cold at once, so he that is contrite and heavy for his sin shall have cause to be, and shall indeed be, both sad and glad, and both twain at once, and shall do as I remember holy Saint Jerome biddeth: "Both be thou sorry," saith he, "and be thou also of thy sorrow joyful."[15]

And thus as I began to say: Of comfort to be given unto him that is in this tribulation, that is to wit, in fruitful heaviness and penance for his sin, shall we none need to give. . . . Remember and consider well [though] the goodness of God's excellent mercy that infinitely passeth the malice of all men's sins, by which He is ready to receive every man, and did spread His arms abroad upon the cross lovingly to embrace all them that will come. [He] even there accepted the thief at his last end that turned not to God till he might steal no longer, and yet maketh more feast in heaven (a[s] one that from sin turneth) than of ninety-nine good men that sinned not at all. And therefore of that first kind[16] will I make no longer tale.

1 I.e., the man willingly performing penance is himself the best judge of how much pain he can bear, and as a matter of common sense will not task himself beyond his own endurance.
2 a fever, with recurrent fits on alternate days.
3 passed through, endured.
4 out of the ordinary.
5 I.e., this incident is hardly a sufficient basis on which to tell the tale with any expectation that it will be believed.
6 medicine.
7 I.e., were it not for Anthony's reliability, Vincent would still not believe the story; testimony given by an unlearned young girl is not sufficient evidence.
8 dare.
9 learned.
10 circumstance.
11 Galen (130-200), citizen of Asia Minor and most famous of ancient medical writers. He was physician to Marcus Aurelius.
12 I.e., that incident proved your point. (More is here having some fun with word-play.)
13 it so happened, it turned out.
14 Her talent has been well used. According to biographer Harpsfield, pp. 90-91, the subject of this story was Margaret Giggs, a close friend of More's daughter Elizabeth Dauncey. In Holbein's Basel sketch (see Plate 3, this edition) of the More family group, Margaret is the second figure from the left, leaning toward More's father, Sir John. See Stanley Morison, *The Likeness of Thomas More* (1963), pp. 18, 20, and Figure 8. In the Nostell painting (see the reproduction in this edition, Plate 4), she has been moved to the extreme left. Margaret would have had a natural interest in fevers, since she married Dr. John Clement, who was also a member of More's household. He was no doubt the "kinsman" who taught her "physic."

15 St. Jerome (340?-420), Latin Church Father who prepared the Vulgate Bible, is also remembered for his letters, selected and translated by F. A. Wright for Loeb Classical Library (1954); and for his *Histories of the . . . Fathers of the Deserts of Egypt between 250 and 400 A.D.*, trans. E. A. Budge (1909). Recent studies include Francis X. Murphy, *A Monument to Saint Jerome* (1952).

16 I.e., the kind of tribulation taken willingly as penance.

Chapter 5

[A Protest against Deathbed Repenters]

VINCENT: Forsooth, uncle, this is unto that kind [of tribulation] comfort very great.[1] And so great also that it may make many a man bold to abide in his sin even unto his end, trusting to be then saved as that thief was.

ANTHONY: Very sooth you say, cousin, that some wretches are there such that in such wise abuse the great goodness of God, that the better that He is, the worse again be they. But, cousin, though there be more joy made of his turning that[2] from the point of perdition cometh to salvation (for pity that God had and His saints all of the peril of perishing that the man stood in), yet is he not set in like state in heaven as he should have been if he had lived better before. Except it so fall that he live so well after and do so much good, that he therein outrun, in the shorter time, those good folk that yet did not so much in much longer—as it proved in the [case of] blessed apostle Saint Paul. Which of a persecutor became an apostle, and *last* of all came in unto that office, and yet in the labor of sowing the seed of Christ's faith outran all the remnant so farforth that he letted not to say of himself: "I have labored more than all the remnant have."[3]

But yet, my cousin, though God, I doubt not, . . . hireth him as well for heaven that cometh to work in His vineyard toward night (at such time as workmen leave work), . . . as He hireth him that cometh in the morning, yet may there no man upon the trust of this parable be bold all his life to lie still in sin.[4] For let him remember that into God's vineyard there goeth no man but he that is called thither. Now, he that in hope to be called toward night will sleep out the morning and drink out the day, is full likely to pass at night unspoken to, and then shall he with shrewd[5] rest go supperless to bed.

They tell of one that was wont alway to say that all the while he lived he would do what he lust, for three words when he died should make all safe enough. But then so happed it that long ere he were old his horse once stumbled upon a broken bridge. And as he labored to recover him, when he saw it would not be, but down into the flood[6] headlong needs he should [slide], in a sudden fright he cried out in the falling: "Have all to the devil!"[7] And there was he drowned with his three words ere he died, whereon his hope hung all his wretched life.

And therefore let no man sin in hope of grace, for grace cometh but at God's will. And that mind may be the let, [so] that grace of fruitful repenting shall never after be offered him, but that he shall either graceless go linger on careless, or with a care fruitless fall into despair.

1 I.e., the Crucifixion and what it signifies constitutes great comfort for those suffering the first kind of tribulation, taken willingly as penance.
2 who. The ambiguous reference is to the thief and similar people.
3 1 Cor. 5:10.
4 The vineyard parable allusion is to Matt. 20:1-16.
5 unsatisfactory.
6 water, river.
7 in modern English, "Go to hell!"

Chapter 6

[A Loud and Sweating Lutheran Preacher]

VINCENT: Forsooth, uncle, in this point methinketh you say very well. But then are there some again that say on the other side that heaviness[1] for our sins we shall need none at all, but only change our intent and purpose to do better, and for all that [sin] that is passed take no thought at all. And as for fasting and other affliction of the body, they say we should not do it, but only to tame the flesh when we feel it wax wanton and begin to rebel.

For fasting, they say, serveth to keep the body in temperance, but for to fast for penance, or to do any other good work, alms deed or other, toward satisfaction for our own sin: this thing they call plain injury to the Passion of Christ, by which only are our sins forgiven freely, without any recompense of our own. And they that would do penance for their own sins, look to be their own Christs, and pay their own ransoms, and save their souls themself.

And with these reasons, in Saxony[2] many cast fasting off and all other bodily affliction, save only where need requireth to bring the body to temperance. For other good, they say, can it none do to ourself, and then to our neighbour can it do none at all, and therefore they condemn it for superstitious folly. Now, heaviness of heart and weeping for our sins, this they reckon shame almost and womanish peevishness. Howbeit, thanked be God, their women were there now so mannish, that they be not so peevish nor so poor of spirit but that they can sin on as men do, and be neither afraid nor ashamed, nor weep for their sins at all.

And surely, mine uncle, I have marvelled the less ever since that I heard the manner of their preachers there. For, as you remember, when I was in Saxony these matters were in a manner but in a mammering,[3] nor Luther[4] was not then wedded yet, nor religious men out of their habit.[5] But suffered were those that would be of the sect freely to preach what they would unto the people.

And forsooth I heard a religious man there myself, one that had been reputed and taken for very good, and which, as far as the folk perceived, was of his own living somewhat austere and sharp. But his preaching was wonderful:[6] methink I hear him yet, his voice was so loud and shrill, his learning less than mean.[7] But whereas his matter was much part against fasting and all affliction for any penance, which he called men's inventions, he cried ever out upon them to keep well the laws of Christ, let go their peevish penance, and purpose then to mend and seek nothing to salvation but the death of Christ.

"For He is our justice," [cried the preacher,] "and He is our Savior and our whole satisfaction for all our deadly sins; He did full penance for us all upon his painful cross. He washed us there all clean with the water of His sweet side, and brought us out of the devil's danger with His dear precious blood. Leave, therefore, leave, I beseech you, these inventions of men, your foolish Lenten fasts and your peevish penances. Minish never Christ's thank,[8] nor look to save yourself. It is Christ's death, I tell you, that must save us all—Christ's death, I tell you yet again, and not our own deeds! Leave your own fasting, therefore, and lean to Christ alone, good Christian people, for Christ's dear bitter Passion."

Now, so loud and so shrill he cried Christ in their ears, and so thick he came forth with Christ's bitter Passion, and that so bitterly spoken with the sweat dropping down his cheeks, that I marvelled not though I saw the poor women weep, for he made my own hair stand up upon my head. And with such preaching were the people so brought in,[9] that some fell to break their fasts on the fasting days, not of frailty or of malice first but almost of devotion, lest they should take from Christ the thank of His bitter Passion. But when they were a while nose-led[10] in that point first, they could abide and endure after many things more—with which had he begun, they would have pulled him down.[11]

ANTHONY: Cousin, God amend that man whatsoever he be, and God keep all good folk from such manner of preachers. Such one preacher much more abuseth the name of Christ and of His bitter Passion than five hundred hazards[12] that in their idle business swear and forswear themself by His holy bitter Passion at dice. They [i.e., heretical preachers] carry the minds of the people from the perceiving of their [the preachers'] craft[13] by the continual naming of the name of Christ. And crying His Passion so shrill into their[14] ears, they[15] forget that the Church hath ever taught them that all our Penance without Christ's Passion were not worth a pea. And they make the people ween that we [Catholics] would [claim to] be saved by our own deeds without Christ's death, where[as] we confess that His only Passion meriteth incomparable more for us than all our own deeds do. But His pleasure is that we shall also take pain our own self with Him. And therefore He biddeth all that will be His disciples take their crosses on their backs as He did, and with their crosses follow him.

And where they say that fasting serveth but for temperance to tame the flesh and keep it from wantonness: I would, in good faith, have weened that Moses had not been so wild, that for the taming of his flesh he should have need to fast whole forty days together![16] No, nor Elijah neither,[17] nor yet our Savior Himself which began, and the apostles followed, and all Christendom have kept, the Lenten forty days' fast that these folk can call now so foolish. King Ahab was not disposed to be wanton in his flesh when he fasted and went clothed in sackcloth and all besprent[18] with ashes. Nor no more was in Nineveh the king and all the city, but they wailed and did painful penance for their sin to procure God to pity them and withdraw His indignation.[19] Anna, that in her widowhood abode so many years with fasting and praying in the temple till the birth of Christ, was not, I ween, in her old age so sore disposed to the wantonness of her flesh that she fasted all therefor.[20] Nor Saint Paul that fasted so much, fasted not all therefore neither.[21] . . . . . .

And therefore I marvel that they take this way against fasting and other bodily penance. And yet much more I marvel that they mislike the sorrow and heaviness and displeasure of mind that a man should take in forethinking[22] of his sin. The prophet saith: "Tear your hearts . . . and not your clothes."[23] And the prophet David saith: "A contrite heart and an humble, that is to say, a heart broken, torn, and with tribulation of heaviness for his sins laid alow under foot, shalt thou not, good Lord, despise."[24] He saith also of his own contrition: "I have labored in my wailing, I shall every night wash my bed with my tears, my couch will I water."[25]

But what should I need in this matter to lay forth one place or twain? The Scripture is full of those places by which it plainly appeareth that God looketh of duty not only that we should amend and be better in the time to come, but also be sorry and weep and bewail our sins committed before. And all the old holy doctors[26] be full and whole of that mind, that men must have for their sins contrition and sorrow in heart.

1 sorrow, contrition.
2 northern Germany, at this period a hotbed of Lutheranism.
3 in a muttering—i.e., just getting started.
4 Martin Luther (1483-1546), was repeatedly excoriated in More's *Dialogue concerning Tyndale* and other controversial works. See above, I, 12, n. 5. The British Museum possesses a letter dated 1526 (*Den wirdigen und vursichtigen heren Burgemeysteren und Rait Manen der Stat Coelln*) in which German merchants operating in London report that Sir Thomas and Cardinal Wolsey had forbidden Lutheran books to be imported into England.
5 clerical garbs.
6 astonishing.
7 mediocre, ordinary.
8 I.e., don't tarnish God's reward (by thinking you can earn it).
9 swindled.
10 The 1557 Rastell and the 1573 Fowler texts read "noseled," which Hallett interprets as a variant spelling of "nousled," the archaic word for "nursed" or "weaned." Though less colorful, Hallett's reading fits the logic and development of the sentence.
11 I.e., by swindling the people on a minor issue (i.e., the rejection of penance), the preacher softened them up for bigger heresies later on.
12 dice players, profligates.
13 trickery.
14 I.e., the people's.
15 I.e., the preachers.
16 Exodus 34:28.
17 In 3 Kings 19:8.
18 spread over, sprinkled; 3 Kings 21:27.
19 Jonas 3:6.
20 Luke 3:37.
21 In 2 Cor. 11:27.
22 contemplating.
23 Joel 2:13.
24 Psalms 50:19.
25 Psalms 6:6.
26 The pre-scholastic Church Fathers, on whom More frequently calls for support.

Chapter 7

[On Men Who Laugh at Their Sins]

[Vincent declares Anthony's verdict, that men should weep for their sins, too harsh. Some men not only find it impossible to weep, but are even inclined to laugh over their more ridiculous escapades. Anthony replies with a paradox: The man who cannot be sorry for his past sins can at least be sorry that he cannot be sorry! Moreover, the man who cannot weep obviously has little faith and an impure soul. Since only pure souls go to heaven, he should therefore stand in great fear of damnation. The non-weeper would do well to follow the counsel of John Gerson.[1] He suggested that men afflict their bodies in inverse ratio to the affliction they feel in their souls.[2] If the non-weeper will severely afflict his body, he will cry soon enough! As for the Lutherans, who argue against sorrow for sin, Anthony will not argue further with them. If they are right and all the church fathers wrong, then Anthony will cheerfully congratulate them for drinking merrily and letting Christ's Crucifixion pay the bill.]

1 John Gerson (1363-1429), French mystic and chancellor of the University of Paris.

2 More quotes Gerson as saying that "the less affliction that [a man] feeleth in his soul, the more pain in recompense let him put upon his body, and purge the spirit by the affliction of the flesh." The "quotation" is apparently a loose paraphrase from Gerson's *Sermo de poenitentia* (see the passage beginning "O quotiens impletur anima nostra limo" and ending with "deposuit vestimenta.") The passage can be found on p. 504 of Vol. V (now in press) of *Oeuvres complètes,* ed. Msgr. Glorieux (1960-). I am indebted to Msgr. Glorieux and Sister M. Thecla for this information. This is one of many examples of More's usually carefree use of sources.

Chapter 8

[The Relation of Temptation to Persecution]

[Anthony now turns to the second kind of tribulation, which he has reserved for last: the kind that is suffered willingly, even though not voluntarily sought out. He divides this tribulation into temptation and persecution. However, these are closely related, because by persecution the devil tempts us to desert Christ. Also, temptation is the devil's underground method of operating, while persecution is merely his more open method for achieving the same ends. Hence Anthony will use the term "temptation" to cover both facets of this second kind of tribulation.]

Chapter 9

[Wrestlers against Satan]

[ANTHONY (continuing):] To speak of every kind of temptation particularly by itself, this were, ye wot well, in manner an infinite thing. For under that, as I told you, fall persecutions and all. And the devil hath of his trains a thousand subtle ways, and of his open fight as many sundry poisoned darts. He tempteth us by the world; he tempteth us by our own flesh; he tempteth us by pleasure; he tempteth us by pains; he tempteth us by our foes; he tempteth us by our friends; and under color of kindred he maketh many times our next friends our most foes. For, as our Savior saith: "A man's own familiar friends are his enemies."[1]

But in all manner of so divers temptations one marvellous comfort is this, that with the more we be tempted the gladder have we cause to be. For, as Saint James saith: "Esteem it and take it, my brethren, for a thing of all joy when you fall into divers and sundry manner of temptations."[2] And no marvel, for there is in this world set up, as it were, a game of wrestling wherein the people of God come in on the one side. And on the other side come mighty strong wrestlers and wily, that is to wit, the devils, the cursed proud damned spirits. For it is not our flesh alone that we must wrestle with, but with the devil too. "Our wrestling is not here," saith Saint Paul, "against flesh and blood, but against the princes and potentates of these dark regions, against the spiritual wicked ghosts of the air."[3] . . . . . .

And then, as holy Saint Bernard saith, how couldest thou fight or wrestle therefore if there were no challenger against thee that would provoke thee thereto?[4] And therefore may it be a great comfort, as Saint James saith, to every man that feeleth himself challenged and provoked by temptation. For thereby perceiveth he that it cometh to his course to wrestle, which shall be (but if he willingly will play the coward or the fool) the matter of his eternal reward.

1 Matt. 10:36.
2 James 1:2.
3 Eph. 6:12. "Ghosts" here refers, of course, to devil-spirits.
4 Re: Bernard, see above, I, 3, n. 3.

Chapter 10

[God As a Mother Hen]

[ANTHONY (continuing):] But now must this needs be to man an inestimable comfort in all temptation (if his faith fail him not), that is to wit, that he may be sure that God is alway ready to give him strength against the devil's might, and wisdom against the devil's trains. For, as the prophet saith: "My strength and my praise is our Lord, He hath been my safeguarder."[1] . . . . . . The prophet in the . . . psalm saith farther: "With His shoulders shall He shadow thee, and under His feathers shalt thou trust."[2]

Lo, here hath every faithful man a sure promise that in the fervent heat of temptation or tribulation . . . God giveth the faithful man that hopeth in Him the shadow of His holy shoulders which are broad and large, sufficient to refrigerate and refresh the man in that heat. And in every tribulation He putteth His shoulders for a defense between. And then what weapon of the evil may give us any deadly wound while that impenetrable avis[3] of the shoulder of God standeth always between?

Then goeth the verse farther, and saith unto such a faithful ıan: "Thine hope shall be under His feathers." That is to wit, or the good hope thou hast in His help, He will take thee so near Iim into His protection that as the hen to keep her young chickens rom the kite nestleth them together under her own wings, so from he devil's claws (the ravenous kite of this dark air) will the God f heaven gather the faithful trusting folk near unto His own sides, nd set them in surety very well and warm, under the covering of is heavenly wings. . . . . . .

Here are, cousin Vincent, words of no little comfort unto every Christian man, by which we may see with how tender affection God of His great goodness longeth to gather [men] under the pro-ection of His wings. And how often like a loving hen He clucketh ome unto him even those chickens of His that willfully walk broad into the kite's danger, and will not come at His clucking. But ever the more He clucketh for them, the farther they go from Iim. And therefore can we not doubt if we will follow Him and vith faithful hope come run to Him, but that He shall in all matter of temptation take us near unto Him, and set us even under His ving. And then are we safe if we will tarry there.

For against our will can there no power pull us thence nor hurt our souls there. Saith [Job]: "Set me near unto thee, and fight gainst me whose hand that will."[4] And to shew the great safe-guard and surety that we shall have while we sit under His heav-enly feathers, the prophet saith yet a great deal farther . . . that we hall not only when we sit by His sweet side under His holy wing it in safeguard, but that we shall also under the covering of His heavenly wings with great exultation rejoice.[5]

1 Psalms 117:14.
2 Ibid., 90:4.
3 This is the first appearance of an image that is to dominate the remainder of the *Dialogue of Comfort.*
4 Job 17:3.
5 Psalms 62:8.

Chapter 11

[The Protecting Shield]

[Anthony now cites Psalms 90:5-6, a passage that is to provide the structure for the remainder of his discussion: "The truth of God shall compass thee about with a pavis [shield]. Thou shalt not be afeard of the night's fear [terror], nor of the arrow flying in the day, nor of the business walking about in the darknesses, nor of the . . . invasion of the devil in the midday." This promised shield of God's will not be a tiny one that permits a man to be protected in one spot and wounded in another. Rather it will protect the soul from all kinds of temptations. This gigantic shield, as St. Bernard observed, is the Spirit of Christ within us.[1]]

1 See St. Bernard's Sermon 5 on the Psalm *Qui habitat* in *Patrologia latina,* 183, col. 196, par. 2: "Non incongrue sane scuto comparatur gratia divinae protectionis, quod in superiori porte amplum et latum est. . . ." Bernard uses similar military metaphor in *De laudibus novae militiae.*

Chapter 12

[The Turkish "Surprise Attack"]

[ANTHONY (continuing):] First he saith: "Thou shalt not be afeard of the fear[1] of the night." By the night is there in Scripture sometime understanden tribulation, as appeareth in the thirty-fourth chapter of Job: "God hath known the works of them, and therefore shall He bring night upon them"[2]—that is to wit, tribulation for their wickedness. And well you wot that the night is of the nature self discomfortable and full of fear.

And therefore by the night's fear here I understand the tribulation by which the devil through the sufferance of God, either by himself or other that are his instruments, tempteth good folk to impatience,[3] as he did Job. But he that (as the prophet saith) dwelleth and continueth faithfully in the hope of God's help, shall so be clipped in on every side with the shield or pavis of God that he shall have no need to be afeard of such tribulation that is here called the night's fear.

And it may be also conveniently called the night's fear for two causes. The one, for that many times the cause of his tribulation is unto him that suffereth dark and unknown, and therein varieth it and differeth from that tribulation by which the devil tempteth a man with open fight and assault. . . . Another cause for which it is called the night's fear may be . . . that the night is so far out of courage[4] and naturally so casteth folk in fear, that of everything whereof they perceive every manner dread, their fantasy doubleth their fear, and maketh them often ween that it were much worse than indeed it is.

The prophet saith in the Psalter: "Thou hast, good Lord, set the darkness, and made was the night, and in the night walken all the beasts of the woods, the whelps of the lions roaring and calling unto God for their meat."[5] Now though that the lions' whelps walk about roaring in the night and seek for their prey, yet can they not get such meat as they would alway, but must hold themself content with such as God suffereth to fall in their way. And though they be not [a]ware thereof, yet of God they ask it, and of Him they have it.

And this may be comfort to all good men in their night's fear, in their dark tribulation, that though they fall into the claws or the teeth of those lions' whelps, yet shall all that they can do not pass beyond the body, which is but as the garment of the soul. For the soul itself, which is the substance of the man,[6] is so surely fenced in round about with the shield or the pavis of God, that as long as he will abide faithfully in the hope of God's help, the lions' whelps shall not be able to hurt it. For the great lion[7] himself could never be suffered to go farther in the tribulation of Job than God from time to time gave him leave.

And therefore the deep darkness of the midnight maketh men that stand out of faith, and out of good hope in God, to be in their tribulation far in the greater fear for lack of the light of faith, whereby they might perceive that the uttermost of their peril is a far less thing than they take it for. But we be so wont to set so much by our body which we see and feel, and in the feeding and fostering whereof we set our delight and our wealth, . . . that the loss of our body we take for a sorer thing and for a greater tribulation a great deal than we do the loss of our soul.

And [therefore] our Savior biddeth us that we should not fear those lions' whelps that can but kill our bodies, and when that is done have no farther thing in their power wherewith they can do us harm. But [He] biddeth us stand in dread of Him which, when He hath slain the body, is able then beside to cast the soul into everlasting fire.[8] [Yet] we be so blind in the dark night of tribulation (for lack of full and fast belief of God's word), that whereas in the day of prosperity we very little fear God for our soul, our night's fear of adversity maketh us very sore to fear the lion and his whelps, for dread of loss of our bodies.

And [yet] Saint Paul in sundry places sheweth us that our body is but as the garment of the soul.[9] Yet the faintness of our faith to the Scripture of God maketh us with the night's fear of tribulation more to dread not only the loss of our body than of our soul, but also of the very outward goods that serve for the clothing of the body. And much more foolish are we in that dark night's fear than were he that would forget the saving of his body for fear of losing his old rain-beaten cloak that is but the covering of his gown or his coat. . . .

Now, wot you well that if a man walk through a wood in the night, many things may make him afeard of which in the day he would not be afeard a whit; for in the night every bush (to him that waxeth once afeard) seemeth a thief. I remember that when I was a young man I was once in the war with the king then my master (God assoil[10] his soul), and we were camped within the Turk's ground many a mile beyond Belgrade—which would God were ours now as well as it was then.[11] But so happed it that in our camp about midnight there suddenly rose a rumor and a scry[12] that the Turk's whole army was secretly stealing upon us, wherewith our whole host was warned to arm them in haste and set themself in array to fight.

And then were scourers[13] of ours that brought those sudden tidings examined more leisurely by the council what surety[14] or what likelihood they had perceived therein. Of whom one shewed that by the glimmering of the moon he had espied and perceived and seen them himself, coming on softly and soberly in a long range all in good order—not one farther forth than the other in the forefront, but as even as a thread, and in breadth farther than he could see in length.

His fellows, being examined, said that he[15] was somewhat pricked[16] forth before them and came so fast back to tell it them, that they thought it rather time to make haste and give warning to the camp than to go nearer unto them. For they were not so far off but that they had yet themself somewhat an unperfect sight of them too.

Thus stood we watching all the remnant of the night, evermore hearkening when we should hear them come, with [whispers of] "Husht," "stand still," "methink I hear a trampling." So that at last many of us thought we heard them ourself also. But when the day was sprungen and that we saw no man, out was our scourer sent again, and some of our captains with him, to shew whereabout the place was in which he perceived them. And when they came thither they found that the great fearful army of the Turks, so soberly coming on, turned (God be thanked) into a fair long hedge standing even stone still!

And thus fareth it in the night's fear of tribulation, in which the devil, to bear down and overwhelm with dread the faithful hope that we should have in God, casteth in our imagination much more fear than cause. . . . The beast that we hear roar in the dark night of tribulation and fear it for a lion, we sometime find well afterward in the day that it was no lion at all but a silly rude roaring ass! And the thing that on the sea seemeth sometime a rock, is indeed nothing else but a mist. Howbeit (as the prophet saith), he that faithfully dwelleth in the hope of God's help, the pavis of His truth shall so fence him round about, that be it an ass, colt, or a lion's whelp, or a rock of stone, or a mist, the night's fear thereof shall he nothing need to dread.

1 terror. See Psalms 90:5.
2 Job 34:25.
3 anxiety (?). See Job 4-5.
4 I.e., is so frightening.
5 Psalms 103:20-21.
6 More here contradicts his own position, made with Gerson's support in II, 7, that "the body and the soul together make the whole man." Although Paul himself emphasized the body as a part of a man's total personality, his figure of the soul's "garment" (2 Cor. 5:1-4) confused many Christians, and lured a number of otherwise orthodox commentators (including Augustine) to accept and espouse the Platonic view that the "soul alone" is the "real man" (cf. Plato's *Republic* IV, 443; *Phaedo* 73; *Timaeus* 41-42). More, who cites Paul's garment figure in the next paragraph, has fallen into a similar dichotomy. See Miles, *John Colet,* pp. 66-70. More reaffirms the orthodox Christian position at the outset of Part III, Chap. 3.
7 Satan. See Job 4:10-11.
8 Luke 12:4-5.
9 2 Cor. 5:14. Even in this garment figure, however, Paul emphasizes that the existence of the soul apart from some type of body is a condition of unnatural "nakedness."
10 save, pardon. "The king then my master" is apparently an allusion to Louis II's father, Vladislav, King of Hungary (1490-1516).
11 See Part I, Intro., n. 19.
12 outcry, shout.
13 scouts, reconnoiterers.
14 I.e., certainty. The Council examined the scouts to determine how valid their reports were.
15 the first scout.
16 spurred, advanced. Note the first line of Spenser's *Faerie Queene*: "A gentle knight was pricking on the plain."

Chapter 13

[Cowardice, Father of Fear]

[One cause of fear is cowardice, says Anthony, whereby men embolden their enemies by running away from them. Cowardice can drive a man not only to fear, but to blasphemous anger against God for placing him in danger. Cowardice is often disguised as a false humility, whereby a man claims himself incompetent to accomplish a task which, with God's help, he could easily perform. Those who take such an attitude should remember the parable of the man who, from a faint heart, stored up his one talent and left it unspent. Cowardice is inspired by the devil, and rectified through trust in God.]

Chapter 14

[The Worry Wart: Daughter of Cowardice]

[ANTHONY (continuing):] This pusillanimity bringeth forth by the night's fear a very timorous daughter, a silly wretched girl and ever puling,[1] that is called Scrupulosity or a scrupulous conscience.[2] This girl is a meetly good posil[3] in an house, never idle but ever occupied and busy. But albeit she hath a very gentle mistress that loveth her well, and is well content with that she doth, . . . yet can this peevish girl never cease whining and puling for fear, lest her mistress be alway angry with her, and that she shall shrewdly be shent.[4] Were her mistress, ween you, like to be content with this condition? Nay, surely.

I knew such one myself, whose mistress was a very wise woman, and (which thing is in women very rare) very mild also and meek, and liked very well such service as she did her in the house. But this continual discomfortable fashion of hers [the mistress] so much misliked, that she would sometime say: "Aye, what aileth this girl? The elvish urchin weeneth I were a devil, I trow. Surely if she did me ten times better service than she doth, yet with this fantastical fear of hers I would be loath to have her in mine house."

Thus fareth, lo, the scrupulous person which frameth himself many times double the fear that he hath cause, and many times [imagines] a great fear where there is no cause at all, and of that

that is indeed no sin maketh a venial [sin], and that that is venial imagineth to be deadly.[5] And yet for all that [he] falleth in them, being namely of their nature such as no man long liveth without.[6] And then he feareth that he be never full confessed nor never full contrite, and then that his sins be never full forgiven him. And then he confesseth and confesseth again, and cumbreth himself and his confessor both. And then every prayer that he saith, though he say it as well as the frail infirmity of the man will suffer, yet is he not satisfied but if he say it again, and yet after that again. And when he hath said one thing thrice, as little is he satisfied with the last as with the first, and then is his heart evermore in heaviness, unquiet, and in fear, full of doubt and dullness,[7] without comfort or spiritual consolation.

With this night's fear the devil sore troubleth the mind of many a right good man, and that doth he to bring him to some great inconvenience. For he will, if he can, drive him so much to the fearful minding of God's rigorous justice, that he will keep him from the comfortable remembrance of God's great mighty mercy, and so make him do all his good works wearily, and without consolation or quickness.[8] . . .   . . .—My mother had, when I was a little boy, a good old woman that took heed[9] to her children; they called her Mother Maud. I trow you have heard of her.

VINCENT: Yea, yea, very much.

ANTHONY: She was wont when she sat by the fire with us to tell us that were children many childish tales. But as Plinius[10] saith that there is no book lightly[11] so bad but that some good thing a man may pick out thereof, so think I that there is almost no tale so foolish but that yet in one matter or other to some purpose it may hap to serve. For I remember me that among other of her fond tales she told us once that the ass and the wolf came upon a time to confession to the fox. The poor ass came to shrift[12] in the Shrovetide a day or two before Ash Wednesday. But the wolf would not come to confession till he saw first Palm Sunday past, and then foded yet forth farther[13] until Good Friday.

The fox asked the ass, before he began "Benedicte,"[14] wherefore he came to confession so soon, before Lent begin. The poor beast answered him again: for fear of deadly sin, if he should lose his part of any of those prayers that the priest in the cleansing days[15] prayeth for them that are confessed already. Then in his shrift he had a marvellous grudge[16] in his inward conscience that he had one day given his master a cause of anger in that that with his rude roaring, before his master arose, he had awaked him out of his sleep and bereaved him of his rest. The fox for that fault, like a good discreet confessor, charged him to do so no more, but lie still and sleep like a good son himself till his master were up and ready to go to work, and so should he be sure that he should not wake him no more.

To tell you all the poor ass's confession, it were a long work, for everything that he did was deadly sin with him, the poor soul was so scrupulous. But his wise, wily confessor accounted them for trifles, as they were, and sware after unto the badger that he was so weary to sit so long and hear him, that saving for the manner's[17] sake he had liefer[18] have sitten all that while at breakfast with a good fat goose. But when it came to the penance giving, the fox found that the most weighty sin in all his [the ass's] shrift was gluttony, and therefore he discreetly gave him in penance that he should never for greediness of his meat do any other beast any harm or hindrance, and then eat his meat and study[19] for no more.

Now, as good Mother Maud told us, when the wolf came to Father Reynard (that was, she said, the fox's name), to confession upon Good Friday, his confessor shook his great pair of beads[20] upon him, almost as big as bowls, and asked him wherefore he came so late. "Forsooth, Father Reynard," quoth he, "I must needs tell you the truth. . . . I durst come no sooner for fear lest you would for any gluttony have given me in penance to fast some part of this Lent." "Nay, nay," quoth the Father Fox, "I am not so unreasonable, for I fast none of it myself. For I may say to thee, son, between us twain here in confession, it is no commandment of God, this fasting, but an invention of man. The priests make folk fast, and put them to pain about the moonshine in the water,[21] and do but make folk fools. But they shall make me no such fool, I warrant thee, son. For I eat flesh all this Lent myself, I. Howbeit, indeed because I will not be occasion of slander, I therefore eat it secretly in my chamber, out of sight of all such foolish brethren as for their weak, scrupulous conscience would wax offended withal. And so would I counsel you to do."

"Forsooth, Father Fox," quoth the wolf, "and so (I thank God) I do as near as I can. For when I go to my meat I take none other company with me, but such sure brethren as are of mine own nature, whose consciences are not weak, I warrant you, but their stomachs as strong as mine." "Well, then, no force,"[22] quoth Father Fox. But [t]hen he heard after by his confession that he [the wolf] was so great a ravener that he devoured and spent[23] sometime so much victual at one meal as the price thereof would well find[24] some poor man with his wife and his children almost all the week. Then he prudently reproved that point in him and preached him a process of his own temperance which never used (as he said) to pass[25] upon himself the value of sixpence at a meal. . . .

"For when I bring home a goose," quoth he, "not out of the poulter's shop (where folk find them out of the feathers ready plucked and see which is the fattest, and yet for sixpence buy and choose the best), but out of the housewife's house, . . . though it be but lean and, I ween, not well worth a groat,[26] serveth it me sometime, for all that, both dinner and supper too. And therefore as for that you live of ravin, therein can I find no fault. You have used it so long that I think you can do none other, and therefore were it folly to forbid it you, and, to say the truth, against good conscience too. For live you must, I wot well, and other craft can you none.[27] And therefore (as reason is) must you live by that. But yet, you wot well, too much is too much, and measure is a merry mean,[28] which I perceive by your shrift you have never used to keep. And therefore surely this shall be your penance: that you shall all this year never pass upon yourself the price of sixpence at a meal, as near as your conscience can guess the price."

1 whining.
2 I.e., a worry-wart: one who worries exessively over whether he is doing the right thing.
3 servant.
4 harshly punished.
5 More refers here to venial or minor sins, as contrasted with the mortal or deadly sins of pride, covetousness, lust, anger, gluttony, envy, and sloth. These latter, if unrepented, send the sinner to hell. See Morton W. Bloomfield, *The Seven Deadly Sins* (1952). Note also Part I, Chap. 6, n. 2; and Part II, Chap. 15, n. 16.
6 I.e., considering the nature of sin (and of man), no one can live for very long without sinning.
7 gloom, melancholy.
8 enthusiasm. In this portrait of the moral worry wart, More might have been thinking of his son-in-law, William Roper, whose religious troubles are similarly described by biographer Harpsfield, p. 85. Note Hallett, *Dialogue,* p. viii.
9 cared for, supervised.
10 Pliny the Elder (23-79), who wrote the *Natural History*. His maxim is quoted in Book III, Epistle 5 of the *Letters* of his nephew and fellow-Roman author, Pliny the Younger (62-113). The most recent edition of the latter is *The Letters of the Younger Pliny,* trans. Betty Radice (1963). One of the few modern studies is Selatie E. Stout, *Scribe and Critic at Work in Pliny's Letters* (1954).
11 frivolously.
12 confession.
13 wasted time by excuses.
14 "Benedicte" is a form of blessing, given upon meeting.
15 Ash Wednesday and the three days following.
16 pain, guilt.
17 custom's.
18 rather.
19 yearn, brood.
20 his rosary.
21 I.e., silly, unimportant matters. Cf. a preface written by Nicholas Udall for the English translation of Erasmus's *Paraphrases* (1548): "Neither is it now any strange thing to hear gentlewomen instead of most vain communication about the moon shining in the water, to use grave and substantial talk in Greek and Latin with their husbands on godly matters."
22 no matter.
23 used up, ate up.
24 supply, furnish the expenses for.
25 exceed.
26 a former English coin worth fourpence.
27 no other technique do you know.
28 I.e., moderation is a happy way (of life). This proverb is first found in *Richard the Redeles,* II, 139, written in 1399.

Chapter 15

[The Fox, Ass, and Wolf: Maud's Tale Concluded]

[ANTHONY (continuing):] Their shrift have I shewed you as Mother Maud shewed it us. But now serveth for our matter the conscience of them both in the true performing of their penance. The poor ass after his shrift, when he waxed anhungered, saw a sow lie with her pigs well lapped in new straw, and near he drew and thought to have eaten of the straw. But anon his scrupulous conscience began therein to grudge him. For while his penance was that for greediness of his meat he should do none other body none harm, he thought he might not eat one straw there, lest for lack of that straw some of those pigs might hap to die for cold. So held he still his hunger till one brought him meat.

But when he should fall thereto, then fell he yet in a far farther scruple. For then it came in his mind that he should yet break his penance if he should eat any of that either, sith he was commanded by his ghostly father[1] that he should not for his own meat hinder any other beast. For he thought that if he eat not that meat some other beast might hap to have it, and so should he by the eating of it peradventure hinder another. And thus stood he still fasting till, when he told the cause, his ghostly father came and informed him better, and then he cast off that scruple and fell mannerly to his meat, and was a right honest ass many a fair day after.

The wolf now coming from shrift, clean soiled[2] from his sins, went about to do as a shrewd[3] wife once told her husband that she would do when she came from shrift. "Be merry, man," quoth she now, "for this day I thank God was I well shriven.[4] And I purpose now therefore to leave of all mine old shrewdness and begin even afresh."

VINCENT: Ah, well, uncle, can you report her so? That word heard I her speak, but she said it in sport to make her goodman laugh.

ANTHONY: Indeed it seemed she spake it half in sport. For that she said she would cast away all her old shrewdness, therein I trow she sported. But in that she said she would begin it all afresh, her husband found that good earnest.

VINCENT: Well I shall shew her what you say, I warrant you.

ANTHONY: Then will you make me make my word good![5] But whatsoever she did, at the least wise so fared now this wolf which had cast out in confession all his old ravin. And then hunger pricked him forward that (as the shrewd wife said) he should begin all afresh. But yet the prick of conscience withdrew and held him back, because he would not for breaking of his penance take any prey for his mealtide that should pass the price of six-pence.

It happed him, then, as he walked prowling for his gear[6] about, he came where a man had in few days before cast off two old lean and lame horses, so sick that no flesh was there left upon them. And the one, when the wolf came by, could scant stand on his legs, and the other already dead and his skin ript off and carried away. And as he looked upon them suddenly, he was first about to feed upon them and whet his teeth on their bones. But as he looked aside he spied a fair cow in a close,[7] walking with her young calf by her side. And as soon as he saw them his conscience began to grudge him against both those two horses. And then he sighed and said unto himself: "Alas, wicked wretch that I am, I had almost broken my penance ere I was [a]ware. For yonder dead horse, because I never saw no dead horse sold in the market, . . . I cannot devise what price I should set upon him. But in my conscience I set him far above sixpence, and therefore I dare not meddle with him. Now then is yonder quick[8] horse of likelihood worth a great deal of money. For horse[s] be dear in this country, specially such soft amblers,[9] for I see by his pace he trotteth not nor can scant shift a foot.[10] And therefore I may not meddle with him, for he very far passeth my sixpence.

But kine this country here hath enough. . . . Yonder peevish cow seemeth unto me in my conscience worth not past a groat, an she be worth so much. Now then, as for her calf, is not so much as she by half. And therefore while the cow is in my conscience worth but fourpence, my conscience cannot serve me for sin of my soul to appraise her calf above twopence; and so pass they not sixpence between them both. And therefore them twain may I well eat at this one meal and break not my penance at all. And so thereupon he did, without any scruple of conscience.

If such beasts could speak now (as Mother Maud said they could then) some of them would, I ween, tell a tale almost as wise as this—wherein save for the minishing[11] of old Mother Maud's tale, else would a shorter process have served. But yet as peevish as the parable is, in this it serveth for our purpose, that the night's fear of a conscience somewhat scrupulous, though it be painful and troublous to him that hath it like as this poor ass had here, is less harm yet than a conscience over large, or such as for his own fantasy the man list to frame himself, now drawing it narrow, now stretching it in breadth, after the manner of a cheverel point,[12] to serve on every side for his own commodity, as did here the wily wolf.

But such folk are out of tribulation, and comfort need they none, and therefore are they out of our matter. But those that are in the night's fear of their own scrupulous conscience, let them be well ware, as I said, that the devil for weariness of the one draw them not into the other, and while he would fly from Scylla dr[a]w him into Charybdis.[13] He must do as doth a ship that should come into an haven in the mouth whereof lie secret rocks under the water on both sides. If he be by mishap entered in among them that are on the one side and cannot tell how to get out, he must get a substantial cunning pilot that so can conduct him from the rocks on that side that yet he bring him not into those that are on the other side, but can guide him in the mid way.

Let them, I say therefore, that are in the troublous fear of their own scrupulous conscience, submit the rule of their own conscience to the counsel of some other good man which after[14] the variety and the nature of the scruples, may temper his advice. Yea, although a man be very well learned himself, yet let him in this case learn the custom used among physicians. For be one of them never so cunning, yet in his own disease and sickness he never useth to trust all to himself, but sendeth for such of his fellows as he knoweth meet, and putteth himself in their hands. For . . . upon some tokens[15] he may conceive in his own passion a great deal more than needeth and than were good for his health. Th[us] for the time [it were better] he know no such thing at all.

I knew once in this town one of the most cunning men in that faculty and the best expert and therewith the most famous too, and he that the greatest cures did upon other men. And yet when he was himself once very sore sick I heard his fellows that then looked unto him . . . wish . . . that for the time of his own sickness, being so sore as it was, he had known no physic at all. He took so great heed unto every suspicious token, and feared so far the worst, that his fear did him sometime much more harm than the sickness gave him cause.

And therefore, as I say, whoso hath such a trouble of his scrupulous conscience, let him for a while forbear the judgment of himself and follow the counsel of some other whom he knoweth for well learned and virtuous, and specially in the place of confession. For there is God specially present with His grace assisting His sacrament.[16] And let him not doubt to acquiet his mind, and follow [w]hat he there is bidden. . . . Then shall he find, without any doubt, that the pavis of God's truth shall, as the prophet saith, so compass him about, that he shall not dread this night's fear of scrupulosity, but shall have afterward his conscience stablished in good quiet and rest.

1 his spiritual father—i.e., the priest or confessor.
2 absolved, pardoned.
3 shrewish, abusive.
4 cleansed (of her sins through the absolution pronounced by the priest).
5 I.e., then you will find out I was telling the truth! According to Harpsfield, p. 94, the wife who, once pardoned for abusiveness, declared she could therefore start all over again, was More's wife, Dame Alice.
6 livelihood, provisions.
7 enclosed pasture.
8 live, as in "the quick and the dead."
9 such easy-riding horses.
10 I.e., the horse is a pacer, whose hooves strike the ground together, rather than a trotter, which provides a rough ride.
11 cutting short, disregarding.
12 a piece of (elastic) kid leather.
13 I.e., those who are wearied by their own excessive worry might be tempted to escape to the other extreme, namely a too lenient conscience which worries over nothing. "Scylla" and "Charybdis" are a rock and whirlpool off the Italian and Sicilian coasts, respectively. Both were personified by the ancients as female monsters. See e.g., Homer's *Odyssey,* Book XII, where Scylla has six heads which yelp terribly, while Charybdis thrice daily sucks down black water and spouts it forth.
14 in accordance with.
15 symptoms.
16 The sacrament of Penance, which consists of: (a) repentance; (b) confession; (c) absolution—i.e., forgiveness and remission of sin; and (d) penance proper—i.e., assignment of temporal punishment to work off demerits which must otherwise be worked off in purgatory. See Part I, Chap. 6, n. 2.

Chapter 16

[The Temptation to Kill Oneself]

VINCENT: Verily, good uncle, you have in my mind well declared these kinds of the night's fear.

ANTHONY: Surely: cousin; but yet are there many more than I can either remember or find. Howbeit, one yet cometh now to my mind, of which I before nothing thought, and which is yet, in mine opinion, of all the other fears the most horrible. That is to wit, cousin, where the devil tempteth a man to kill and destroy himself.

VINCENT: Undoubtedly this kind of tribulation is marvellous and strange, and the temptation is of such a sort that some men have opinion that such as once fall in that fantasy can never full cast it off.

ANTHONY: Yes, yes, cousin, many an hundred, and else God forbid. But the thing that maketh men so say is because, that of those which finally do destroy themself, there is much speech and much wondering—as it is well worthy.[1] But many a good man and woman hath sometime, yea divers years each after other,[2] continually been tempted thereto, and yet have by grace and good counsel well and virtuously withstood it, and been in conclusion clearly delivered of it, and their tribulation nothing known abroad, and therefore nothing talked of. But surely, cousin, an horrible sore trouble it is to any man or woman that the devil tempteth therewith. Many have I heard of, and with some have I talked myself, that have been sore [en]cumbered with that temptation, and marked have I not a little the manner of them.

VINCENT: I require you, good uncle, shew me somewhat of such things as you perceive therein. For first, where you call this kind of temptation the daughter of pusillanimity, and thereby so near of sib[3] unto the night's fear, methinketh on the other side that it is rather a thing that cometh of a great courage and boldness, when they dare [with] their own hands put themself to death. From [death] we see almost every man shrink and fly, and that many such as we know by good proof and plain experience for men of great heart and excellent hardy courage.

ANTHONY: I said, cousin Vincent, that of pusillanimity cometh this temptation, . . . but yet I meant it not that of only faint heart and fear it cometh and groweth alway. For the devil tempteth sundry folks by sundry ways. But the cause wherefore I spake of none other kind of that temptation than of only that which is the daughter that the devil begetteth upon pusillanimity, was . . . that those other kinds of the temptation fall not under the nature of tribulation and fear. And therefore fall they far out of our matter here. . . . The persons therewith tempted be with that kind of temptation not troubled in their mind, but verily well content, both in the tempting and following.

For some hath there been, cousin, such that they have been tempted thereto by mean of a foolish pride, and some by the mean of anger without any dread at all, and very glad to go thereto. To this I say not nay. But where you ween that none fall thereto by fear, but that they have all a strong mighty stomach, that shall you well see the contrary, and that peradventure in those of whom you would ween the stomach most strong and their heart and courage most hardy.

VINCENT: Yet is it marvel, uncle, unto me that it should be as you say it is: that this temptation is unto them that do it for pride or for anger no tribulation, nor that they should need in so great a distress (and peril both of body and soul to be lost) no manner of good ghostly comfort.

ANTHONY: Let us therefore, cousin, consider a sample or two, for thereby shall we the better perceive it. There was in Buda-[pest],[4] in King Ladislaus's days, a good, poor, honest man's wife. This woman was so fiendish that the devil, perceiving her nature, put her in the mind that she should anger her husband so sore that she might give him occasion to kill her, and then should he be hanged for her.

VINCENT: This was a strange temptation indeed. What the devil should she be the better then?

ANTHONY: Nothing, but that it eased her shrewd stomach[5] before to think that her husband should be hanged after. And peradventure if you look about the world and consider it well, you shall find more such stomachs than a few. Have you never heard no furious body plainly say that to see some such man have a mischief he would with goodwill be content to lie as long in hell as God liveth in heaven?

VINCENT: Forsooth, and some such have I heard of.

ANTHONY: This mind of his was not much less mad than hers, but rather haply[6] the more mad of the twain. For the woman peradventure did not cast so far peril therein.[7] But to tell you now to what good pass her charitable[8] purpose came: As her husband (the man was a carpenter) stood hewing with his chip-axe upon a piece of timber, she began after her old guise so to revile him that the man waxed wroth at last and bade her get her in, or he would lay the helm of his axe about her back. And [he] said also that it were little sin even with that axe-head to chop off that unhappy head of hers that carried such an ungracious tongue therein. At that word the devil took his time, and whetted her tongue against her teeth.[9] And when it was well sharped she sware to him in very fierce anger: "By the mass, whoreson husband, I would thou wouldest; here lieth mine head, lo!" And therewith down she laid her head upon the same timber log. "If thou smite it not off, I beshrew[10] thine whoreson's heart."

With that, likewise as the devil stood at her elbow, so stood (as I heard say) his good angel at his, and gave him ghostly courage, and bade him be bold and do it. And so the good man up with his chip-axe, and at a chop chopped off her head indeed. There were standing other folk by, which had a good sport to hear her chide, but little they looked for this chance till it was done ere they could let it. They said they heard her tongue babble in her head, and call "Whoreson, whoreson," twice after that the head was from the body. At the least wise, afterward unto the king thus they reported all—except only one, and that was a woman, and she said that she heard it not.

VINCENT: Forsooth, this was a wonderful work. What came, uncle, of the man?

ANTHONY: The king gave him his pardon.

VINCENT: Verily he might in conscience do no less.

ANTHONY: But then was it farther almost at another point.[11] . . . There should have been a statute made[12] that in such case there should never after[wards] pardon be granted, but the truth being able to be proved, none husband should need any pardon, but should have leave by the law to follow the sample of that carpenter and do the same.

VINCENT: How happed it, uncle, that that good law was left unmade?

ANTHONY: How happed it? As it happeth, cousin, that many more be left unmade as well as it, and within a little as good as it too, both here and in other countries, and sometime some worse made in their stead. But, as they say, the let[13] of that law was the queen's grace (God forgive her soul). It was the greatest thing, I ween, good lady, that she had to answer for when she died. For surely, save for that one thing, she was a full blessed woman.

But letting now that law pass, this temptation in procuring her own death was unto this carpenter's wife no tribulation at all, as far as ever men could perceive. For it liked her well to think thereon, and she even longed therefor. And therefore if she had before told you or me her mind, and that she would so fain bring it so to pass, we could have had none occasion to comfort her as one that were in tribulation. But, marry, counsel her (as I told you before) we might to refrain and amend that malicious devilish mind.

VINCENT: Verily that is truth. But such as are well willing to do any purpose that is so shameful will never tell their mind to nobody for very shame.

ANTHONY: Some will not indeed. And yet are there some again

that, be their intent never so shameful, find some[one] yet whom their heart serveth them to make of their counsel therein. Some of my folk here can tell you that no longer ago than even yesterday, one that came out of Vienna shewed us among other talking that a rich widow (but I forgot to ask him where it happed), having all her life an high proud mind and a fell[14]—as those two virtues are wont alway to keep company together—was at debate with another neighbor of hers in the town. And on a time she made of her counsel a poor neighbor of hers whom she thought for money she might induce to follow her mind.

With him she secretly brake,[15] and offered him ten ducats for his labor, to do so much for her as in a morning early to come to her house and with an axe unknown privily strike off her head. And when he had so done, [he was] then [to] convey the bloody axe into the house of him with whom she was at debate, in some such manner wise as it might be thought he had murdered her for malice. And then she thought she should be taken for a martyr. And yet had she farther devised that another sum of money should after be sent to Rome, and there should be means made to the Pope that she might in all haste be canonized.

This poor man promised but intended not to perform it. Howbeit, when he deferred it she provided the axe herself; and he appointed with her the morning when he should come and do it, *and thereupon into her house he came.*[16] But then set he such other folk as he would should know her frantic fantasy in such place appointed as they might well hear her and him talk together. And after that he had talked with her thereof what he would, so much as he thought was enough, he made her lie down and took up the axe in his own hand. And with the other hand he felt the edge and found a fault that it was not sharp, and [said] that therefore he would in no wise do it till he had grounden it sharp. He would not else, he said, for pity it would put her to so much pain.

And so full sore against her will, for that time she kept her head still. But because she would no more suffer any more [people to] deceive her so and fode her forth with delays, ere it was very long after she hung herself with her own hands.

VINCENT: Forsooth, here was a tragical story whereof I never heard the like.

ANTHONY: Forsooth, the party that told it me sware that he knew it for a truth. And himself is, I promise you, such as I reckon for right honest and of substantial truth. . . . And here I wot well that her temptation came not of fear but of high malice and pride. But then was she so glad in the pleasant device[17] thereof that, as I shewed you, she took it for no tribulation, and therefore comforting of her could have no place.[18]

1 as is well justified.
2 many years in succession.
3 kin.
4 This sentence clearly establishes the place-setting of the *Dialogue of Comfort*. Budapest was near the northern border of early sixteenth-century Hungary, about 200 miles from the fallen fortress of Belgrade. Budapest fell to the Turks in 1529, when Suleiman invaded the country to reinstate his vassal king John Zapolya of Transylvania. "King Ladislaus" is apparently Vladislav, King of Hungary. See Part II, Chap. 12, n. 10.
5 nasty disposition.
6 indeed possibly (the more mad of the two).
7 I.e., the woman probably did not so greatly endanger her soul (as did the man who would accept eternal hell in return for misfortune to his enemy).
8 More is of course being ironic.
9 I.e., the devil retreated briefly, while he sharpened her tongue (for worse abuse) against her teeth.
10. curse.
11 I.e., but then the case almost developed beyond the mere giving of a pardon.
12 there was (vainly) proposed that a statute be made.
13 blocker.
14 cruel.
15 broke bread—i.e., ate by way of conferring (?)
16 The italicized words have been added by Rastell. They are not found in the 1553 printed version. See Part I, Chap. 13, n. 2.
17 planning, scheming.
18 I.e., would be out of place, not warranted.

Chapter 17

[Suicide and the Devil]

[ANTHONY (continuing):] But lest you might reject both these samples, weening they were but feigned[1] tales, I shall put you in remembrance of one which I reckon yourself have read in the *Collations* of Cassianus.[2] And if you have not, there you may soon find it. For myself have half forgotten the thing, it is so long since I read it. But this much I remember: that he telleth there of one that was many days a very special holy man in his living, and among the other virtuous monks and anchors[3] that lived there in wilderness[4] was marvellously much esteemed—saving that some were not all out of fear of him,[5] lest his revelations, whereof he told many by himself, would prove illusions of the devil. And so proved it after indeed.

For the man was by the devil's subtle suggestions brought into such an high spiritual pride, that in conclusion the devil brought him to that horrible point that he made him go kill himself. And as far as my mind giveth me now without new sight of the book,[6] he brought him to it by this persuasion, that he made him believe that it was God's will he should so do and that thereby should he go straight to heaven. And then if it were by that persuasion, with which he took very great comfort in his own mind himself, then was it (as I said) out of our case,[7] and needed not comfort but counsel against giving credence to the devil's persuasion.

But marry, if he [the devil] made him first perceive how he had been deluded, and then tempted him to his own death by shame and by despair, then was it within our matter, lo. For then was his temptation fallen down from pride to pusillanimity and was waxen that kind of the night's fear[8] that I spake of, wherein a good part of the counsel that were to be given him should have need to stand in good comforting. For then was he brought into right sore tribulation.

But, as I was about to tell you, strength of heart and courage is is there none therein,[9] [and] not only for that[10] very strength (as it hath the name of virtue in a reasonable creature) can never be without prudence. But also for that (as I said) even in them that seem men of most hardiness, it shall well appear to them that well weigh the matter that the mind whereby they be led to destroy themself groweth of pusillanimity and very foolish fear.

Take for example Cato Uticensis, which in Africa killed himself after the great victory that Julius Caesar had. Saint Austin well declareth in his work *The City of God* that there was no strength nor magnanimity therein, but plain pusillanimity and impotency of stomach.[11] . . . He was forced to the destruction of himself because his heart was too feeble for to bear the beholding of another man's glory, or the suffering of other worldly calamities that he feared should fall on himself. So that, as Saint Austin well proveth, that horrible deed is none act of strength. But [it is] an act of a mind either drawn from the consideration of itself with some devilish fantasy, wherein the man hath need to be called home with good counsel; or else oppressed by faint heart and fear, wherein a good part of the counsel must stand in lifting up his courage with good consolation and comfort.

And therefore [suppose] we found any such religious person, as was that father which Cassian writeth of, that were of such austerity and apparent ghostly living that he were with such as well knew him reputed for a man of singular virtue. [Suppose] it were perceived that he had many strange visions appearing unto him. If it should now be perceived after that, that the man went about secretly to destroy himself, whoso should hap to come to the knowledge thereof and intended to do his devoir in the let,[12] first must he find the means to search and find out whether the man be in his manner and his countenance lightsome, glad, and joyful, or dumpish, heavy, and sad. . . . [Does] he go thereabout as one that were full of the glad hope of heaven, or as one that had his breast farced[13] full of tediousness and weariness of the world?

If he were founden of the first fashion, it were a token that the devil hath by his fantastical apparitions puffed him up in such a peevish pride, that he hath finally persuaded him by some illusion, shewed him for the proof, that God's pleasure is that he shall for His sake with his own hands kill himself.

VINCENT: Now, if a man so found it, uncle, what counsel should a man give him then?

ANTHONY: That were somewhat out of our purpose, cousin, sith (as I told you before) the man were not then in sorrow and tribulation, whereof our matter speaketh, but in a perilous merry mortal tentation.[14] So that if we should, beside our own matter that we have in hand enter into that too, we might make a longer work between both than we could well finish this day.

Howbeit, to be short, it is soon seen that therein the sum and effect of the counsel must in manner rest in giving him warning of the devil's sleights. And that must be done under such sweet pleasant manner, as the man should not abhor to hear it. For while it could lightly[15] be none other but that the man were rocked and sungen asleep by the devil's craft and his mind occupied as it were in a delectable dream, he should never have good audience of him that would rudely and boisterously shog[16] him and wake him and so shake him out thereof. Therefore must you fair and easily touch him, and with some pleasant speech awake him, so that he wax not wayward as children do that are waked ere they list to rise.

But when a man hath first begun with his praise . . . , then after favor won therewithal, a man may little and little insinuate the doubt of such revelations—not at the first as it were for any doubt of his, but of some other that men in some other places talk of. And peradventure it shall not miscontent himself to shew great perils that may fall therein in another man's case than his own. . . . Or [maybe] you were a man that had not so very great scrupulous conscience of an harmless lie, devised to do good withal—which kind Saint Austin, though he take alway for sin, yet he taketh but for venial; and Saint Jerome, as by divers places in his books appeareth, taketh not fully for so much.[17]

Then may you feign some secret friend of yours to be in such case, and that yourself somewhat fear his peril and have made of charity this voyage for his sake, to ask this good father's counsel. And in the communication upon these words of Saint John: "Give not credence to every spirit, but prove the spirits whether they be of God,"[18] and these words of Saint Paul: "The angel of Satan transfigureth himself into the angel of light,"[19] you shall take occasion the better if they hap to come in on his side. But yet [you shall] not lack occasion neither if those texts, for lack of his offer, come in upon your own.[20]

PLATE 5. Sir Thomas with his daughter, Margaret Roper, in the Tower of London. They are watching as the Carthusian monks are dragged off to Tyburn to be executed. Engraving by J. Outrim from a painting by the nineteenth-century Royal Academy artist, J. R. Herbert. Original painting owned by Mrs. Richard O'Sullivan of London.

Occasion, I say, shall you not lack to inquire by what sure and undeceivable tokens a man may discern the true revelations from the false illusions, whereof a man shall find many both here and there in divers other authors, and whole together divers goodly treatises of that good godly doctor, Master John Gerson, entitled *The Examination of Spirits.*[21] As[k] whether the party[22] be natural wise or anything seem fantastical;[23] whether the party be poor-spirited or proud—which will somewhat appear by his delight in his own praise. . . . Any little fault found in himself, or diffidence declared and mistrust of his own revelations, and doubtful tokens told wherefore himself should fear lest they be the devil's illusion —such things, as Master Gerson saith, will make him spit out somewhat of his [evil] spirit, if the devil lie in his breast.

Or if the devil be yet so subtle that he keep himself close in his warm den and blow out never an hot word, yet is it to be considered what end his [the visionary's] revelations draw to: whether to any spiritual profit to himself or other folk, or only to vain marvels and wonders. Also whether they withdraw him from such other good virtuous business as by the common rules of Christendom or any rules of his profession he was wont to use, or were bounden to be ocupied in. Or whether he fall into any singularity of opinions against the Scripture of God or against the common faith of Christ's Catholic Church. Many other tokens are there in the work of Master Gerson spoken of to consider by,[24] whether the person, neither having revelations of God nor illusions from the devil, do either for winning of money or worldly favor, feign his revelations himself and delude the people withal.

But now for our purpose: If among any of the marks by which the true revelations may be known from false illusions, that man himself bring forth for one mark the doing or teaching of anything against the Scripture of God or the common faith of the Church, then have you an entry made you, by which when you list you may enter into the special matter wherein he can never well flit from you.

Or else may you yet, if you list, feign that your secret friend, for whose sake you come to him for counsel, is brought in that mind by a certain apparition shewed unto him (as himself saith by an angel, as you fear by the devil) that he can be by you none otherwise persuaded. [He thinks] that the pleasure of God is that he shall go kill himself, and that if he so do then shall he be thereby so specially participant of Christ's Passion that he shall forthwith be carried up with angels into heaven. For which he is so joyful, that he firmly purposeth upon it, no less glad to do it than another man would be glad to avoid it. And therefore may you desire his [the visionary's] good counsel to instruct you with some substantial good advice, wherewith you may turn him [the secret friend] from this error [so] that he be not, under hope of God's true revelation, in body and soul destroyed by the devil's false illusion.

If he will in this thing study and labor to instruct you, the things that himself shall find of his own invention (though they be less effectual) shall peradventure more work with himself toward his own amendment, sith he shall of likelihood better like them than [he] shall [like] double so substantial[25] told him by another man. If he be loath to think upon that side, and therefore shrink from the matter, then is there none other way but adventure after the plain fashion to fall into the matter,[26] and shew what you hear, and to give him counsel and exhortation to the contrary—but if you list to say that thus and thus hath the matter been reasoned already between your friend and you. And therein may you rehearse such things as should prove that the vision which moveth him is no true revelation, but a very false illusion.

1 imaginary.
2 See the *Collations* of John Cassian, Part II, Chap. 5, "On the Death of the Old Man Heron."
3 Anchorites.
4 I.e., the Egyptian desert. See *The Wisdom of the Desert Fathers of the Fourth Century,* trans. Thomas Merton (1960).
5 not wholly in awe of him.
6 This statement would suggest that in the summer of 1534 More's cell-library was meager or non-existent.
7 out of our scope (of discussion).
8 I.e., terrifying tribulation. See Psalms 90:5.
9 I.e., in committing suicide.
10 because.
11 The *City of God,* Book I, Chaps. 22 and 23.

12 to do his duty by stopping him.
13 stuffed.
14 temptation, trouble.
15 hardly, surely.
16 shake.
17 As e.g., in Jerome's *Ad Consent. de Mendac.* (*In Consent of Lying*).
18 1 John 4:1.
19 2 Cor. 11:14.
20 I.e., it will be a happy occasion if the Scriptural texts turn out to support the visionary's position. If, however, the visionary remains silent, the texts can be used by the friend to pursue the inquiry.
21 See John Gerson's *De probatione spirituum* in Mallers, *Maleficarum* (1620), II, i, 71-80. A key study of this work is Paschal Boland, *The Concept of "descretio spirituum" in John Gerson's "De probatione spirituum" and "De distinctione verarum visionum a falsis"* (1959). In the two works treated by Boland, Gerson lays down tests by which to distinguish true (divine) from false (devilish) visions and spirits.
22 the person involved—i.e., the visionary.
23. deranged.
24 to determine.
25 (arguments) twice as good.
26 I.e., to make a direct frontal attack (on his views).

Chapter 18

[The Carver Who Was Almost Crucified]

VINCENT: Verily, uncle, I well allow this, that a man should as well in this thing as every other wherein he longeth to do another man good, seek such a pleasant way as the party should be likely to like . . . his communication, and not so to enter in thereunto as he whom he would help should abhor him, and be loath to hear him, and therefore take no profit by him. But now, uncle, if it come by the one way or the other to the point that hear me he will or [must], what be the reasons effectual with which I should by my counsel convert him?

ANTHONY: All those by which you may make him perceive that himself is deceived and that his visions be no godly revelations but very devilish illusion. And those reasons must you gather of the man, of the matter,[1] and of the law of God, or of some one of these. Of the man, . . . you can peradventure shew him that in such a point or such he is waxen worse since such revelations have haunted him than he was before, as in those that are deluded whoso be well acquainted with them shall well mark and perceive. For they wax more proud, more wayward, more envious, suspicious—misjudging and depraving[2] other men with the delight of their own praise, and such other spiritual vices of the soul.

Of the matter may you gather, if it have happed his revelations before to prove false, or that they be things rather strange than profitable. For that is a good mark[3] between God's miracles and the devil's wonders. For Christ and His saints have their miracles alway tending to fruit and profit. The devil and his witches and necromancers, all their wonderful works draw to no fruitful end, but to a fruitless ostentation and shew, as it were a juggler that would for a shew before the people play masteries[4] at a feast.

Of the law of God, you must draw your reasons in shewing by the Scripture that the thing which he weeneth God by His angel biddeth, God hath [by] his own mouth forbidden. And that is, you wot well, in the case that we speak of so easy to find, that I need not to rehearse it to you, sith there is plain among the ten commandments forboden the unlawful killing of any man, and therefore of himself (as Saint Austin saith[5] all the Church teacheth), except himself be no man.

VINCENT: This is very true, good uncle, nor I will not dispute upon any glossing[6] of that prohibition. But [yet] we find not the contrary but that God may dispense with that commandment Himself, and both license and command also (if Himself list) any man to go kill either another man or himself. . . . This man . . . is now by such a marvellous vision induced to believe that God so biddeth him, and therefore thinketh himself in that case of that prohibition discharged, and charged with the contrary commandment. With what reason may we make him perceive that his vision is but an illusion and not a true revelation?

ANTHONY: Nay, cousin Vincent, ye shall in this case not need to require those reasons of me. But taking the Scripture of God for a ground for this matter, you know very well yourself you shall go somewhat a shorter way to work if you ask [one] question of him. . . . God hath forboden once the thing Himself, though He may dispense therewith if He will. Yet . . . the devil may feign himself God and with a marvellous vision delude one and make as though God did it. And [further,] the devil is also more likely to speak against God's commandment than God against His own. You shall [therefore] have good cause, I say, to demand of the man himself whereby he knoweth that his vision is God's true revelation and not the devil's false delusion?

VINCENT: Indeed, uncle, I think that would be an hard question to him. May a man, uncle, have in such a thing even a very sure knowledge of his own mind?

ANTHONY: Yea, cousin, God may cast into the mind of a man, I suppose, such an inward light of understanding that he cannot fail but be sure thereof. And yet he that is deluded by the devil may think himself as sure and yet be deceived indeed. And such a difference is there in a manner between them as is between the sight of a thing while we be waking and look thereon, and the sight with which we see a thing in our sleep while we dream thereof.

VINCENT: This is a pretty similitude, uncle, in this thing. And then is it easy for the monk that we speak of to declare how he knoweth his vision for a true revelation and not a false delusion, if there be so great difference between them.

ANTHONY: Not so easy, cousin, yet as you ween it were. For how can you now prove unto me that you be awake?

VINCENT: Marry, lo, do I not now wag my hand, shake my head, and stamp with my foot here in the floor?

ANTHONY: Have you never dreamed ere this, that you have done the same?

VINCENT: Yes, that have I, and more too than that. For I have ere this in my sleep dreamed that I doubted whether I were asleep or awake; and have in good faith thought that I did thereupon even the same things that I do now indeed, and thereby determined that I was not asleep. And yet have I dreamed in good faith, farther, that I have been afterward at dinner, and there making merry with good company have told the same dream at the table and laughed well thereat, that while I was asleep I had by such means of moving the parts of my body . . . thought myself waking.

ANTHONY: And will you not now soon, trow you, when you wake and rise, laugh as well at yourself when you see that you lie now in your warm bed asleep again, and dream all this time while you ween so verily that you be waking and talking of these matters with me?

VINCENT: Good Lord, uncle, you go now merrily to work with me indeed when you look and speak so sadly[7] and would make me ween I were asleep.

ANTHONY: It may be that you be so, for anything that you can say or do whereby you may (with any reason that you make) drive me to confess that yourself be sure of the contrary. [For] you can do nor say nothing now whereby you be sure to be waking, but that you have ere this (or hereafter may) think yourself as surely to do the selfsame things indeed while you be all the while asleep, and nothing do but lie dreaming.

VINCENT: Well, well, uncle, though I have ere this thought myself awake while I was indeed asleep, yet for all this I know well enough that I am awake now, and so do you too, though I cannot find the words by which I may with reason force you to confess it. . . . Alway you may drive me off, by the sample of my dream.

ANTHONY: This is, cousin, as meseemeth, very true. And likewise seemeth me the manner and difference between some kind of true revelations and some kind of false illusions, as it standeth between the things that are done waking and the things that in our dreams seem to be done. . . . He which hath that kind of revelation from God is as sure of the truth as we be of our own deed while we be waking. And he that is [de]luded by the devil, is in such wise deceived, and worse too, than be they by their dream. . . . . . .

VINCENT: Yet then may this religious man of whom we speak, when I shew him the Scripture against his revelation and therefore call it an illusion, bid me with reason go care for myself. For he knoweth well and surely himself that his revelation is very good and true and not any false illusion, sith for all the general commandment of God in the Scripture, God may dispense[8] where He will and when He will, and may command him do the contrary.

[So] He commanded Abraham to kill his own son, and [so] Samson had by inspiration of God commandment to kill himself with pulling down the house upon his own head at the feast of the Philistines.... ...

ANTHONY: This is well said, cousin; but yet could he not [e]scape you so. For the dispensation . . . he hath by his private revelation is a thing of such sort as sheweth itself naught and false. For it never hath had any sample like since the world began unto now, that ever man hath read or heard of. . . . First in Abraham touching the death of his son, God intended it not, but only tempted the towardness[10] of the father's obedience. In Samson all men make not the matter very sure, whether he be saved or not; but yet therein some matter and cause appeareth.[11] For the Philistines, being enemies to God and using Samson for their mocking-stock in scorn of God, it is well likely that God gave him the mind to bestow his own life upon the revenging of the displeasure that those blasphemous Philistines did unto God.[12] . . . . . .

Saint Austin also rehearseth that certain holy virtuous virgins in time of persecution, being by God's enemies (infidels) pursued upon to be deflowered by force, ran into a water and drowned themself rather than they would be bereaved of their virginity.[13] . . . He thinketh it is not lawful for any other maid to follow their sample, but rather [that she should] suffer other to do her any manner violence by force, and commit sin of his own upon her against her will, than willingly and thereby sinfully herself become an homicide of herself. Yet he thinketh that in them it happed [that] the special instinct of the Spirit of God, for causes seen unto Himself, would rather that they should avoid it with their own temporal death than abide the defiling and violation of their chastity.

But now this good man neither hath any of God's enemies to be by his own death revenged on, nor any woman that violently pursue him by force to bereave him of his virginity! Nor never find we that God proved any man's obedient mind, by the commandment of his own slaughter of himself. Therefore is his case both plain against God's open precept, and the dispensation strange and without sample. . . . . . .

VINCENT: [But] then shall he peradventure say to me again, that whether I believe him or not maketh him no matter. The thing toucheth himself and not me, and himself is in himself as sure that it is a true revelation as that he can tell that he dreameth not but talketh with me waking.

ANTHONY: Cousin, [suppose] he abide at that point and can be by no reason brought to do so much as doubt, nor can by no mean be shogged out of his dead sleep, but will needs take his dream for a very truth, and (as some by night rise and walk about their chamber in their sleep) will so rise and hang himself. I can then none other way see but either bind him fast in his bed, or else assay whether that might hap to help him with which the common tale goeth that a carver's[14] wife in such a frantic fantasy[15] holp her husband.

To whom, when he would upon a Good Friday needs have killed himself for Christ's sake as Christ was killed for him, *she would not in vain plead against his mind, but well and wisely put him in remembrance that if he would die for Christ as Christ died for him,*[16] it were then convenient for him to die even after the same fashion. And that might not be by his own hands, but the hand of some other. For Christ, pardie, killed not Himself. . . . She offered him that for God's sake she would secretly crucify him herself upon a great cross that he had made to nail a new-carved crucifix upon. Whereof when he was very glad, yet she bethought her that Christ was bounden to a pillar and beaten first, and after crowned with thorn.

Whereupon, when she had by his own assent bound him fast to a post, she left not beating with holy exhortation to suffer so much and so long, that ere ever she left work and unbound him, [she] pray[ed] him nevertheless that she might put on his head, and drive it well down, a crown of thorn that she had wreathed for him. . . . [But] he said he thought this was enough for that year! He would pray God forbear him of the remnant till Good

Friday come again. But when it came again the next year, then was his lust past; he longed to follow Christ no farther.

VINCENT: Indeed, uncle, if this help him not, then will nothing help him, I trow.

ANTHONY: And yet, cousin, the devil may peradventure make him toward such a purpose first gladly suffer other pain—yea, and minish his feeling too therein, that he may thereby the less fear his death. . . . But for conclusion: If the man be surely proved so inflexibly set upon the purpose to destroy himself, as commanded thereto by God, that no good counsel that men can give him nor any other thing that men may do to him can refrain him, . . . then (except only good prayer by his friends made for him) I can find no farther shift[17] but either have him ever in sight, or bind him fast in his bed.

And so must he needs of reason be content to be ordered. For though himself take his fantasy for a true revelation, yet . . . he cannot make us perceive it for such. Likewise, as he thinketh himself by his secret commandment bounden to follow it, so must he needs agree that sith it is against the plain open prohibition of God, we be by the plain open precept bounden to keep him from it.

1 circumstances.
2 demeaning, speaking evil of.
3 distinction.
4 tricks.
5 See *The City of God*, Book I, Chap. 19—"That there is no authority which allows Christians to be their own deaths in what cause soever."
6 explaining away.
7 An allusion to More's famous habit of telling a joke with a solemn face.
8 waive (the prohibition against killing, including killing oneself).
9 Judges 16:27-30.
10 degree, or pliancy.
11 I.e., there is some dispute over whether Samson acted on God's inspiration or simply committed suicide; but the evidence seems to favor the former.
12 This argument, like Anthony's preceding comments on Abraham, are paraphrased from *The City of God*, Book I, Chap. 20: "Of some sorts of killing men which . . . are not murder." Note especially Augustine's observation: "Nor could Samson be excused pulling down the house upon himself and his enemies, but that the Spirit within him, which wrought miracles by him, did prompt him unto this act."
13 *City of God*, Book I, Chap. 25: "Of some unlawful acts done by the saints."
14 one who carves in wood, ivory, or stone: a sculptor.
15 (the husband's) derangement.
16 The italicized words, necessary for the sense, have been inserted from the 1553 edition. They are not found in the Rastell text.
17 solution.

Chapter 19

[How to Prevent a Suicide]

[Anthony now turns to the man who is not deluded by the devil, but who seeks suicide because he has fallen into some terrible sin or had some secret sin exposed. Thus he despairs of salvation, or is ashamed of his loss of reputation. This man's friends should stress that his despair is a blessing, because through it God teaches him not to be proud. They should stress that they regard him now as far wiser than before, because he has had such a close brush with the devil. Vincent objects that such tactics might make the man proud again. Anthony replies that the first step is to get the man out of despair. A physician must first extract a man from a near fatal fever before worrying about minor ailments. A pilot must first keep from wrecking on the rock Scylla. We can always worry about Charybdis (the whirlpool of pride) later. Vincent suggests that despair at sin or exposed sin is not the only reason for suicide. Anthony agrees: He once knew a man who wanted to kill himself because he (wrongly) thought people disliked him.

The devil works in clever ways. He assesses not only a man's social status, but also his temperament as determined by the bodily fluids or humors. Indeed, the two factors most conducive to suicide are upset humors and the devil. Thus a man needs both bodily and spiritual physicians. As St. James said, a sick soul can hurt the body. A man who dreads killing himself will probably do so, just as a man who dreads falling from a bridge will fall. In fighting temptation to commit suicide, laughing at the devil (who cannot stand scorn) and praying to God (through his saints) are the most effective methods of all. Anthony concludes: "I doubt not by God's grace but he that in such a temptation will use good counsel and prayer . . . shall have the truth of God . . . so compass him about with a pavis, that he shall not need to dread.

. . . And thus will I finish this piece of the night's fear; and glad am I that we be . . . comen once unto the day, to those other words of the prophet: 'For the arrow flying in the day.' For methinketh I have made it a long night."]

Chapter 20

[The Arrow of Pride]

VINCENT: Forsooth, uncle, so have you; but we have not slept in it, but been very well occupied. But now I fear that, except you make here a pause till you have dined, you shall keep yourself from your dinner overlong.

ANTHONY: Nay, nay, cousin, for both brake I my fast even as you came in, and also you shall find this night and this day like a winter day and a winter night. For as the winter hath short days and long nights, so shall you find that I made you not this fearful night so long but I shall make you this light courageous day as short. . . . For in these words of the prophet: "The truth of God shall compass thee round about with a pavis, from the arrow fleeing in the day," I understand the arrow of pride with which the devil tempteth a man not in the night (that is to wit, in tribulation and adversity), . . . but in the day (that is to wit, in prosperity). For that time is full of lightsome lust[1] and courage.

But surely this worldly prosperity, wherein a man so rejoiceth and whereof the devil maketh him so proud, is but even a very short winter day. For we begin, many [of us,] full poor and cold. And up we fly like an arrow that were shot up into the air. And yet when we be suddenly shot up into the highest, ere we be well warm there, down we come unto the cold ground again. And then even there stick we still. And yet for the short while that we be upward and aloft, Lord, how lusty and how proud we be—buzzing above busily, like as a bumble bee flieth about in summer, never [a]ware that she shall die in winter. And so fare many of us, God help us. For in the short winter day of worldly wealth and prosperity this flying arrow of the devil, this high spirit of pride, shot out of the devil's bow and piercing through our heart, beareth us up in our affection aloft into the clouds. [T]here we ween we sit on the rainbow and overlook the world under us, accounting in the regard of our own glory such other poor souls as were peradventure wont to be our fellows for silly poor pismires and ants.

But this arrow of pride, fly it never so high in the clouds, and be the man that it carrieth up so high never so joyful thereof, yet . . . it hath yet an heavy iron head. And therefore, fly it never so high, down must it needs come and on the ground must it light, and falleth sometime not in a very cleanly place. [Then] the pride turneth into rebuke and shame; and there is then all the glory gone. Of this arrow speaketh the wise man in the fifth chapter of Sapience where he saith, in the person of them that in pride and vanity passed the time of this present life and after that so spent, passed hence into hell: "What hath pride profited us, or what good hath the glory of our riches done unto us?"[2] . . . . . .

Here shall you, good cousin, consider that . . . the proud man himself hath no certain purpose or appointment[3] at any mark, butt,[4] or prick[5] upon earth whereat he determineth to shoot and there to stick and tarry. But ever he shooteth as children do, that love to shoot up a cop high[6] to see how high their arrow can fly up. But now doth the devil intend and appoint a certain prick surely set in a place into which he purposeth (fly this arrow never so high and the proud heart thereon) to have them light both at last. And that place is in the very pit of hell. There is set the devil's well-acquainted prick and his very just mark. Down upon which prick with his pricking[7] shaft of pride he hath by himself a plain proof and experience that (but if it be stopped by some grace of God in the way), the soul that flieth up therewith can never fail to fall. For when himself was in heaven, [he] began to fly up a cop high with the lusty light[8] flight of pride, saying: "I will fly up above the stars, and set my throne on the sides of the north, and will be like unto the highest."[9] [But] long ere he could fly up half so high as he said in his heart he would, he was turned from a bright glorious angel into a dark deformed devil. And from flying any farther upward, down was he thrown into the deep dungeon of hell.

Now may it peradventure, cousin, seem that sith this kind of temptation of pride is no tribulation or pain, all this that we speak of this arrow of pride flying forth in the day of prosperity were beside our matter.

VINCENT: Verily, mine uncle, and so seemed it unto me. And somewhat was I minded so to say to you too, saying that were it properly pertaining to the present matter or somewhat disgressing therefrom, good matter methought it was and such as I had no lust to let.[10]

ANTHONY: But now must you, cousin, consider that though prosperity be contrary to tribulation, yet unto many a good man the devil's temptation unto pride in prosperity is a greater tribulation, and more need hath of good comfort and good counsel both, than he that never felt it would ween. And that is the thing, cousin, that maketh me speak thereof as of a thing proper to this matter.

For cousin, . . . it is a thing right hard to touch pitch and never file[11] the fingers, to put flax unto fire and yet keep them from burning, to keep a serpent in thy bosom and yet be safe from stinging, to put young men with young women without danger of foul fleshly desire. So is it hard for any person (either man or woman) in great worldly wealth and much prosperity so to withstand the suggestions of the devil and occasions given by the world, that they keep themself from the deadly desire of ambitious glory. Whereupon there followeth (if a man fall thereto) an whole flood of all unhappy mischief: arrogant manner; high, sullen, solemn port; overlooking the poor in word and countenance; displeasant and disdainous behavior; ravin, extortion, oppression, hatred, and cruelty.

Now many a good man, cousin, comen into great authority, casting in his mind the peril of such occasions of pride, . . . be sore troubled therewith. And some fall so feard thereof, that even in the day of prosperity they fall into the night's fear of pusillanimity and, doubting overmuch lest they should misuse themself, leave the things undone wherein they might use themself well. And mistrusting the aid and help of God in holding them upright in their temptations, [they] give place to the devil in the contrary temptation, whereby for faint heart they leave off good business wherein they were well occupied. And under pretext (as it seemeth to themself) of humble heart and meekness, and serving God in contemplation and silence, they seek their own ease and earthly rest unware.[12] Wherewith (if it so be) God is not well content.

Howbeit, [suppose] that a man . . . perceiveth that in wealth and authority he doth his own soul harm and cannot do therein the good that to his part appertaineth,[13] but seeth the things that he should set his hands to sustain decay through his default,[14] and fall to ruin under him. And th[en] to the amendment [of his soul] he leaveth his own duty undone. Then would I in any wise advise him to leave off that thing, be it spiritual benefice that he have, parsonage, or bishopric, or temporal room and authority, and rather give it over quite and draw himself aside and serve God. . . .

But on the other side, if he see not the contrary, but that he may do his duty conveniently[15] well and feareth nothing but that the temptations of ambition and pride may peradventure turn his good purpose and make him decline unto sin, I say not nay but that well done it is to stand in moderate fear alway. Whereof the Scripture saith: "Blessed is the man that is alway fearful."[16] And St. Paul saith: "He that standeth, let him look that he fall not."[17] Yet is overmuch fear perilous, and draweth toward the mistrust of God's gracious help, which immoderate fear and faint heart Holy Scripture forbiddeth, saying: "Be not feeble-hearted or timorous."[18] Let such a man, therefore, temper his fear with good hope, and think that sith God hath set him in that place . . . , God will assist him with His grace to the well using thereof.

Howbeit, if he came thereto by simony or some such other evil mean, then were the thing one good reason wherefore he should the rather leave it off. But else let him continue in his good business, and against the devil's provocation unto evil bless himself and call unto God and pray, and look [that] what[ever] thing the devil tempteth him, [he] lean the more toward the contrary.

Let him be piteous and comfortable to those that are in distress and affliction. I mean not to let every malefactor pass forth unpunished and freely run out and rob at rovers,[19] but in his heart be sorry to see that of necessity, for fear of decaying the commonweal, men are driven to put malefactors to pain. And yet where he findeth good tokens and likelihood of amendment, therein all that he may, [let him] help that mercy may be had.[20] There shall never lack desperately disposed wretches enow[21] beside, upon whom for ensample justice may proceed. Let him think in his own heart every poor beggar his fellow.

VINCENT: That will be very hard, uncle, for an honorable man to do, when he beholdeth himself richly apparelled and the beggar rigged in his rags.

ANTHONY: [Suppose] here were, cousin, two men that were beggars both. And afterward a great rich man would take yet one unto him and tell him that for a little time he would have him in his house, and thereupon arrayed him in silk, and give him a great bag by his side filled even full of gold—but giving him this knot[22] therewith: that within a little while, out he should in his old rags again and bear never a penny with him. If this beggar met his fellow now while his gay gown were on, might he not for all his gay gear,[23] take him for his fellow still? And were he not a very fool if for a wealth of a few weeks he would ween himself far his better?

VINCENT: Yes, uncle, if the difference of their state were none other.

ANTHONY: Surely, cousin, methinketh that in this world, between the richest and the most poor the difference is scant so much. For let the highest look on the most base and consider how poor they came both into this world. And then consider further therewith [that,] how rich soever he be now, he shall yet within a while (peradventure less than one week) walk out again as poor as that beggar shall. And then, by my troth, methinketh this rich man much more than mad if for the wealth of a little while, haply less than one week, he reckon himself in earnest any better than the beggar's fellow. And less than this can no man think that hath any natural wit and well useth it.

But now a Christian man, cousin, that hath the light of faith, he cannot fail to think in this thing much farther. For he will think not only upon his bare coming hither and his bare going hence again, but also upon the dreadful judgment of God, and upon the fearful pains of hell and the inestimable joys of heaven. And in the considering of these things he will call to remembrance that peradventure when this beggar and he both departed hence, the beggar may be suddenly set up in such royalty, that well[24] were himself that ever was he born if he might be made his fellow.

And he that well bethinketh him, cousin, upon these things, I verily think that the arrow of pride flying forth in the day of worldly wealth shall never so wound his heart that ever it shall bear him up one foot. But now, to the intent he may think on such things the better, let him use often to resort to confession and there open his heart, and by the mouth of some virtuous ghostly father[25] have such things oft renewed in his remembrance.

Let him also choose himself some secret solitary place in his own house, as far from noise and company as he conveniently can.[26] And thither let him sometime secretly resort alone, imagining himself as one going out of the world even straight into the giving up his reckoning unto God of his sinful living. Then let him there before an altar or some pitiful image of Christ's bitter Passion . . . kneel down or fall prostrate as at the feet of Almighty God, verily believing Him to be there invisibly present—as without any doubt He is.

There let him open his heart to God and confess his faults such as he can call to mind, and pray God of forgiveness. Let him call to remembrance the benefits that God hath given him, either in general among other men or privately to himself, and give Him humble hearty thanks therefor. There let him declare unto God the temptations of the devil, the suggestions of the flesh, the occasions of the world and of his worldly friends—much worse many times in drawing a man from God than are his most mortal enemies. Which thing our Savior witnessed Himself where He saith: "The enemies of a man are they that are his own familiars."[27]

There let him lament and bewail unto God his own frailty, negligence, and sloth in resisting and withstanding of temptation, his readiness and pronity to fall thereunto. There let him lamentably beseech God of His gracious aid and help to strength his infirmity withal—both in keeping him from falling and, when he by his own fault misfortuneth to fall, then with the helping hand of His merciful grace to lift him up, and set him on his feet in the state of His grace again. And let this man not doubt but that God heareth him and granteth him gladly His boon.

And so, dwelling in the faithful trust of God's help, he shall well use his prosperity and persevere in his good profitable business, and shall have therein the truth of God so compass him about with a pavis of His heavenly defense, that of the devil's arrow flying in the day of worldly wealth he shall not need to dread.

VINCENT: Forsooth, uncle, I like this good counsel well, and I would ween that such as are in prosperity and take such order therein may do both to themself and other folk about[28] much good.

ANTHONY: I beseech our Lord, cousin, put this and better in the mind of every man that needeth it. And now will I touch one word or twain of the third temptation whereof the prophet speaketh in these words, "from the business walking in the darknesses."[29] And then will we call for our dinner, leaving the last temptation (that is to wit "from the incursion and the devil of the midday") till after noon. And then shall we therewith (God willing) make an end of all this matter.

VINCENT: Our Lord reward you, good uncle, for your good

labor with me. But, for our Lord's sake, take good heed, uncle, that you forbear not your dinner overlong.

ANTHONY: Fear not that, cousin, I warrant you; for this piece will I make you but short.

1 cheerful pleasure.
2 Book of Wisdom 5:8.
3 plan (to remain at, or be satisfied with).
4 a mound or other backstop for catching arrows shot at a target.
5 target.
6 above their heads, to a great height.
7 piercing.
8 merrily nimble.
9 Isaias 14:14.
10 no desire to stop or interrupt.
11 defile, dirty.
12 unwittingly, without realizing it.
13 I.e., cannot perform the duties expected of his office.
14 lack of attention, preoccupation (with his soul's condition).
15 in good conscience.
16 Proverbs 28:14.
17 1 Cor. 10:12.
18 Eccles. 7:9.
19 at random.
20 I.e., where the criminal gives some sign of rehabilitation, the Godly man should strive to see mercy applied. More seems to be returning here to a major theme of Book I in *Utopia*, where he pleaded for a more humane treatment of criminals.
21 enough.
22 proviso, condition.
23 apparel.
24 lucky.
25 spiritual father—i.e., the priest.
26 Hallett, in his Intro. to the *Dialogue*, p. vii, suggests that this is an allusion to "the new building, with an oratory," that More "erected on his grounds" at Chelsea; and that the prayer which follows is a rendition of More's own prayer which he said before the crucifix there.
27 Matt. 10:36.
28 around—i.e., one's neighbors.
29 Psalms 90:6.

Chapter 21

[The Corset of Covetousness]

[ANTHONY:] The prophet saith in the said psalm: . . .   . . . "Shall the truth of Him so compass [thee] about with a pavis that thou shalt not be afeard of the business walking about in the darknesses."[1] "Business" is here, cousin, the name of a devil that is ever full of business in tempting folk to much evil business. His time of tempting is in the darknesses. For you wot well that beside the very full night which is the deep dark, there are two times of darknesses: the one ere the morning wax light, the other when the evening waxeth dark.

Two times of like manner darkness are there also in the soul of man: the one ere the light of grace be well in the heart sprungen up; the other when the light of grace out of the soul beginneth to walk fast away. In these two darknesses this devil that is called business busily walketh about, and such fond folk as will follow him, he carrieth about with him and setteth them a-work with many manner [of] bumbling[2] business.

He setteth, I say, some to seek the pleasures of the flesh in eating, drinking, and other filthy delight. And some he setteth about incessant seeking for these worldly goods. And of such busy folk whom this devil . . . setteth a-work with such business our Savior saith in the gospel: "He that walketh in darknesses wotteth not whither he goeth."[3] And surely in such case are they. They neither wot which way they go nor whither. For verily they walk round about, as it were, in a round maze.[4] When they ween themself at an end of their business they be but at the beginning again.

For is not the going about the serving of the flesh a business that hath none end, but evermore from the end cometh to the beginning again? Go they never so full fed to bed, yet evermore on the morrow as new be they to be fed again as they were the day before. Thus fareth it by the belly; thus fareth it by those parts that are beneath the belly. And as for covetise, [it] fareth like the fire: The more wood that cometh thereto, the more fervent and the more greedy it is.

But now hath this maze a center, or a middle place, into which sometime they be conveyed suddenly when they ween they were not yet far from the brink.[5] The center or middle place of this maze is hell, and into that place be these busy folk, that with this devil of business walk about in this busy maze in the darknesses, suddenly sometime conveyed, nothing [a]ware whither they be going. . . . But of these fleshly folk walking in this busy pleasant maze the Scripture declareth the end: "They lead their life in pleasure, and at a pop down they descend into hell."[6] . . . . . .

[Take] the covetous rich man also that our Savior speaketh of in the gospel, that had so greatly plenty of corn that his barns would not receive it, but intended to make his barns larger and said unto himself that he would make merry many days. [He] had weened, you wot well, that he had had a great way yet to walk. But God said unto him: "Fool, this night shall they take thy soul from thee, and then all this good that thou hast gathered, whose shall it be?"[7] Here you see that he fell suddenly into the deep center of this busy maze, so that he was fallen full therein long ere ever he had weened he should have come near thereto.

Now, this wot I very well, that those that are walking about in this busy maze take not their business for any tribulation. And yet are there many of them forwearied [very] sore, and as sore panged[8] and pained therein, their pleasures being so short, so little, and so few, and their displeasures and their griefs so great, so continual, and so many. . . . It maketh me think upon a good worshipful man which . . . divers times beheld his wife, what pain she took in strait binding up her hair to make her a fair large forehead, and with strait bracing in her body to make her middle small, both twain[9] to her great pain for the pride of a little foolish praise. He said unto her: "Forsooth, madam, if God give you not hell, He shall do you great wrong; for it must needs be your own of very right. For you buy it very dear and take very great pain therefor." . . . . . .

So help me God and none other wise but as I verily think that many a man buyeth hell here with so much pain, that he might have bought heaven with less than the one-half. But yet, as I say, while these fleshly and worldly busy folk are walking about in this round busy maze of this devil that is called business (that walketh about in these two times of darkness), their wits are so by the secret enchantment of the devil bewitched, that they mark not the great long miserable weariness and pain that the devil maketh them take and endure about nought. And therefore they take it for no tribulation, so that they need no comfort.

And therefore is it not for their sakes that I speak all this. . . . But there are very good folk and virtuous that are in the daylight of grace. And yet because the devil tempteth them busily to such fleshly delight, and sith they see plently of worldly substance fall unto them, [they] feel the devil in like wise busily tempt them to set their heart thereupon. . . . . . . And very troublous fear doth there oftentimes arise thereof in the hearts of very good folk when the world falleth fast unto them, because of the sore words and terrible threats that God in Holy Scripture speaketh against those that are rich. As where Saint Paul saith: "They that will be rich fall into temptation, and into the grin[10] of the devil."[11] And where our Savior saith Himself: 'It is more easy for a camel or (as some say for *camelus* so signifieth in the Greek tongue) for a great cable rope to go through a needle's eye, than for a rich man to enter into the kingdom of God."[12]

No marvel now though good folk that fear God take occasion of great dread at so dreadful words, when they see the worldly goods fall to them. And some stand in doubt whether it be lieful[13] for them to keep any good or no. But evermore in all those places of Scripture, the having of the worldly goods is not the thing that is rebuked and threatened, but the affection that the haver unliefully beareth thereto. For where Saint Paul saith: "They that will be made rich," he speaketh not of the having, but of the will and the desire and affection to have, and the longing for it. For that cannot be lightly[14] without sin. For the thing that folk sore long for they will make many shifts[15] to get, and jeopard themself therefor.

And to declare that the having of riches is not forboden, but the inordinate affection of the mind sore set thereupon, the prophet saith: "If riches flow unto you, set not your heart thereupon."[16] And albeit that out Lord by the said ensample of the camel or cable rope to come through the needle's eye said that it is not only hard but also impossible for a rich man to enter into the kingdom of heaven, . . . yet God (He said) can get him in well enough. For unto men, He said, it was impossible, but not unto God. For unto God, He said, all things are possible. And yet, over that, He told of which manner rich men He meant that could not get into the kingdom of heaven, saying: "My babes, how hard is it for them that put their trust and confidence in their money to enter into the kingdom of God."[17]

VINCENT: This is, I suppose, uncle, very true, and else God forbid. For else were the world in a full hard case,[18] if every rich man were in such danger and peril.

ANTHONY: That were it, cousin, indeed; and so I ween is it yet. For I fear me that to the multitude there be very few but that they long sore to be rich. And of those that so long to be, very few reserved[19] also but that they set their heart very sore thereon.

VINCENT: This is, uncle, I fear me, very true, but yet not the thing that I was about to speak of. But the thing that I would have said was this: that I cannot well perceive (the world being such as it is, and so many poor people therein) how any man may be rich and keep him rich without danger of damnation therefore. For all the while that he seeth poor people so many that lack, while himself hath [money] to give them, [their] necessity . . . he is bounden in such case of duty to relieve. So far forth that holy Saint Ambrose sayeth that whoso that die for default where we might help them, we kill them.[20] I cannot see but that every rich man hath great cause to stand in great fear of damnation. Nor I cannot perceive, as I say, how he can be delivered of that fear as long as he keepeth his riches.

And therefore, though he might keep his riches if there lacked poor men and yet stand in God's favor therewith (as Abraham did and many another holy rich man since), yet in such abundance of poor men as there be now in every country, any man that keepeth any riches, it must needs be that he hath an inordinate affection thereunto. [For] he giveth it not out unto the poor needy persons that the duty of charity bindeth and straineth him to. And thus, uncle, in this world at this day, meseemeth your comfort unto good men, that are rich and troubled with fear of damnation for the keeping, can very scantly serve.

ANTHONY: . . . . . . To peruse every circumstance that might, cousin, in this matter be touched, and were to be considered and weighed, would indeed make this part of this devil of business a very busy piece of work and a long. But I shall a little open the point that you speak of, and shall shew you what I think therein with as few words as I conveniently can, and then will we go to dinner.

1 Psalms 90:6.
2 humming like bumble bees.
3 John 12:35.
4 One of the favorite Renaissance games was the maze. It consisted of a confusing and intricate network of passages, laid out in a pattern of concentric fences or hedges. The purpose was to find one's way from the entrance to the exit. Most players got so confused that they wound up back where they started, or else arrived at a *cul de sac* in the center. One of the most beautifully preserved mazes, dating from the reign of George I, is at Hampton Court Palace in Surrey, England.
5 outside edge or perimeter (of the maze).
6 Job 21:13.
7 Luke 12:20.
8 tormented.
9 "both twain": both of the two actions. The anecdote treats More's second wife, Dame Alice. See Harpsfield, p. 94.
10 snare, trap.
11 1 Tim. 6:9.
12 Luke 18:25.
13 permissible.
14 easily.
15 underhanded schemes—i.e., go to any extremity to get.
16 Psalms 61:11.
17 Mark 10:23.
18 in a very unfortunate condition.
19 left over, remaining.
20 In *Treatises on the Gospel of St. Luke,* Book VIII, Chap. 18, by St. Ambrose (340?-397), bishop of Milan. The most recent edition is *Traité sur l'Evangile de S. Luc.* Texte latin, traduction, et notes de G. Tissot (1956-8). Ambrose's *Letters* (trans. Sister Mary Beyenka) and his *Theological and Dogmatic Works* (trans. Roy J. Deferrari) have been published by Fathers of the Church, 1954 and 1963.

Chapter 22

[A Defense of Capitalism]

[ANTHONY:] First, cousin, he that is a rich man and keepeth all his good[s], he hath, I think, very good cause to be very feard indeed. And yet I fear me that such folk fear it least. For they be very far from the state of good men, sith if they keep still all, then are they very far from charity, and do (you wot well) [give] alms either little or none at all.

But now is our question, cousin, not in what case that rich man standeth that keepeth all, but whether we should suffer men to stand in a perilous dread and fear for the keeping of any great part. For if that by the keeping still of so much as maketh a rich man, still they stand in the state of damnation, then are the curates bounden plainly to tell them so according to the commandment of God given unto them all in the person of Ezekiel.[1] . . . . . .

But, cousin, though God invited men unto the following of Himself in willful poverty, . . . [that] they may the more speedily get and attain the state of spiritual perfection and the hungry desire and longing for celestial things, yet doth He not command every man so to do upon the peril of damnation. For where He saith: "He that forsaketh not all that ever he hath cannot be my disciple,"[2] He declareth well by other words of His own in the selfsame place a little before what He meaneth. For there saith He more: "He that cometh to me, and hateth not his father and mother, and his wife and his children and his brethren and his sisters—yea, and his own life too—cannot be my disciple."[3]

Here meaneth our Savior Christ that none can be His disciple but if he love Him so far above all his kin and above his own life too, that for the love of Him rather than to forsake Him, he shall forsake them all. And so meaneth He by those other words, that whosoever do not so renounce and forsake all that ever he hath in his own heart and affection, that he will rather lose it all and let it go every whit than deadly displease God with the reserving of any one part thereof, he cannot be Christ's disciple. . . . . . . But, as I said, to give away all, or that no man should be rich or have substance, that find I no commandment of. There are, as our Savior, saith, in the house of His Father many mansions.[4] And happy shall he be that shall have the grace to dwell even in the lowest.

It seemeth verily by the gospel[5] that those which for God's sake patiently suffer penury shall not only dwell above those in heaven that live here in plenty in earth, but also that heaven in some manner of wise more properly belongeth unto them, and is more specially prepared for them than it is for the rich. . . . . . . But now, although this be thus in respect of the riches and the poverty compared together, yet they being good men both, there may be some other virtue beside wherein the rich man may . . . peradventure excel. Th[en] he may in heaven be far above that poor man that was here in earth in other virtues far under him—as the proof appeareth clear in Lazarus and Abraham.

Nor I say not this to the intent to comfort rich men in heaping up of riches. For a little comfort is bent[6] thereto for them. They be not so proud-hearted and obstinate but that they would, I ween, to that counsel be with right little exhortation very conformable. But I say this for those good men to whom God giveth substance and the mind to dispose it well, and yet not the mind to give it all away at once, but for good causes to keep some substance still. [They] should not despair of God's favor for the not doing of the thing which God hath given them no commandment of nor drawn by any special calling thereunto.

Zacchaeus, lo, [he] climbed up into the tree for desire that he had to behold our Savior at such time as Christ called aloud unto him and said: "Zacchaeus, make haste and come down, for this day must I dwell in thy house."[7] . . . All the people murmured much that Christ would call him and be so familiar with him as of His own offer to come unto his house. [For] they knew him for the chief of the publicans that were customers[8] or toll gatherers of the emperor's duties—all which whole company were among the people sore infamed[9] of ravin, extortion, and bribery. And then Zacchaeus [was] not only the chief of the fellowship, but also grown greatly rich, whereby the people accounted him in their own opinion for a man very sinful and naught.

[But] he forthwith by the instinct of the Spirit of God, in reproach of all such temerarious, bold, and blind judgment given upon a man whose inward mind and sudden change they cannot see, shortly proved them all deceived. . . . Our Lord had at those few words outwardly spoken to him[10] so wrought in his heart within, that whatsoever he was before, he was then, unware[11] unto them all, suddenly waxen good. For he made haste and came down, and gladly received Christ and said: "Lo, Lord, the one half of my good[s] here I give unto poor people; and yet over that, if I have in anything deceived any man, here am I ready to recompense him fourfold as much."[12]

VINCENT: This was, uncle, a gracious hearing.[13] But yet I marvel me somewhat wherefore Zacchaeus used his words in that manner of order. For methinketh he should first have spoken of making restitution unto those whom he had beguiled, and then speak of giving his alms after. For restitution is (you wot well) duty and a thing of such necessity that in respect of restitution, alms deed is but voluntary. Therefore it might seem that, to put men in mind of their duty in making restitution first and doing their alms after, Zacchaeus should have said more conveniently, if he had said first that he would make every man restitution whom he had wronged, and then give half in alms of that that remained after. For only that might he call clearly his own.

ANTHONY: This is true, cousin, where a man hath not enough to suffice for both. But he that hath is not bounden to leave[14] his almsgiving to the poor man that is at his hand and peradventure calleth upon him, till he go seek up all his creditors and all those that he hath wronged. [They are] so far peradventure asunder,[15] that leaving the one good deed undone the while, he may, before they come together, change that good mind again, and do neither the one nor the other. It is good alway to be doing some good out of hand while we think thereon; grace shall the better stand with us, and increase also to go the farther in the other after.[16] . . . . . .

But his words declared that he was deep enough in his reckoning,[17] that if half his good were given away, yet were he well able to yield every man his duty with the other half, and yet leave himself no beggar neither. For he said not he would give away all. . . . . . . Yet forasmuch as he might both lawfully use his substance that he minded to reserve, and lawfully might use his office too, . . . our Lord well allowing his good purpose, and exacting no further forth of him concerning his worldly behavior, answered and said: "This day is health comen to this house, for that he too is the son of Abraham."[18]

But now forget I not, cousin, that in effect thus far you condescended unto me, that a man may be rich, and yet not out of state of grace nor out of God's favor. Howbeit, you think that though it may be so in some time or in some place, yet at this time and in this place (or any such other like), wherein be so many poor people upon whom they be (you think) bounden to bestow their good, they can keep no riches with conscience.

Verily, cousin, if that reason would hold, I ween the world was never such anywhere in which any man might have kept any substance without the danger of damnation. As for since Christ's days to the world's end, we have the witness of His own word that there hath never lacked poor men nor never shall. For He said Himself: "Poor men shall you alway have with you, whom when you will you may do good unto."[19] So that, as I tell you, if your rule should hold, then were there, I ween, no place in no time since Christ's days hitherto (nor as I think in as long before that neither, nor never shall there hereafter), in which there could any man abide rich without the danger of eternal damnation—even for his riches alone, though he demeaned it never so well.

But, cousin, men of substance must there be, for else shall you have more beggars (pardie) than there be, and no man left able to relieve another. For this I think in my mind a very sure conclusion, that if all the money that is in this country were tomorrow next brought together out of every man's hand and laid all upon one heap, and then divided out unto every man alike, it would be on the morrow after worse than it was the day before. For I suppose when it were all equally thus divided among all, the best should be left little better then than almost a beggar is now. And yet he that was a beggar before, all that . . . he should thereby receive shall not make him much above a beggar still. But many one of the rich men, if their riches stood but in movable substance,[20] shall be safe enough from riches haply for all their life after.

Men cannot, you wot well, live here in this world but if that some one man provide a mean of living for some other many. Every man cannot have a ship of his own, nor every man be a merchant without a stock . . . , nor every man cannot have a plough by himself. And who might live by the tailor's craft if no man were able to put a gown to make?[21] Who by the masonry, or who could live a carpenter, if no man were able to build neither church nor house? Who should be the makers of any manner cloth if there lacked men of substance to set sundry sorts a-work? Some man that hath not two ducats in his house were better forbear them both and leave himself not a farthing (but utterly lose all his own), than that some rich man by whom he is weekly set a-work should of his money lose the one half.

For then were himself like to lack work. For surely the rich man's substance is the wellspring of the poor man's living. And therefore here would it fare by the poor man as it fared by the woman in one of Aesop's fables.[22] [She] had an hen that laid her every day a golden egg, till on a day she thought she would have a great many eggs at once. And therefore she killed her hen and found but one or twain in her belly, so that for a few she lost many.

1 Ezech. 33:8.
2 Luke 14:33.
3 Ibid., 14:46.
4 John 14:2.
5 Luke 16:9.
6 pasture, comfortable grassland.
7 Luke 19:5.
8 custom agents.
9 notorious for (plundering, etc.).
10 The 1553 edition here inserts *so touched him, that his grace* after "spoken to him." The Rastell text seems clearer.
11 unnoticed.
12 Luke 19:8.
13 I.e., a gracious thing to hear spoken.
14 leave off, ignore.
15 scattered (geographically).
16 I.e., giving alms to the poor now will better put us in the mood to make restitution later to those we have wronged.
17 careful enough in computing (his financial position).
18 Luke 19:9. In reference to the last sentence of this paragraph, note also Luke 16:22 and Vincent's observation in Part I, Chap. 15, p. 45.
19 Matt. 26:11.
20 I.e., unless their riches stood only in liquid assets like money (as distinguished from solid assets like property), they will still have enough wealth to remain secure, etc.
21 to request (place an order for) a gown to be made.
22 The Greek fabulist Aesop (c. 620-c. 560 B.C.). Caxton in 1484 published an English edition of *Aesop's Fables,* including supplementary fables by Avian, Alfonso, and Poggio. In the Caxton text, "The Goose and Her Lord" is presented as the 24th fable of Avian (not Aesop). During the sixteenth and seventeenth centuries the story got transformed into a woman killing her hen, probably through confusion with Aesop's fable about a woman who gave her hen extra corn in an effort to get it to lay twice as many (normal) eggs. See "A Woman and a Fat Hen," Aesop Fable #87, in Sir Roger L'Estrange's 5th (1708) edition.

Chapter 23

[Philanthropy Begins at Home]

[ANTHONY (continuing):] But now, cousin, to come to your doubt how it may be that a man may with conscience keep riches with him when he seeth so many poor men upon whom he may bestow it.... ... Our Savior saith: "Give every man that asketh thee."[1] [According to this,] he[2] be bounden to give out still to every beggar that will ask him, as long as any penny lasteth in his purse. But verily, cousin, that saying hath (as Saint Austin saith other places in Scripture hath) need of interpretation.[3] For, as holy Saint Austin saith, though Christ say give every man that asketh thee, He saith not yet give them all that they will ask thee. But surely all were one if he meant to bind me by commandment to give every man without exception somewhat, for so should I leave myself nothing!

Our Savior in that place of the sixth chapter of Saint Luke, speaketh both of the contempt that we should in heart have of these worldly things and also of the manner that men should use toward their enemies.... And among these things He biddeth us to give every man that asketh, meaning that in the thing that we may conveniently do a man we should not refuse it, what manner of man soever he be, though he were our mortal enemy—namely[4] where we see that, but if we help him ourself, the person of the man should stand in peril of perishing. And therefore saith Saint Paul: "If thine enemy be in hunger give him meat."[5]

But now, though I be bounden to give every manner man in some manner of his necessity, were he my friend or my foe, Christian man or heathen, yet am I not unto all men bounden alike nor unto any man in every case alike. But (as I began to tell you) the differences of the circumstances make great change in the matter. Saint Paul saith: "He that provideth not for those that are his, is worse than an infidel."[6] Those are ours that are belonging to our charge either by nature or by law or any commandment of God. By nature as our children, by law as our servants in our household.

So that, albeit these two sorts be not ours all alike, yet would I think that the least ours of the twain (that is to wit, our servants), if they need and lack, we be bounden to look to and provide for their need, and see so far forth as we may that they lack not the things that should serve for their necessity while they dwell in our service.[7] Meseemeth also that if they fall sick in our service, so that they cannot do the service that we retain them for, yet may we not in any wise turn them then out of doors and cast them up comfortless while they be not able to labor and help themself. For this were a thing against all humanity.

[Take even] a wayfaring man that I received into my house as a guest. If he f[e]ll sick therein and his money gone, I [would] reckon myself bounden to keep him still, and rather to beg about for his relief than cast him out in that case[8] to the peril of his life, what loss soever I should hap to sustain in the keeping of him. For when God hath by such chance sent him to me and there once matched me with him, I reckon myself surely charged with him till I may without peril of his life be well and conveniently discharged of him.

[Further,] . . . Saint Paul saith it is not the children's part to provide for the parents, but the parents' to provide for the children.[9] Provide, I mean, conveniently good learning or good occupations to get their living by with truth and the favor of God, but not make provision for them of such manner living as to Godward they should live the worse for. But rather, if they see by their manner that too much would make them naught, the father should then give them a great deal the less. . . . But the order of nature also compelleth that the children should both in reverent behavior honor their father and mother, and also in all their necessity maintain them. And yet as much as God and nature both bindeth us to the sustenance of our own father, his need may be so little, though it be somewhat, and a fremd[10] man's so great, that both nature and God also would [decree that] I should in such unequal need relieve that urgent necessity of a stranger—yea, [even were he] my foe, and God's enemy too, the very Turk or Saracen. . . . . . .

But now, cousin, out of my case of[11] such extreme needs well perceived and known unto myself, I am not bounden to give every beggar that will ask, nor to believe every faitour[12] that I meet in the street that will say himself that he is very sick, nor to reckon all the poor folk committed by God only so to my charge alone, that none other man should give them nothing of his, till I have first given out all mine. Nor am [I] not bounden neither to have so evil opinion of all other folk save myself, as to think that but if I help, the poor folk shall all fail at once, for God hath left in all this quarter no more good folk now but me. I may think better by my neighbors and worse by myself than so, and yet come to heaven by God's grace well enough.

VINCENT: Marry, uncle, but some man will peradventure be right well content in such cases to think his neighbors very charitable, to the intent that he may think himself at liberty to give nothing at all.

ANTHONY: That is, cousin, very true. So will there some be content either to think or make as though they thought; but those are they that are content to give nought because they be naught. But our question is, cousin, not of them, but of good folk that by the keeping of worldly good[s] stand in great fear to offend God. For the acquieting of their conscience speak we now, to the intent that they may perceive what manner of having of worldly good[s] and keeping thereof may stand with[13] the state of grace. Now think I, cousin, that if a man keep riches about him for a glory and royalty of the world,[14] in the consideration whereof he taketh a great delight and liketh himself therefor, taking the poorer for the lack thereof as one far worse than himself—such a mind is very vain foolish pride, and such a man is very naught indeed.

But on the other side, [suppose] there be a man (such as would God there were many) that hath unto riches no love, but having it fall abundantly unto him, taketh to his own part no great pleasure thereof but as though he had it not. [He] keepeth himself in like abstinence and penance privily as he would do in case he had it not. And in such things as he doth openly, [he] bestow[s] somewhat more liberally upon himself in his house after some manner of the world,[15] lest he should give other folk occasion to marvel and muse and talk of his manner and misreport him for an hypocrite. . . .

He doth it not for any desire thereof in the satisfying of his own pleasure, but would with as goodwill or better forbear the possession of riches—saving for the commodity that other men have by his disposing thereof. As percase in keeping a good household in good Christian order and fashion, and in setting other folk a-work with such things as they gain their living the better by his means. This man's having of riches I might, methinketh, in merit match in a manner with another man's forsaking of all, if there were none other circumstance more pleasant unto God added farther unto the forsaking beside.[16]

Now if he that have this good[17] and riches by him have not haply fully so perfect a mind, but somewhat loveth to keep himself from lack . . . well, what will you more? The man is so much the less perfect than I would he were, and haply than himself would wish if it were as easy to be it as to wish it. But yet [he is] not by and by in state of damnation for all that, no more than *every man is forthwith in state of damnation*[18] that, forsaking all and entering into religion, is not yet alway so clear depured[19] from all worldly affections as himself would very fain he were, and much bewaileth that he is not. . . .

Some man that hath in the world willingly forsaken the likelihood of right worshipful rooms hath afterward had much ado to keep himself from the desire of the office of cellarer,[20] or sexton, to bear yet at the least wise some rule and authority, though it were but among the bellies. But God is more merciful to man's imperfection, if the man know it and knowledge it and mislike it and little and little labor to mend it. . . .

And therefore, cousin, to make an end of this piece withal: . . . . . . Let every man fear and think in this world that all the good that he doth or can do is a great deal too little. But yet for all that fear, let him dwell therewith in the faithful hope of God's help, and then shall the truth of God so compass him about, as the prophet saith, with a pavis, that he shall not so need to dread the trains and the temptations of this devil that the prophet calleth "business" walking about in the darknesses. But th[en] he shall, for all the having of riches and worldly substance, so avoid his trains and temptations, that he shall in conclusion, by the great grace and almighty mercy of God, get into heaven well enough.

And now was I (cousin) about, lo, after this piece thus ended, to bid them bring in our dinner;[21] but now shall I not need, lo, for here they come with it already.

[Servants enter with trays of food.]

VINCENT: Forsooth, good uncle, God disposeth and timeth your matter[22] and your dinner both, I trust. For the end of your good tale (for which our Lord reward you) and the beginning here of your good dinner too (from which it were more than pity that you should any longer have tarried) meet even at the close together.

ANTHONY: Well, cousin, now will we say grace, and then for a while will we leave talking and assay how our dinner shall like us, and how fair we can fall to feeding. Which done, you know my customable guise (for manner I may not call it, because the guise is unmannerly) to bid you not farewell, but steal away from you to sleep. But you wot well I am not wont at afternoon to sleep long, but even a little to forget the world.[23] And when I wake I will again come to you, and then is (God willing) all this long day ours, wherein we shall have time enough to take much more than shall suffice for the finishing of this one part of our matter which only now remaineth.[24]

VINCENT: I pray you, good uncle, keep your customable manner, for manner may you call it well enough. For . . . it were against good manner to look that a man should kneel down for courtesy when his knee is sore. So is it very good manner that a man of your age, aggrieved with such sundry sicknesses beside[s] that suffer you not alway to sleep when you should, [should] let his sleep not slip away, but take it when he may. And I will, uncle, in the meanwhile steal from you too, and speed[25] a little errand and return to you again.

ANTHONY: Tarry while you will, and when you have dined go at your pleasure, but I pray you tarry not long.

VINCENT: You shall not need, uncle, to put me in mind of that, I would so fain have up the remnant of our matter.

1 Luke 6:30.
2 I.e., the rich man.
3 See *City of God,* Book XI, Chaps. 19, 34; Book XX, Chap. 20; and Book XVII, Chap. 3. In these and other sections, Augustine stresses the need for careful interpretation of difficult passages.
4 especially.
5 Rom. 12:20.
6 1 Tim. 5:28.
7 More's love for his servants is amply demonstrated in the Nostell copy of Holbein's More family painting, for which More insisted on including his jester, Henry Patenson, and his secretary, John Harris. See Plate 4.
8 condition.
9 2 Cor. 12:14.
10 unrelated, not of kin.
11 apart from, over and beyond.
12 cheater, faker.
13 be compatible with.
14 I.e., for mere ostentatious display.
15 to some extent as the rest of the world does.
16 I.e., if there were no particular motivation for forsaking the riches other than the mere feeling that one ought not to possess them.
17 these (material) goods.
18 The italicized words are found in Rastell but not in the 1553 edition. See Part I, Chap. 13, n. 2.
19 purified.
20 monastic official in charge of provision.
21 the midday meal—i.e., lunch.
22 discussion.
23 This is possibly an allusion to More's own latter day habit of taking an afternoon nap.
24 Anthony alludes here to the final part of the discussion, which is to be built around Psalm 90:6—"the incursion of the devil in the midday"—i.e., persecution.
25 take care of.

[PART III]

[*Setting*: Anthony's home, a few hours later]

Introduction

[News from Constantinople]

VINCENT: Somewhat have I tarried the longer, uncle, partly for that I was loath to come over soon, lest my soon coming might have happed to have made you wake too soon. But specially did I tarry by the reason that I was letted with[1] one that shewed me a letter dated at Constantinople—by which letter it appeareth that the great Turk prepareth a marvellous mighty army. And yet whither he will therewith, that can there yet no man tell; but I fear in good faith, uncle, that his voyage shall be hither. Howbeit, he that wrote the letter saith that it is secretly said in Constantinople that great part of his army shall be shipped and sent either into Naples or into Sicily.

ANTHONY: It may fortune, cousin, that the letter of the Venetian[2] dated at Constantinople was devised at Venice. From thence come there some among, and sometime from Rome too, and sometime also from some other places, letters all farced[3] full of such tidings that the Turk is ready to do some great exploit. [These] tidings they blow about for the furtherance of some such affairs as they then have themself in hand. The Turk hath also . . . many men of arms in his retinue at his continual charge. . . . Lest they should lie still and do nothing, but peradventure fall in devising of some novelties[4] among themself, he is fain[5] yearly to make some assemblies and some changing of them from one place unto another. [He] part[s] some sort asunder,[6] that they wax not over well acquainted by dwelling overlong together.

By these ways also he maketh those that he mindeth suddenly to invade indeed the less to look therefor, and thereby the less preparation to make before, while they see him so many times make a great visage of war when he mindeth it not. But then at one time or other they suddenly feel it when they fear it not. Howbeit, full likely (cousin) it is of very truth that into this realm of Hungary he will not fail to come. For neither is there any country through Christendom that lieth for him so meet, nor never was there any time till now in which he might so well and surely win it. For now call we him in ourself,[7] God save us, as Aesop telleth that the sheep took in the wolf unto them to keep them from the dogs.[8]

VINCENT: Then are there very like, good uncle, all those tribulations to fall upon us here that I spake of in the beginning of our first communication here the other day.

ANTHONY: Very truth it is, cousin, that so there will of likelihood in a while, but not forthwith all at the first. For while he cometh under the color of aid for the one against the other,[9] he will somewhat see the proof before he fully shew himself.[10] But in conclusion, if he be able to get it for him, you shall see him so handle it that he shall not fail to get it from him, and that forthwith out of hand, ere ever he suffer him settle himself over-sure therein.[11]

VINCENT: Yet say they, uncle, that he useth not to force any man to forsake his faith.

ANTHONY: Not any man, cousin? They say more than they can make good that tell you so. He maketh a solemn oath among the ceremonies of that feast,[12] in which he first taketh upon him his authority, that he shall—in all that he possible may—minish the faith of Christ and dilate the faith of Mahomet.[13] But yet hath he not used to force every whole country at once to forsake their faith. For of some countries hath he been content only to take a tribute yearly, and let them then live as they list. Out of some he taketh the whole people away, dispersing them for slaves among many sundry countries of his very far from their own, without any sufferance of regret.[14]

[In] some country, so great and populous that they cannot well be carried and conveyed thence, he destroyeth the gentlemen and giveth the lands, part to such as he bringeth, and part to such as willingly will reney[15] their faith. [He] keepeth the other in such misery that they were in manner as good be dead at once. In rest[16] he suffereth else no Christian man almost, but those that resort as merchants or those that offer themself to serve him in his war.

But [consider] those Christian countries that he useth not for only tributaries (as he doth Chios,[17] Cyprus, Crete), but reckoneth for clear conquest and utterly taketh for his own, as Morea,[18] Greece, and Macedonia and such other like—and as I verily think he will Hungary if he get it. In all those, useth he Christian people after sundry fashions. He letteth them dwell there indeed, because they were too many to carry all away, and too many to kill them all too. . . . There, lo, those that will not be turned from their faith, of which God keepeth (lauded be His holy name) very many, he suffereth to dwell still in peace.

But yet is their peace for all that not very peaceable. For lands he suffereth them to have none of their own. Office or honest room they bear none. With occasions of his wars he pilleth[19] them with taxes and tallages[20] unto the bare bones. Their children he chooseth where he list in their youth and taketh them from their parents, conveying them whither he list where their friends never see them after. And [he] abuseth them as he list: some young maidens [he] maketh harlots, some young men he bringeth up in war, and some young children he causeth to be gelded—not their stones cut out as the custom was of old, but cutteth off their whole members [from] the body. How few [e]scape and live he little forceth,[21] for he will have enough. And all that he so taketh young to any use of his own are betaken unto such Turks or false renegades to keep, that they be turned from the faith of Christ every one, or else so handled that as for this world they come to an evil cheving.[22]

For beside many other contumelies[23] and despites that the Turks and the false renegade Christians many times do to good Christian people that still persevere and abide by the faith, they find the mean[s] sometime to make some false shrews[24] say that they heard such a Christian man speak opprobrious words against Mahomet. And upon that point falsely testified will they take occasion to compel him forsake the faith of Christ and turn to the profession of their shameful superstitious sect, or else will they put him unto death with cruel intolerable torments.

VINCENT: Our Lord, uncle, for His mighty mercy keep those wretches hence. For, by my troth, if they hap to come hither, methink I see many more tokens than one that we shall have [many] of our own folk here ready to fall in unto them. For like as before a great storm the sea beginneth sometime to work and roar in itself ere ever the winds wax boisterous, so methink I hear at mine ear some of our own here among us, which within these few years could no more have borne the name of a Turk than the name of the devil, begin now to find little fault therein. Yea, and some . . . praise them[25] too, little and little as they may, [and are] more glad to find faults at every state of Christendom, priests, princes, rites, ceremonies, sacraments, laws, and customs spiritual, temporal, and all.

ANTHONY: In good faith, cousin, so begin we to fare here indeed, and that but even now of late. For since the title of the crown hath comen in question the good rule of this realm hath very sore decayed, as little while as it is.[26] And undoubtedly Hungary shall never do well as long as it standeth in this case, that men's minds hearken after novelty and have their hearts hanging upon a change. And much the worse I like it when their words walk so large toward the favor of the Turk's sect, which they were ever wont to have in so great abomination—as every true-minded Christian man, and Christian woman too, must have.

I am of such age as you see, and verily from as far as I can remember it hath been marked and often proved true that when children have in Buda[27] fallen in a fantasy by themself to draw together, and in their playing make as it were corpses carried to church, and sing after their childish fashion the tune of the dirge, there hath great death there shortly followed after. And twice or thrice I may remember in my days when children in divers parts of this realm have gathered themself in sundry companies and made as it were [war] parties and battles. And after their battles in sport, wherein some children have yet taken great hurt, there hath fallen very battle and deadly war indeed.

These tokens were somewhat like your ensample of the sea, sith they be of things that after follow tokens foregoing,[28] through some secret motion or instinct whereof the cause is unknown. But by Saint Mary, cousin, these tokens like I much worse—these tokens I say, not of children's plays nor of children's songs, but old shrews' large open words so boldly spoken in the favor of Mahomet's sect in this realm of Hungary (that hath been ever hitherto a very sure key of Christendom). And, out of doubt, if Hungary be lost and that the Turk have it once fast in his possession, he shall (ere it be long after) have an open ready way into almost the remnant of all Christendom. Though he win it not all in a week, the great part will be won after, I fear me, within very few years.

VINCENT: But yet evermore I trust in Christ, good uncle, that He shall not suffer that abominable sect of His mortal enemies in such wise to prevail against His Christian countries.

ANTHONY: That is very well said, cousin. Let us have our sure hope in Him, and then shall we be very sure that we shall not be deceived. For either shall we have the thing that we hope for, or a better thing in the stead. For as for the thing itself that we pray for and hope to have, God will not alway send [it to] us. And therefore (as I said in our first communication), in all thing save only for heaven, our prayer nor our hope may never be too precise, although the thing be lieful to require.[29]

Verily, if we people of the Christian nations were such as would God we were, I would little fear all the preparations that the great Turk could make. No, nor yet being as bad as we be, I nothing doubt at all but that in conclusion, how base[30] soever Christendom be brought, ... this ungracious[31] sect of Mahomet shall have a foul fall and Christendom spring and spread, flower and increase again. Howbeit, the pleasure and the comfort shall they see that shall be born after that we be buried, I fear me, both twain.[32]

For God giveth us great likelihood that for our sinful wretched living He goeth about to make these infidels, that are His open professed enemies, the sorrowful scourge of correction over evil Christian people that should be faithful, and are of truth His falsely professed friends.[33] And surely, cousin, albeit that methinketh I see divers tokens of this misery coming to us, yet can there not in my mind be a worse[34] prognostication thereof than this ungracious token that you note here yourself. For undoubtedly, cousin, this new manner here of men's favorable fashion in their language toward these ungracious Turks declareth plainly that not only their minds give them that hither in shall he come, but also that they can be content . . . to live under him. . . .

VINCENT: . . . Many of these fellows that are meet[35] for the war first were wont as it were in sport and, in a while after, half between game and earnest, and (by our Lady) now not far from fair flat earnest indeed, talk as though they looked for a day when with a turn unto the Turk's faith they should be made masters here of true Christian men's bodies, and owners of all their goods.

ANTHONY: Though I go little abroad,[36] cousin, yet hear I sometime, when I say little, almost as much as that. But while there is no man to complain to for the redress, what remedy [is there] but patience, and fain[37] to sit still and hold my peace? For of these two[38] that strive whether[39] of them both shall reign upon us, . . . each of them calleth himself king, and both twain put the people to pain. The one is, you wot well, too far from our quarters here[40] to help us in this behalf, and the other, while he looketh for the Turk's aid, either will not or I ween well dare not find any fault with them that favor the Turk and his sect.[41] For of Turks natural this country lacketh none now, which are here conversant under divers pretexts,[42] and of every thing advertise the great Turk full surely.

And therefore, cousin, . . . I would advise every man pray still and call unto God to hold His gracious hand over us, and keep away this wretchedness if His pleasure [so] be. Yet would I farther advise every good Christian body to remember and consider that it is very likely to come, and therefore make his reckoning and cast his pennyworths before.[43] [Let] every man and every woman both, appoint with God's help in their own mind beforehand, what thing they intend to do if the very worst fall.

1 held up by.
2 I.e., the man who showed Vincent the letter. Renaissance Venice was a center of intrigue and conspiracy.
3 stuffed.
4 unauthorized actions (e.g., insurrection).
5 prompted.
6 I.e., he periodically splits up and reorganizes various military units.
7 John Zapolya, one of the two claimants to the Hungarian throne, had appealed to Suleiman I for aid after being expelled from the capital by his rival claimant, Ferdinand of Austria, in 1527. See above, Part I, Intro., ns. 21, 22.
8 Possibly More's faulty recollection, or deliberate adaptation, of Aesop's Fable 23, Book III ("Of the Wolves and of the Sheep") as printed in Caxton's 1484 edition. A variation of the same story is presented as Fable 45 ("A League betwixt the Wolves and the Sheep") in the L'Estrange text (5th ed., 1708). In both versions the wolves agree to a truce with the sheep, if the latter will give over their dog-protectors as hostages. When the sheep agree, the wolves kill the dogs and devour the sheep. The obvious moral of the story, as presented by Anthony, is that any alliance with the wolfish Turks will be disastrous for the naively sheep-like Hungarians. Re: Anthony's distrust of Turkish promises and pledges, see Part III, Chapter 14.
9 I.e., on behalf of Zapolya and against Ferdinand.
10 I.e., he (Suleiman) will look over the situation carefully before he shows his hand.
11 Even if Suleiman gets the crown for Zapolya, says Anthony, he will grab it back before Zapolya can get en-

trenched in the job. Anthony is implying that, should Suleiman invade Hungary to reinstate Zapolya, it will be only in order to usurp the whole country himself eventually. This in effect happened in 1547, when Turkey annexed the whole southcentral portion of Hungary.

12 The reference is to the ceremonies by which Suleiman became Sultan in 1520.

13 Anthony's attitude of fear and antipathy for "Suleiman the Magnificent" was typical of Renaissance Christians, and was partly justified. The Great Turk was not, e.g., above harem intrigue: apparently as a result of his wife Roxelana's influence, he murdered two of his own sons, and executed his own grand visier. On the other hand, his own people considered him just, courteous, and wise. The Turks called him "Lawgiver," partly for his organization of a learned class. He began his reign by freeing all prisoners of war and restoring goods confiscated from merchants by Selim I. Quite contrary to the impression Anthony gives, some of his legal enactments even ameliorated the condition of his Christian subjects.

14 This is a just accusation. In an earlier invasion (which More for dramatic purposes ignores in constructing his narrative framework), Suleiman had carried 105,000 Hungarians away into captivity and forced labor.

15 renege, renounce.

16 among the remainder—i.e., among those other than the nobility (whose land the Turk usurps) and the peasants (whom he keeps in misery).

17 An island in the Aegean off the west coast of Turkey.

18 Peloponnesus: the peninsula forming the southern part of the mainland of Greece.

19 For the support of his wars he strips.

20 tolls.

21 cares.

22 end.

23 harsh words—instances of contemptuous language or treatment.

24 malicious persons.

25 I.e., the Turks.

26 In defiance of the Turkish appointment of Zapolya, Ferdinand had gotten himself crowned king of Hungary in 1527. The resulting civil war, complicated by Suleiman's intervention on behalf of Zapolya, continued until 1538, when the two men finally agreed to partition the country. Anthony's statement that the crown has been disputed for only a "little while," combined with the fact that Suleiman invaded Hungary in 1529, clearly establishes 1528 as the time-setting for the *Dialogue of Comfort.*

27 The two medieval towns "Buda" and "Pest" have now merged into the modern city.

28 I.e., the roaring sea and the children's mock-battles are symbolic foreshadowings of (dire) events to come.

29 permissible to request.

30 low.

31 I.e., outside the pale of God's grace. Anthony had used the same term in reference to witchcraft in Part I, Chap. 18. Note also the reference to "ungracious Turks" in the next paragraph.

32 both of us.

33 More here reflects the standard view of Renaissance Christians, that the Turk was the scourge of God, sent to punish Christians for their sins. See C. A. Patrides, "The Bloody and Cruell Turke: The Background of a Renaissance Commonplace," *Studies in the Renaissance,* X (1963), 126-135.

34 more ominous.

35 anxious for war—i.e., pleased at the prospect of Turkish invasion.

36 outside the house.

37 (a reluctant) willingness.

38 Zapolya and Ferdinand.

39 which.

40 Ferdinand was of course based in Austria, and, as archduke, had heavy responsibilities there.

41 A reference to the fact that Zapolya was obviously a puppet of the Turks and would therefore take no action against the pro-Turkish element in the country.

42 I.e., in addition to the pro-Turkish Hungarians, there are many real Turks who have infiltrated the country under various diplomatic or commercial pretexts.

43 I.e., decide where he stands in advance (of the invasion).

Chapter 1

[Should We Anticipate Persecution?]

[Vincent questions whether it is wise to think too much about persecution in advance. If a man promises not to desert Christ, he might later (as St. Peter did) find it necessary to break his word. If on the other hand a man decides that he will forsake Christ if persecuted, he has already sinned, despite the fact that he might never be put to the test. Anthony argues that St. Peter did not displease God in his promise, but only in his later performance. Moreover, though a man might never fall into the peril of persecution, he can be bolstered all his life by a promise to remain faithful.

Besides, it is absurd to counsel a man not to think about persecution, when he will hear people discussing it on all sides. Indeed, priests and parents should raise the issue with their parishioners and children. They should remind them of the pain Christ suffered for them, and should urge them to pray to God for the strength to withstand physical torment. Many men who think they will never be in danger, soon are. Certainly Anthony and Vincent are in for trouble. Under the circumstances, it is unfortunate that they did not begin sooner to reflect on persecution. Vincent urges Anthony to move on quickly to the fourth and final temptation.]

Chapter 2

[The Invasion of the Devil]

[ANTHONY:] The fourth temptation, cousin, that the prophet speaketh of in the fore-remembered psalm,[1] is plain open persecution. Which is touched in these words: "The invasion of the devil in the midday." And of all his temptations this is the most perilous, the most bitter sharp, and the most rigorous. . . . In other temptations he useth either pleasant allectives[2] unto sin, or other secret sleights and trains, and cometh in the night, and stealeth on in the dark unware.[3] . . . [But] in this temptation, this plain open persecution for the faith, he cometh even in the very midday, that is to wit, even upon them that have an high light of faith shining in their heart. And [he] openly suffereth himself so plainly [to] be perceived by his fierce malicious persecution against the faithful Christians, for hatred of Christ's true Catholic faith, that no man having faith can doubt what he is. . . . . . . In other of his temptations he stealeth on like a fox, but in this Turk's persecution for the faith he runneth on roaring with assault like a ramping[4] lion.

This temptation is of all temptations also the most perilous. For . . . in temptations of prosperity he useth only delectable allectives to move a man to sin, and in other kinds of tribulation and adversity he useth only grief and pain to pull a man into murmur,[5] impatience,[6] and blasphemy. [But] in this kind of persecution for the faith of Christ he useth both twain: that is to wit, both his allectives of quiet and rest (by deliverance from death and pain, with other pleasures also of this present life) and beside that, the terror and infliction of intolerable pain and torment.

In other tribulation (as loss, or sickness, or death of our friends), though the pain be peradventure as great and sometime greater too, yet is not the peril nowhere nigh half so much. For in other tribulations (as I said before) that necessity that the man must of fine force[7] abide and endure the pain, wax he never so wroth and impatient therewith, is a great reason to move him to keep his patience therein and be content therewith, and thank God thereof, and of necessity to make a virtue[8] that he may be rewarded for. But in this temptation, this persecution for the faith, . . . he is taken and in hold[9] and may for the forswearing or the denying of his faith be delivered and suffered to live in rest, and

PLATE 6. More on his way to the scaffold. Probably by Antoine Caron (c. 1590). Depicts Margaret Roper breaking through a cordon of guards (clad in pseudo-Roman armor) as More comes out of the Tower. Actually, Margaret performed this action a few days earlier, as More was returning from Westminster after the trial. She was not present at the execution. In the background can be seen, as in a double exposure, Sir Thomas on the scaffold. Reproduced, with permission, from the collection of the Chateau de Blois, France.

some in great worldly wealth also. In this case, I say, this thing that he needeth not to suffer this trouble and pain but he will,[10] is a marvellous great occasion for him to fall into the sin that the devil would drive him to: that is to wit, the forsaking of the faith. . . .

VINCENT: The more perilous, uncle, that this temptation is, . . . the more need have they that stand in peril thereof to be before with substantial advice and good counsel well armed against it. Then we may with the comfort and consolation thereof the better bear that tribulation when it cometh, and the better withstand the temptation.

ANTHONY: You say, cousin Vincent, therein very truth, and I am content to fall therefore in hand therewith.[11] But . . . methinketh that of this tribulation somewhat you be more feard than I. And of truth somewhat more excusable it is in you than it were in me, mine age considered and the sorrow that I have suffered already, with some other considerations upon my part beside.[12] Rehearse you therefore the griefs and the pains that you think in this tribulation possible to fall unto you, and I shall against each of them give you counsel and rehearse you such occasion of comfort and consolation as my poor wit and learning can call unto my mind.

VINCENT: In good faith, uncle, I am not all thing afeard in this case only for myself, but well you wot I have cause to care also for many more, and that folk of sundry sorts, men and women both, and that not all of one age.[13]

ANTHONY: All that you have cause to fear for, cousin, for all them have I cause to fear with you too, sith all your kinsfolk and allies within a little be likewise unto me. Howbeit, to say the truth, every man hath cause in this case to fear, both for himself and also for every other. For [surely] the Scripture saith, "God hath given every man cure[14] and charge of his neighbor."[15] There is no man that hath any spark of Christian love and charity in his breast, but that in a matter of such peril as this is, wherein the soul of man standeth in so great danger to be lost, he must needs care and take thought not for his friends only, but also for his very foes.

We shall therefore, cousin, not rehearse your harms or mine that may befall in this persecution, but all the great harms in general, as near as we can call to mind, that may hap unto any man.

1 Psalms 90:5-6, around which Anthony is building his discussion in Parts II and III.
2 allurements.
3 unbeknown (to the victim).
4 rampaging, raging. The lion is one of More's favorite Scriptural symbols for Satan. Note e.g., Part II, Chap. 12 re: Job 4:10-11; and Part III, Chap. 29 re: 1 Peter 5:8.
5 protest, complaint.
6 restlessness, rebelliousness (against God).
7 no matter what. I.e., we have no control over loss or sickness of friends.
8 An echo of the famous proverb "Make a virtue of necessity." See also paragraph five of I, 8. It originated with Quintillian and St. Jerome, and is found in Chaucer (Troilus IV) and Shakespeare (e.g., *Two Gentlemen of Verona,* IV, i, 61. See under "Necessity" in Morris P. Tilley's *A Dictionary of the Proverbs in England in the 16th and 17th Centuries* (1950).
9 (placed) in prison, held forcibly.
10 unless he wishes it.
11 I.e., agree with you.
12 Probably another allusion to More's difficulties with Henry VIII prior to imprisonment in the Tower. See Part I, Intro., n. 8.
13 Almost certainly an allusion to More's large household, which, in addition to his own wife and children, included servants, in-laws, children of friends, and long-term guests like Holbein. Some idea of the cosmopolitan character of the More household can be gained by examining Holbein's painting of the More family (see Plate 4).
14 care (in sickness); responsibility for restoring to health if ill.
15 Eccles. 17:12.

Chapter 3

[Rooted and Rootless Trees]

[ANTHONY:] Sith a man is made of the body and the soul, all the harm that any man may take, it must needs be in one of these two—either immediately[1] or by the mean of some such thing as serveth for the pleasure, weal, or commodity of the one of these two. As for the soul first, we shall need no rehearsal of any harm that by this kind of tribulation may attain thereto, but if that by some inordinate love and affection that the soul bear to the body she consent to slide from the faith, and thereby do her harm herself.[2] Now remain there the body, and these outward things of fortune[3] which serve for the maintenance of the body. . . . Consider, then, first the loss of those outward things as somewhat the less in weight than is the body itself. In them what may a man lose, and thereby what pain may he suffer?

VINCENT: He may lose, uncle, of which I should somewhat lose myself, money, plate, and other movable substance; then offices, authority; and finally all the lands of his inheritance for ever that himself and his heirs perpetually might else enjoy. And of all these things, uncle, you wot well that myself have some—little in respect of that that some other have here, but somewhat more yet than he that hath most here would be well content to lose.

Upon the loss of these things follow neediness and poverty, the pain of lacking, the shame of begging . . . , beside the grief and heaviness of heart in beholding good men and faithful and his dear friends bewrapped[4] in like misery. And ungracious wretches and infidels and his mortal enemies [would then] enjoy the commodities that himself and his friends have lost. Now for the body, very few words shall serve us. For therein I see none other harm but loss of liberty, labor, imprisonment, painful and shameful death.

ANTHONY: There needeth not much more, cousin, as the world is now. For I fear me that less than a fourth part of this will make many a man sore stagger in his faith and some man fall quite therefrom, that yet at this day, before he come to the proof, weeneth himself that he would stand very fast. And I beseech our Lord that all they that so think . . . may get of God the grace to ween still as they do, and [yet] not to be brought to the assay where pain or fear should shew them, as it shewed Saint Peter,[5] how far they be deceived now.

But now, cousin, against these terrible things what way shall we take in giving men counsel of comfort? If the faith were in our days as fervent as it hath been ere this in time before passed, little counsel and little comfort would suffice. We should not much need with words and reasoning to extenuate and minish the vigor and asperity of the pains. But the greater and the more bitter that the passion were, the more ready was of old time the fervor of faith to suffer it.

And surely, cousin, I doubt it little in my mind, but that if a man had in his heart so deep a desire and love, longing to be with God in heaven, to have the fruition of His glorious face as had those holy men that were martyrs in old time, he would no more now stick at the pain that he must pass between than at that time those old holy martyrs did.[6] But alas, our faint and feeble faith, with our love to God less than lukewarm by the fiery affection that we bear to our own filthy flesh, maketh us so dull in the desire of heaven, that the sudden dread of every bodily pain woundeth us to the heart, and striketh our devotion dead.

And therefore hath there every man, cousin (as I said before), much the more need to think upon this thing many a time and oft aforehand, ere any such peril fall, and by much devising thereupon before they see cause to fear it. While the thing shall not appear so terrible unto them reason shall better enter, and through grace working with their diligence engender and set sure not a sudden slight affection of sufferance for God's sake, but by a long continuance a strong deep-rooted habit. [Then they will] not be like a reed ready to wave with every wind, nor like a rootless tree scant set up on end in a loose heap of light sand, that will with a blast or two be blown down.

1 directly.
2 This was a common view in patristic writings. St. Chrysostom (347-407), for example, asserted in his *Moral Essays to Olympias* that "None can hurt the man who will not hurt himself." The idea was further developed in Chrysostom's *In Galatians* 720, where he argued that the body is good so long as it is subordinated to the soul. Responsibility for keeping the body subordinate lies not with the flesh but with the soul, which by its indolence can allow its delegated power of restraint to sink away. See Paul E. More, *The Religion of Plato* (1921), p. 255. This notion of the "indolence" or laziness of the soul was apparently adapted by the Church Fathers from Plato. (See e.g., *Laws* X, 903-4, where the soul's "energy" and "marvelous watchfulness" is said to be necessary if the soul is to remain supreme in its "immortal conflict" with the body. More mentions Chrysostom in the *Dialogue concerning Tyndale* (Campbell ed.), p. 302.
3 Lady Fortune. See Part I, Chap. 1, n. 2.
4 caught, involved.
5 An allusion to Peter's denial of Christ, after boasting that he would never forsake Him. See Mark 14:66-72.
6 The perseverance of martyrs under unspeakable torture is a frequent theme of the *Ecclesiastical History* by Eusebius (c. 260-c. 341), bishop of Caesarea in Palestine. Note e.g., Eusebius' description of martyrdom by drowning (Book VIII, Chaps. 9, 12, 13, 14); by slow burning (VIII, 6, 10); and by crucifixion (III, 32; VIII, 9).

Chapter 4

[Turkish Terror Overrated]

[Anthony insists that the terror of persecution is exaggerated. He will prove it in the ensuing discussions.]

Chapter 5[1]

[The Vanity of Empire]

ANTHONY: For first, [let us] begin at the outward goods (that neither are the proper goods of the soul nor of the body but are called the goods of fortune) that serve for the sustenance and commodity of man for the short season of this present life—as worldly substance, offices, honor, and authority. What great good is there in these things of themself, for which they were worthy so much as to bear the name by which the world of a worldly favor[2] customably calleth them?

For if the having of strength make a man strong, and the having of heat make a man hot, and the having of virtue make a man virtuous, how can those things be verily and truly good which he that hath them may by the having of them, as well be the worse [for] as the better? And, as experience proveth, more oft is [he] the worse than the better.

What should a man greatly rejoice in that, that he daily seeth most abound in the hands of many that be naught? Do not now this great Turk and his bashaws,[3] in all these advancements of fortune, surmount very far above any Christian estate,[4] and any lords living under him? And was there not yet hence upon twenty years the great sultan of Syria, which many a year together bare as great a port[5] as the great Turk? And after in one summer unto the great Turk that whole empire was lost. And so may all his[6] empire now (and shall hereafter by God's grace) be lost into Christian men's hands likewise, when Christian people shall be mended and grow in God's favor again.

But when that whole kingdoms and mighty great empires are of so little surety to stand, but be so soon translated[7] from one man unto another, what great thing can you or I, yea or any lord the greatest in this land, reckon himself to have by the possession of an heap of silver or gold? For white and yellow metal[s are] not so profitable of their own nature, save for a little glittering, as the rude rusty metal of iron.[8]

1 Compare this Chap. 5 through Chap. 12 with *The Consolation of Philosophy,* ed. Irwin Edman (1943), Book III, pp. 45-55. Therein Boethius discusses the vanity of riches, high office, kingdoms, fame, and sensual pleasure.
2 prejudice.
3 governors, pashas.
4 dignitary, high-ranking person.
5 bore as haughty a demeanor.
6 the Turk's.
7 transferred.
8 An echo from More's *Utopia,* Book II. See H. V. S. Ogden's edition (1949), p. 43: "Since they [the Utopians] keep gold and silver only for grave contingencies, they take care that in the meantime no one shall value these metals more than they deserve. Iron is obviously greatly superior to either. Men can no more do without iron than without fire and water. But gold and silver have no indispensable qualities. Human folly has made them precious only because of their scarcity."

Chapter 6

[If the Land Had a Soul]

[ANTHONY (continuing):] Lands and possessions many men yet much more esteem than money, because the lands seem not so casual[1] as money is or plate, for that though their other substance may be stole and taken away, yet evermore they think that their land will lie still where it lay. But what are we the better that our land cannot be stirred,[2] but will lie still where it lay, while ourself may be removed and not suffered to come near it? What great difference is there to us whether our substance be movable or unmovable, sith we be so movable ourself, that we may be removed from them both, and lose them both twain? Saving that sometime in the money is the surety somewhat more. For when we be fain ourself to flee we may make shift to carry some of our money with us—whereof our land we cannot carry one inch.

If our land be a thing of more surety than our money, how happeth it then that in this persecution we be more feard to lose it? For if it be a thing of more surety, then can it not so soon be lost. In the translation[3] of these two great empires, Greece first sith myself was born, and after Syria since you were born too, the land was lost before the money was found.

Oh, cousin Vincent, [suppose] the whole world were animated with a reasonable soul (as Plato had weened it were), and that it had wit and understanding to mark and perceive all thing.[4] Lord God, how the ground on which a prince buildeth his palace would loud laugh his lord to scorn when he saw him proud of his possession, and heard him boast himself that he and his blood are for ever the very lords and owners of the land! For then would the ground think the while in himself: "Ah, thou silly poor soul, that weenest thou were half a god, and art amid thy glory but a man in a gay gown. I, that am the ground here over whom thou art so proud, have had an hundred such owners of me as thou callest thyself—more than ever thou hast heard the names of. And some of them that proudly went over mine head lie now low in my belly, and my side lieth over them. And many one shall, as thou dost now, call himself mine owner after thee, that neither shall be sib[5] to thy blood nor any word hear of thy name."—Who ought[6] your castle, cousin, three thousand year ago?

VINCENT: Three thousand, uncle? Nay, nay, in the case of any king, Christian or heathen, you may strike off a third part of that well enough, and, as far as I ween, half of the remnant too. In far fewer years than three thousand it may well fortune that a poor plowman's blood may come up to a kingdom, and a king's right royal kin on the other side fall down to the plow and cart. And neither that king [will] know that ever he came from the cart, nor that carter know that ever he came from the crown!

ANTHONY: We find, cousin Vincent, in full authentic[7] stories many strange changes as marvellous as that come about in the compass of very few years in effect. And be such things then in reason so greatly to be set by that we should esteem the loss at so great, when we see that in keeping our surety is so little?

VINCENT: Marry, uncle, but the less surety that we have to keep it, . . . the more loath we be to forgo it.

ANTHONY: That reason shall I, cousin, turn against yourself. For . . . on the other side, the more that a thing is of his nature such that the commodity thereof bringeth a man little surety and much fear, that thing of reason the less have we cause to love. And then the less cause that we have to love a thing, the less cause have we to care therefor, or fear the loss thereof, or be loath to go therefrom.

1 uncertain—i.e., not so subject to the exigencies of fortune.
2 moved, taken away.
3 See Part I, Intro., ns. 17, 18, particularly with reference to the ages of Vincent and Anthony.
4 Plato's World-Soul was presented in *Timaeus* 36 and 54 and in *Laws* X,893-8, as the immanent governor and guide of the World-Body. Because its reason partition was always dominant over its other faculties, it served as a model for individual souls. See Friedrich Solmsen, *Plato's Theology* (1942), p. 90 and *passim*.
5 kin, related.
6 owned.
7 Although the Rastell edition here reads "antique," the other two early texts read "antentique" (1553) and "autentique" (1573). In the same sentence, the 1553 and 1573 versions read "chances" for Rastell's "changes." The latter has been retained as on the whole more appropriate for the context.

Chapters 7 *and* 8

[The Problems of Being Rich]

[The convenience of riches is overrated, argues Anthony. Riches give us expensive apparel to wear, but plain cloth is just as warm.

They give us gourmet food, but we can stay healthier with plainer fare. Also, we have the exhausting labor of getting the riches, then the fear of retaining them, and often the pain of losing them. In losing riches we sometimes lose our life too, because many a rich man is slain. All these tribulations more than counterbalance any pleasure derived from riches. Many rich people have no pleasure at all in their money. Instead, they hoard it in a buried pot and live in needless poverty. Such people are in effect thieves of their own money.]

Chapter 9

[Fame: A Blast of Men's Mouths]

[ANTHONY:] Let us now consider good name, honest estimation, and honorable fame. For these three things are of their own nature one and take their difference, in effect, but of the manner of the common speech in diversity of degrees.[1] For a good name may a man have, be he never so poor. Honest estimation in the common taking of the people[2] belongeth not unto any man, but [unto] him that is taken for one of some countenance[3] and havior,[4] and among his neighbors had in some reputation. In the word of honorable fame folk conceive the renown of great estates,[5] much and far spoken of by reason of their laudable acts.

Now all this gear,[6] used as a thing pleasant and commodious for this present life, pleasant it may seem to him that fasteneth his fantasy[7] therein. But of the nature of the thing itself, I perceive no great commodity that it hath. I say of the nature of the thing itself because it may be by chance some occasion of commodity. As if it hap that for the good name the poor man hath, or for the honest estimation that a man of some havior and substance standeth in among his neighbors, or for the honorable fame wherewith the great estate is renowned—if it hap, I say, that any man bearing them the better will therefore do them therefor any good. And yet . . . so may it hap sometime on the other side, . . . that such folk are of some other envied and hated, and as readily by them that envy them and hate them take harm, as they take by them that love them good.

But now to speak of the thing itself in his own proper nature, what is it but a blast of another man's mouth, as soon passed as spoken? Whereupon he that setteth his delight feedeth himself but with wind. Whereof be he never so full, he hath little substance therein, and many times shall he much deceive himself. For he shall ween that many praise him that never speak word of him—and they that do, say yet much less than he weeneth, and far more seldom too. For they spend not all the day, he may be sure, in talking of him alone. And whoso commend him most will yet, I ween, in every four and twenty hours wink[8] and forget him once. Besides this, that while one talketh well of him in one place, another sitteth and saith as shrewdly[9] of him in another. And finally, some that most praise him in his presence, behind his back mock him as fast and loud laugh him to scorn—and sometime slyly to his own face too.

And yet are there some fools so fed with this fond fantasy of fame, that they rejoice and glory to think how they be continually praised all about. As though all the world did nothing else day nor night but ever sit and sing, "Holy, Holy, Holy"[10] upon them!

1 I.e., popular habit distinguishes among various types of fame on the basis of social classes. Thus a poor man may have a "good name," but "honest estimation" applies to a merchant or the like, etc.
2 as the people commonly use, or understand, the term.
3 bearing, deportment.
4 property. Although More usually employs "havior" as a contraction of "behavior" or "deportment," he apparently uses it here (and in another instance in the next paragraph) to mean property or possessions. See the abridged OED, II, 873.
5 nobleman.
6 all these goods or trappings—i.e., all these facets of fame.
7 fancy, liking.
8 doze off. Intended here humorously and metaphorically.
9 abusively.
10 From the *Te deum,* sung in Catholic, Anglican, and some other liturgies. The impact of More's comic irony is appreciated only if one is familiar with some of the phrases: "We praise Thee, O God; we acknowledge Thee to be the Lord. / All the earth doth worship Thee. . . . / To Thee all angels cry aloud: . . . / Holy, Holy, Holy, . . . ; / Heaven and earth are full of the majesty of Thy glory. . . ."

Chapter 10

[A Great Man of the Church][1]

[ANTHONY (continuing):] And into this pleasant fantasy of much foolish vainglory be there some men brought sometime by such as themself do in a manner hire to flatter them. . . .

VINCENT: Forsooth, uncle, this is very truth. I have been ere this, and not very long ago, where I saw so proper experience of this point, that I must stop your tale for so long while I tell you mine.

ANTHONY: I pray you, cousin, tell on.

VINCENT: When I was first in Almaine,[2] uncle, it happed me to be somewhat favored with a great man of the church, and [of] great state[3]—one of the greatest in all that country there. And indeed, whosoever might spend as much as he might in one thing and other, were a right great estate[4] in any country of Christendom. But glorious[5] was he very far above all measure; and that was great pity, for it did harm and made him abuse many great gifts that God had given him. Never was he satiate of hearing his own praise.

So happed it one day that he had in a great audience made an oration in a certain manner wherein he liked himself so well, that at his dinner he sat (him thought) on thorns till he might hear how they that sat with him at his board would commend it. . . . He had s[a]t musing awhile, devising (as I thought after) upon some pretty proper way to bring it in withal. At the last, for lack of a better (lest he should have letted the matter too long), he brought it even bluntly forth, and asked us all that sat at his board's end—for at his own mess in the midst there sat but himself alone—how well we liked his oration that he had made that day.

But in faith, uncle, when that problem was once propo[s]ed, till it was full answered no man, I ween, eat one morsel of meat more. Every man was fallen in so deep a study for the finding of some exquisite praise. For he that should have brought out but a vulgar and a common commendation would have thought himself shamed for ever. Then said we our sentence by row as we sat, from the lowest unto the highest in good order, as it had been a great matter of the commonweal in a right solemn council. When it came to my part (I will not say it, uncle, for no boast), methought, by our Lady, for my part I quit myself meetly well.

And I liked myself the better because methought my words, being but a stranger, went yet with some grace in the Almaine tongue, wherein letting my Latin alone me listed to shew my cunning.[6] And I hoped to be liked the better because I saw that he that sat next me and should say his sentence after me was an unlearned priest, for he could speak no Latin at all. But when he came forth for his part with my lord's commendation, the wily fox had been so well accustomed in court with the craft of flattery that he went beyond me to too far. And then might I see by him what excellence a right mean wit may come to in one craft, that in all his whole life studieth and busieth his wit about no more but that one. But I made after a solemn vow unto myself that if ever he and I were matched together at that board again, when we should fall to our flattery, I would flatter in Latin, that he should not contend with me no more. For though I could be content to be outrun of an horse, yet would I no more abide it to be outrun of an ass!

But, uncle, here began now the game. He that sat highest and was to speak last was a great beneficed man, and not a doctor only but also somewhat learned indeed in the laws of the Church. A world it was to see how he marked every man's word that spake before him. And it seemed that every word the more proper it was the worse he liked it, for the cumbrance that he had to study out a better to pass it. The man even sweat with the labor, so that he was fain in the while now and then to wipe his face. Howbeit, in conclusion, when it came to his course, we that had spoken before him had so taken up all among us before, that we had not left him one wise word to speak after.

ANTHONY: Alas, good man! Among so many of you some good fellow should have lent him one.

VINCENT: It needed not as hap was,[7] uncle, for he found out such a shift[8] that in his flattering he passed us all the many.[9]

ANTHONY: Why, what said he, cousin?

VINCENT: By our Lady, uncle, not one word! . . . Plinius telleth that . . . Apelles the painter, in the table that he painted of the sacrifice and the death of Iphigenia, had in the making of the sorrowful countenances of the other noblemen of Greece that beheld it, spent out so much his craft and his cunning, that when he came to make the countenance of King Agamemnon her father . . . , he could devise no manner of new heavy cheer.[10] . . . [For] he had made there already in some of the other a much more heavy [countenance] before. And therefore, to the intent that no man should see what manner countenance it was that her father had, the painter was fain to paint him holding his face in his handkercher!

The like pageant[11] in a manner played us there this good ancient honorable flatterer. For when he saw that he could find no words of praise that would pass all that had been spoken before already, the wily fox would speak never a word. But as he that were ravished[12] unto heavenward with the wonder of the wisdom and eloquence that my lord's grace had uttered in that oration, he set a long sigh with an "Oh!" from the bottom of his breast. [He] held up both his hands, and lift up his head, and cast up his eyes into the welkin[13] and wept.

ANTHONY: Forsooth, cousin, he played his part very properly. But was that great prelate's oration, cousin, anything praiseworthy? For you can tell, I see well. For you would not, I ween, play as Juvenal merrily describeth the blind senator, one of the flatterers of Tiberius the emperor, that among the remnant[14] so magnified the great fish that the emperor had sent for them to shew them.[15] Which this blind senator (Montanus I trow they called him) marvelled of as much as any that marvelled most, and many things he spake thereof with some of his words directed thereunto

—looking himself toward his left side while the fish lay on his right side! You would not, I trow, cousin, have take upon you to praise it so but if you had heard it.[16]

VINCENT: I heard it, uncle, indeed, and to say the truth, it was not to dispraise.[17] Howbeit, surely somewhat less praise might have served it, by more a great deal than the half. But this am I sure: Had it been the worst that ever was made, the praise had not been the less of one hair. For they that used to praise him to his face never considered how much the thing deserved, but how great a laud and praise themself could give his good grace.

ANTHONY: Surely, cousin, as Terence saith, such folk make men of fools even stark mad,[18] and much cause have their lords to be right angry with them.[19]

VINCENT: God hath indeed and is, I ween. But as for their lords, uncle, if they would after wax angry with them therefor, they should in my mind do them very great wrong, when it is one of the things that they specially keep them for. For those that are of such vainglorious mind (be they lords or be they meaner men) can be much better contented to have their devices commended than amended. And require they their servant and their friend never so specially to tell them the very truth, yet shall he better please them if he speak them fair than if he telleth them truth.

For they be in the case that Martial speaketh of in an epigram unto a friend of his that required his judgment how he liked his verses. But he prayed him [Martial] in any wise to tell him even the very truth. To whom Martial made answer in this wise:

> The very truth of me thou dost require.
> The very truth is this, my friend dear:
> The very truth thou wouldst not gladly hear.[20]

And in good faith, uncle, the selfsame prelate that I told you my tale of (I dare be bold to swear it, I know it so surely) had on a time made of his own drawing[21] a certain treaty that should serve for a league between that country and a great prince. In which treaty himself thought that he had devised his articles so wisely and indited[22] so well, that all the world would allow them. Whereupon longing sore to be praised, he called unto him a friend of his, a man well learned and of good worship and very well expert in those matters. . . . [He] had been divers times ambassador for that country and had made many such treaties himself.

When he [the prelate] took him the treaty and that he had read it, he asked him how he liked it and said: "But I pray you heartily, tell me the very truth." . . . He [the prelate] spake so heartily that the other had weened he would fain have heard the truth. And in trust thereof he told him a fault therein, at the hearing whereof he sware in great anger: "By the mass, thou art a very fool." The other afterward told me that he would never tell him truth again.

ANTHONY: Without question, cousin, I cannot greatly blame him. And thus themself make every man mock them, flatter them, and deceive them—those, I say, that are of such vainglorious mind. For if they be content to hear the truth, let them then make much of those that tell them the truth, and withdraw their ear from them that falsely flatter them. [Then] they shall be more truly served than with twenty requests praying men to tell them true. King Ladislaus[23] (our Lord assoil[24] his soul) used much this matter among his servants. When one of them praised any deed of his or any condition in him, if he perceived that they said but the truth, he would let it pass by uncontrolled. But when he saw that they set a gloss[25] upon it for his praise of their own making beside, then would he shortly[26] say unto them: "I pray thee, good fellow, when thou sayest grace at my board, never bring in *Gloria Patri* without a *sicut erat*.[27] Any act that ever I did, if thou report it again to mine honor with a *Gloria Patri,* never report it but with a *sicut erat:* that is to wit, even as it was and none otherwise. And lift me not up with no lies, for I love it not."

If men would use this way with them that this noble king used, it would minish much of their false flattery. I can well allow that men should commend (keeping them within the bonds of truth) such things as they see praiseworthy in other men, to give them the greater courage to the increase thereof. For men keep still in that point one condition of children, that praise must prick[28] them forth. But better it were to do well and look for none.

Howbeit, they that cannot find in their heart to commend another man's good deed, shew themself either envious or else of nature very cold and dull. But out of question, he that putteth his pleasure in the praise of the people hath but a fond fantasy. For if his finger do but ache of an hot blain,[29] a great many men's mouths blowing out his praise will scantly do him among them all half so much ease, as to have one little boy blow upon his finger.

1 The two hilarious anecdotes related in this chapter are usually thought to refer to Cardinal Wolsey, whom More succeeded as Lord Chancellor. The setting of the anecdotes is probably Hampton Court, the luxurious palace which Wolsey built for himself and then, in a desperate effort to save his career, gave as a gift to Henry VIII. See R. W. Chambers, "The Continuity of English Prose," in Harpsfield's *Life* (Hitchcock ed.), p. clii.

2 Germany. The alleged geographical locale is probably a disguise.

3 estate, wealth.

4 dignitary.

5 vain.

6 knowledge, skill.

7 it was not necessary, as it turned out.

8 device.

9 he surpassed the whole company.

10 See Pliny the Elder (23-79 A.D.), Roman scholar, in his *Natural History,* Book XXXV, Chap. 36, sec. 73 (ed. H. Rackham for Loeb, 1952). More has confused two famous Greek painters. Pliny tells the tale not of Apelles, but of Timanthes (c. 400 B.C.), whose masterpiece was "The Sacrifice of Iphigenia."

11 scene. In More's day the term "pageant" often referred to a dramatic scene, illustrating Biblical or other history, enacted by players (as in the medieval craft plays) or depicted on tapestry. As a youth, More himself wrote some verses to describe nine "pageants" depicted on a "fine painted cloth" in his father's London house. See "Early Poems," in More's *English Works,* I, 332-5, ed. W. E. Campbell.

12 enraptured—i.e., as if he were swept up into heaven.

13 sky, heaven.

14 among those standing around.

15 See the *Satires,* IV, lines 116-121, by Juvenal (60?-140?), Roman poet and satirist.

16 unless you had (so) heard it—i.e., unless you had thought it was really worth praising.

17 not unworthy of some praise.

18 I.e., such flatterers drive foolish men crazy.

19 See *The Eunuch,* Act II, Scene 2, by the Roman dramatist Terence (185-159 B.C.).

20 See Book VIII, Epigram 76 ("To Gallicus") by the Roman epigrammist Martial (c. 40-102 A.D.):

> Pray tell me plainly what you think of it,
> You always say: "I love a frank report."
> Thus when you read the products of your wit,
> Thus when you plead a client's case in court,
> You pester me a verdict to extort.
> And since a flat refusal seems uncouth,
> Here is the truth you seek for, plain and short—
> That truth is that you do not want the truth!

(From *The Twelve Books of Epigrams,* trans. J. Pott and F. Wright. London: Routledge.)

21 of his own execution—i.e., unilaterally, without consulting others.

22 composed.

23 Vladislav, King of Bohemia (1471-1516) and of Hungary (1490-1516),

and father of the courageous boy-king, Louis II, killed at Mohacs in 1526 (see Part I, Intro., n. 20). Anthony's reverent portrait, which makes Vladislav sound like King Utopus, is highly idealized. Actually, Vladislav was so notoriously weak that his council refused to recognize his decrees unless confirmed by them. He got himself into a scandal with the French princess, Anne de Candale, whom he finally married in order to beget lawful issue. He was so inept that the diet of 1505 passed a resolution never again to accept a foreign king.

24 pardon, bless.

25 (flattering) commentary.

26 curtly.

27 A humorous reference to the Doxology: "Glory be to the Father, . . . As it was in the beginning. . . ." In effect Ladislaus is saying: "Don't ever praise me unless the unadorned facts justify it."

28 spur.

29 infected blister.

Chapter 11

[To Rule or Be Ruled]

[ANTHONY:] Let us now consider in like wise what great worldly wealth ariseth unto men by great offices, rooms, and authority—to those worldly disposed people, I say, that desire them for no better purpose. For of them that desire them for better we shall speak after anon. The great thing that they[1] chief like all therein is that they may bear a rule, command and control other men, and live uncommanded and uncontrolled themself. And yet this commodity took I so little heed of, that I never was ware it was so great till a good friend of ours merrily told me once that his wife once in a great anger taught it him. For . . . her husband had no list to grow greatly upward in the world, nor neither would labor for office of authority, and over that forsook a right worshipful room when it was offered him.

[So] she fell in hand with him (he told me) and all-to rated[2] him and asked him: "What will you do that you list not to put forth yourself as other folk do? Will you sit still by the fire and make goslings[3] in the ashes with a stick as children do? Would God I were a man, and look what I would do." "Why wife," quoth her husband, "what would you do?" "What?" [she said.] "By God, go forward with the best. For as my mother was wont to say (God have mercy on her soul), it is evermore better to rule than to be ruled. And therefore, by God, I would not, I warrant you, be so foolish to be ruled where I might rule." "By my troth, wife," quoth her husband, "in this I dare say you say truth. For I never found you willing to be ruled yet!"[4]

VINCENT: Well, uncle, I wot where you be now well enough;[5] she is indeed a stout master woman. And in good faith, for aught that I can see, even that same womanish mind of hers is the greatest commodity that men reckon upon in rooms and offices of authority.

ANTHONY: By my troth, and methinketh very few there are of them that attain any great commodity therein. For first there is in every kingdom but one man that can have an office of such authority that no man may command him or control him. None officer can there stand in that case but the king himself. [He] only, uncontrolled or uncommanded, may control and command all. Now of all the remnant each is under him. And yet beside him almost every one is under more commanders and controllers too than one. And some man that is in a great office commandeth fewer things and less labor to many men that are under him, than someone that is over him commandeth him alone.

VINCENT: Yet it doth them good, uncle, that men must make courtesy to them, and salute them with reverence, and stand barehead before them, or unto some of them kneel peradventure too.

ANTHONY: Well, cousin, in some part they do but play at gleek,[6] receive reverence, and to their cost pay honor again therefor. For except (as I said) only a king, the greatest in authority under him receiveth not so much reverence of no man, as according to reason himself doth honor to him.[7] Nor twenty men's courtesies do him not so much pleasure as his own once kneeling doth him pain, if his knee hap to be sore. And I wist once a great officer of the king's say (and in good faith I ween he said but as he thought) that twenty men standing barehead before him, keep not his head half so warm as to keep on his own cap. Nor he never took so much ease with their being barehead before him, as he caught once grief with a cough that came upon him by standing barehead long before the king.

But let it be that these commodities be somewhat such as they be, yet then consider whether that any incommodities be so joined therewith that a man were almost as good lack both as have both. Goeth all thing evermore as every one of them would have it? That were as hard as to please all the people at once with one weather, while in one house the husband would have fair weather for his corn, and his wife would have rain for her leeks. So while they that are in authority be not all evermore of one mind, . . . it cannot be that both the parties can have their own mind. Nor often are they content which see their conclusion quail,[8] but ten times they take the missing of their mind[9] more displeasantly than other poor men do.

And this goeth not only to men of mean authority but unto the very greatest. The princes themself cannot have, you wot well, all their will. For how were it possible while each of them almost would, if he might, be lord over all the remnant? Then many men under their princes in authority are in that case that privy malice and envy many bear them in heart, falsely speak them full fair, and praise them with their mouth. [Yet these underlings,] when there happeth any great fall unto them,[10] bawl and bark and bite upon them like dogs.

Finally, [in] the cost and charge, the danger and peril of war, . . . their part is more than a poor man's is, sith that matter more dependeth upon them. And many a poor plowman may sit still by the fire while they must arise and walk. And sometime their authority falleth by change of their master's mind. And of that see we daily in one place or other ensamples such and so many, that the parable of the philosopher can lack no testimony which likened the servants of great princes unto the counters[11] with which men do cast account. For . . . that counter that standeth sometime for a farthing is suddenly set up and standeth for a thousand pound, and after as soon set down eftsoon[12] beneath to stand for a farthing again. So fareth it, lo, sometime with those that seek the way to rise and grow up in authority by the favor of great princes, that as they rise up high so fall they down again as low.[13]

Howbeit, though a man escape all such [mis]adventures and abide in great authority till he die, yet then at the least wise every man must leave it at the last. And that which we call "at last" hath no very long time to it. Let a man reckon his years that are passed of his age ere ever he can get up aloft, and let him when he hath it[14] first in his fist reckon how long he shall be like to live after, and I ween that then the most part shall have little cause to rejoice. . . . And then, when they see that they must needs leave it, the thing which they did much more set their heart upon than ever they had reasonable cause—what sorrow they take therefor, that shall I not need to tell you.

And thus it seemeth unto me, cousin, in good faith, that . . . in the having[15] the profit is not great and the displeasures neither small nor few, and of the losing [there are] so many sundry chances. And [since] by no mean a man can keep it long, and that to part therefrom is such a painful grief, I can see no very great cause for which as an high worldly commodity men should great desire it.

1 I.e., the "worldly disposed people."
2 took issue with him and thoroughly berated him.
3 draw geese—i.e., doodle.
4 As Vincent's remark indicates, the subject of this anecdote is a person well known to both speakers. On Harpsfield's authority, p. 95, we assume that More is here poking fun at his wife, Dame Alice.
5 I.e., I know very well to whom you are alluding.
6 cards—i.e., they (the famous men) are just playing meaningless games.
7 I.e., to the king. The point is that a man of high station has to give more reverence to a king than he receives from others, so that in terms of reverence he is always the loser.
8 their decisions break down (in the face of opposition), their judgments disputed.
9 thwarting of their ambitions or intentions.
10 I.e., the princes.
11 pieces of metal, ivory, or the like, used in financial and business computations. These sentences possibly adapt the merchantile metaphor in Boethius' *Consolation of Philosophy* (Edman, ed., 1943), Book II, p. 25: "While Fortune then favored you . . ., she cherished you as her own darling. Will you then balance accounts with Fortune?" The key phrase in the Latin text, "cum fortuna calculum ponere," would literally translate as "with fortune lay down (or discard) counters." A much closer parallel is the Greek historian Polybius (205?-125? B.C.). See Robert Burton's *Anatomy of Mel-*

ancholy, ed. Floyd Dell and Paul Jordan-Smith (New York: Farrar & Rinehart, 1927), "Democritus to the Reader," p. 94: "If great men live in Court, they are up and down, ebb and flow with their Prince's favors; . . . as Polybius describes them, 'Like so many casting counters, now of gold, tomorrow of silver, that vary in worth as the computant will; now they stand for units, tomorrow for thousands; now before all, and anon behind.' " I am indebted for this source to D. J. Barr of Toronto, Canada. Cf. Polybius' *The Histories,* trans. W. R. Paton (Loeb Classical Library, Cambridge: Harvard University Press; London: Heinemann, 1960), Book V, Chap. 26, secs. 12-13, wherein courtiers are said to be "like counters on a reckoning board. For these at the will of the reckoner are now worth a copper and now worth a talent. . . ."

12 again, afterwards.

13 This statement, obviously inspired at least partly by More's own experiences, takes on special poignancy in view of his fluctuating relationship with Henry VIII. It was after all Henry who had insisted that More enter royal service, and who had later elevated More to the Lord Chancellorship.

14 I.e., authority, high rank.

15 I.e., the having of high office.

Chapter 12

[Some Dangers of Fortune's Gifts]

[ANTHONY (continuing):] And thus far have we considered hitherto in these outward goods that are called the gifts of fortune no farther but the slender commodity that worldly-minded men have by them. But now, if we consider farther what harm to the soul they take by them that desire them but only for the wretched wealth of this world, then shall we well perceive how far more happy is he that well loseth them than he that evil findeth them.

These [worldly] things . . . be such as are of their own nature indifferent: that is to wit, of themself things neither good nor bad. But [they] are matter that may serve to the one or the other, after as men will use them. Yet need we little to doubt it but that they that desire them but for their worldly pleasure and for no farther godly purpose, the devil shall soon turn them[1] from things indifferent . . . and make them things very naught. For though that they be indifferent of their nature, yet cannot the use of them lightly stand indifferent, but determinately must either be good or bad. And therefore he that desireth them but for worldly pleasure desireth them not for any good. And for better purpose than he desireth them, to better use is he not likely to put them, and therefore not unto good but consequently to naught.

As, for ensample, first consider it in riches. He that longeth for them as for things of temporal commodity and not for any godly purpose, what good they shall do him Saint Paul declareth, where he writeth unto Timothy: "They that long to be rich fall into temptation and into the grin[2] of the devil and into many desires unprofitable and noyous,[3] which drown men into death and into perdition."[4] And the Holy Scripture saith also in the twenty-first chapter of the Proverbs: "He that gathereth treasures shall be shoved into the grins of death."[5] So that whereas by the mouth of Saint Paul God saith that they shall fall into the devil's grin, He saith in the other place that they shall be pushed and shoved in by violence.

And of truth, while a man desireth riches not for any good godly purpose but for only worldly wealth, it must needs be that he shall have little conscience in the getting, but by all evil ways that he can invent shall labor to get them. And then shall he either niggardly heap them up together (which is you wot well damnable) or wastefully misspend them about worldly pomp, pride, and gluttony, with occasion of many sins more. And that is yet much more damnable.

As for fame and glory desired but for worldly pleasure, [it] doth unto the soul inestimable harm. For that setteth men's hearts upon high devices and desires of such things as are immoderate and outrageous, and by help of false flatterers puff[s] up a man in pride. And make[s] a brittle man (lately made of earth, and that shall again shortly be laid full low in earth, and there lie and rot and turn again into earth) take himself in the meantime for a god here upon earth, and ween to win himself[6] to be lord of all the earth. This maketh battles between these great princes, and with much trouble to much people, and great effusion of blood, one king to look to reign in five realms that cannot well rule one. For how many hath now this great Turk, and yet aspireth to more? And those that he hath he ordereth evil,[7] and yet himself worst.

Then offices and rooms of authority: If men desire them only for their worldly fantasies, who can look that ever they shall occupy them well, but abuse their authority and do thereby great hurt? For then shall they fall from indifferency[8] and maintain false matters of their friends, [and] bear up[9] their servants and such as depend upon them, with bearing down of other innocent folk [who are] not so able to do hurt, as easy to take harm. Then the laws that are made against malefactors shall they make, as an old philosopher said,[10] to be much like unto cobwebs, in which the little gnats and flies stick still and hang fast, but the great humble-bees break them and fly quite through. And then the laws that are made as a buckler in the defense of innocents, those shall they make serve for a sword to cut and sore wound them with, and therewith wound they their own souls sorer.

And thus you see, cousin, that of all these outward goods which men call the goods of fortune, there is never one that unto them which long therefor (not for any godly purpose but only for their worldly wealth) hath any great commodity to the body. And yet are they all in such case besides that, very deadly destruction unto the soul.

1 I.e., worldly goods.
2 trap.
3 troublesome.
4 1 Tim. 6:9.
5 Proverbs 21:6.
6 imagine that he can make himself lord, etc.
7 administers badly.
8 impartiality.
9 bolster, give patronage to.
10 The "old philosopher" is Solon, the Greek law-giver (late 6th c. B.C.). See Diogenes Laertius, *Lives of Eminent Philosophers*, ed. R. D. Hicks (1938), Book I, sec. 59. The gnats-flies-bees imagery is apparently appropriated from a similar passage in Ariosto's *Orlando Furioso*, Book XXXII. The newest edition, selected from the 1591 Harington translation, is edited by Rudolf Gottfried (1963).

Chapter 13

[A Magic Touchstone]

VINCENT: Verily, good uncle, this thing is so plainly true that no man may with any good reason deny it. But I ween, uncle, also, that there will no man say nay. For I see no man that will for very shame confess that he desireth riches, honor, and renown, offices and rooms of authority for his only worldly pleasure. For every man would fain seem as holy as an horse. And therefore will every man say, and would it were so believed too, that he desireth these things (though for his worldly wealth a little so), yet principally to merit thereby through doing some good therewith.

ANTHONY: This is, cousin, very sure so. . . . . . . Many men will say so too that have principal respect unto their worldly commodity, and unto Godward therein little or nothing at all. And yet they pretend the contrary, and that unto their own harm. [For] God cannot be mocked.[1] And some peradventure know not well their own affection[2] themself. But there lieth more imperfection secret in their affection than themself are well aware of, which only God beholdeth. And therefore saith the prophet unto God: "Mine imperfection have Thine eyes beholden."[3] For which the prophet prayeth: "From mine hid sins cleanse Thou me, good Lord."[4]

But now, cousin, this tribulation of the Turk . . . so persecute[s] us for the faith that those that will forsake their faith shall keep their goods, and those shall lose their goods that will not leave their faith. This manner of persecution, lo, shall like a touchstone try them and shew the feigned from the true-minded—and teach also them that ween they mean better than they do indeed, better to discern themself. For some there are that ween they mean well while they frame themself a conscience.[5] [They] ever keep still a great heap of superfluous substance by them, thinking ever still that they will bethink themself upon some good deed whereon they will well bestow it once, or that else their executors shall. But now if they lie not unto themself, but keep their goods for any good purpose to the pleasure of God indeed, then shall they in this persecution, for the pleasure of God in keeping of His faith, be glad for to depart from them.

And therefore, as for all these things—the loss (I mean) of all these outward things that men call the gifts of fortune . . .—[there is] consolation great and sufficient, sith every man that hath them either setteth by them for the world or for God. He that setteth by them for the world hath, as I have shewed you, little profit by them to the body and great harm unto the soul, and therefore may well (if he be wise) reckon that he winneth by the loss. . . . And on the other side, he that keepeth them for some good purpose, intending to bestow them for the pleasure of God, the loss of them in this Turk's persecution for keeping of the faith can be no manner grief unto him. . . .

For though it had be peradventure better to have bestowed them well before, yet sith he kept them for some good purpose, he would not have left them unbestowed if he had foreknown the chance.[6] But being now prevented so by persecution that he cannot bestow them in that other good way that he would, yet while he parteth from them because he will not part from the faith, though the devil's escheator[7] violently take them from him, yet willingly giveth he them to God.

1 Gal. 6:7.
2 feelings.
3 Psalms 138:16.
4 Ibid., 18:13.
5 fabricate a conscience for themselves.
6 if he had earlier known of some opportunity.
7 depriver—i.e., one who seizes or deprives others of legally held property.

Chapter 14

[The Treachery of Sultans]

VINCENT: I cannot in good faith, good uncle, say nay to none of this. And indeed unto them that by the Turk's overrunning of the country were happed to be spoiled and robbed and all their substance movable and unmovable bereft and lost already, their persons only fled and safe, I think that these considerations . . . might unto them be good occasion of comfort and cause them (as you said) make a virtue of necessity.[1]

But [take] the case, uncle, that we now speak of. That is to wit, where they have yet their substance untouched in their own hands, and that the keeping or the losing shall hang both in their own hands by the Turk's offer upon the retaining or the renouncing of the Christian faith. Here, uncle, I find it (as you said) that this temptation is more sore and most perilous. For I fear me that we shall find few, of such as have much to lose, that shall find in their hearts so suddenly to forsake their goods. . . . . . .

ANTHONY: And yet they being even such, this would I fain ask one of them; and I pray you, cousin, take you his person upon you and in this case answer for him.[2] What letteth . . . your lordship, that you be not gladly content without any deliberation at all in this kind of persecution, rather than to leave your faith, to let go all that ever you have at once?

VINCENT: . . . You put it, uncle, unto me, to make the matter the more plain, that I should play that great man's part that is so wealthy and hath so much to lose. . . . And therefore to your question I answer, that there letteth me the thing that yourself may lightly guess, the losing of the manifold commodities which I now have: riches and substance, lands and great possessions of inheritance, with great rule and authority here in my country. All which things the great Turk granteth me to keep still in peace, and have them enhanced too, so[3] that I will forsake the faith of Christ.

Yea, I may say to you, I have a motion secretly made me farther, to keep all this yet better cheap.[4] That is to wit, [I will] not be compelled utterly to forsake Christ nor all the whole Christian faith, but only some such parts thereof as may not stand with Mahomet's law. And only granting Mahomet for a true prophet and serving the Turk truly in his wars against all Christian kings, I shall not be letted to praise Christ also and to call Him a good man and worship Him and serve Him too.

ANTHONY: Nay, nay, my lord, Christ hath not so great need of your lordship as rather than to lose your service He would fall at such covenants with you to take your service at halves to serve Him and His enemy both. He hath given you plain warning already by Saint Paul that He will have in your service no parting fellow:[5] "What fellowship is there between light and darkness? Between Christ and Belial?"[6] And He hath also plainly shewed you Himself by His own mouth: "No man may serve two lords at once."[7] He will have you believe all that He telleth you and do all that He biddeth you and forbear all that He forbiddeth you, without any manner exception. Break one of His commandments and break all. Forsake one point of His faith and forsake all, as for any thanks you get of Him for the remnant.

And therefore . . . you [cannot] devise as it were indentures between God and you, what thing you will do for Him and what thing you will not do, as though He should hold Him content with such service of yours as yourself list appoint Him. If you make, I say, such indentures you shall seal both the parts yourself, and you get thereto none agreement of Him.

And this I say, though the Turk would make such an appointment[8] with you as you speak of, and would when he had made it keep it. Whereas he would not, I warrant you, leave you so when he had once brought you so far forth, but would little and little after ere he left you make you deny Christ altogether and take Mahomet in His stead. And so doth he in the beginning when he will not have you believe him [Mahomet] to be God. For surely if he were not God he were no good man neither, while he plainly said he was God.

But though he would never go so far forth with you, yet Christ will, as I said, not take your service to halves, but will that you shall love Him with all your whole heart. . . . While He was living here 1500 year ago He foresaw this mind of yours that you have now, with which you would fain serve Him in some such fashion as you might keep your worldly substance still, but rather forsake His service than put all your substance from you. He telleth you plain 1500 year ago [out of] His own mouth, that He will [accept] no such service of you, saying: "You cannot serve both God and your riches together."[9]. . . . . .

Sith the promise of the Turk made unto you for the keeping of [riches] is the thing that moveth you and maketh you thus to doubt, I ask you first whereby you wot that when you have done all that he will have you do against Christ to the harm of your soul, . . . he will keep you his promise in these things that he promiseth you, concerning the retaining of your well-beloved wealth for the pleasure of your body?

VINCENT: What surety can a man have of such a great prince but his promise, which for his own honor it cannot become him to break?

ANTHONY: I have known him, and his father afore him too, break more promises than five as great as this is that he should here make with you.[10] Who shall come and cast it in his teeth, and tell him it is a shame for him to be so fickle and so false of his promise? And then what careth he for those words that he wotteth well he shall never hear? Not very much, although they were told him too. If you might come after and complain your grief unto his own person yourself, you should find him as shamefast as a friend of mine, a merchant, found once the sultan of Syria.

To whom, being certain years about his merchandise in that country, he gave a great sum of money for a certain office meet for him there for the while. Which he scant had granted and put in his hand but that ere ever it was aught worth unto him, the sultan suddenly sold it to another of his own sect and put our Hungarian out. Then came he to him and humbly put him in remembrance of his grant passed [from] his own mouth and signed with his own hand. Whereunto the sultan answered him with a grim countenance: "I will thou wit it, losel,[11] that neither my mouth nor mine hand shall be master over me to bind all my body at their pleasure. But I will so be lord and master over them both, that whatsoever the one say or the other write, I will be at mine own liberty to do what me list myself, and ask them both no leave. And therefore go get thee hence out of my countries, knave!"

Ween you now, my lord,[12] that that sultan and this Turk being both of one false sect, you may not find them both like, false of their promise?

VINCENT: That must I needs jeopard, for other surety can there none be had.

ANTHONY: An unwise jeoparding, to put your soul in peril of damnation for the keeping of your bodily pleasures, and yet without surety thereof [you] must jeopard them too. But yet go a little farther, lo. Suppose me that you might be very sure that the Turk would break no promise with you. Are you then sure enough to retain all your substance still?

VINCENT: Yea, then. . . . . . .

ANTHONY: May he not lose this country again unto Christian men, and you with the taking of this way fall in the same peril then that ye would now eschew?

VINCENT: Forsooth, I think that if he get it once he will never lose it after again in our days.

ANTHONY: Yes, by God's grace. But yet if he lose it after your days, there goeth your children's inheritance away again. But be it now that he could never lose it, could none take your substance from you then?

VINCENT: No, in good faith, none.

ANTHONY: No? None at all? Not God?

VINCENT: God? What yes, pardie, who doubteth of that?

ANTHONY: Who? Marry, he that doubteth whether there be any God or no. . . . . . . But unto you, my lord, . . . you believe and confess, like as a wise man should, that . . . God, whose faith you forsake and therein do Him displeasure, may so take [riches] from you that the great Turk with all the power he hath is not able to keep you them.[13] Why [then] will you be so unwise with the loss of your soul to please the great Turk for your goods, while you wot well that God (whom you displease therewith) may take them from you too?

Besides this: Sith you believe there is a God, you cannot but believe therewith that the great Turk cannot take your goods from you without His will or sufferance, no more than the devil could from Job. And think you then that if He will suffer the Turk take away your goods (albeit that by the keeping and confessing of His faith you please Him), He will (when you displease Him by forsaking His faith) suffer you of those goods that you get or keep thereby to rejoice or enjoy any benefit?

VINCENT: God is gracious, and though that men offend Him, yet He suffereth them many times to live in prosperity long after.

ANTHONY: Long after? Nay, by my troth, my lord, that doth He no man! For how can that be that He should suffer you live in prosperity long after, when your whole life is but short in all together? And either almost half thereof, or more than half (you think yourself, I dare say) spent out already before? Can you burn out half a short candle and then have a long one left of the remnant? . . . . . . [Also,] as Saint Austin saith, the longer that He tarrieth ere He strike, the sorer is the stroke when He striketh.[14] And therefore if ye will well do, reckon yourself very sure that when you deadly displease God for the getting or the keeping of your goods, God shall not suffer those goods to do you good. But either shall He take them shortly from you, or suffer you to keep them for a little while to your more harm.

And after shall He, when you least look therefore, take you away from them. And then what a heap of heaviness will there enter into your heart, when you shall see that you shall so suddenly go from your goods and leave them here in the earth in one place. And that your body shall be put in the earth in another place. And (which then shall be most heaviness of all) . . . you shall fear (and not without great cause) that your soul shall first forthwith, and after that at the final judgment your body, be driven down deep toward the center of the earth, into the fiery pit and dungeon of the devil of hell, there to tarry in torment world without end. . . . . . .

Our Saviour in few words concluded and confuted all these follies of them that for the short use of this worldly substance forsake Him and His faith and sell their souls unto the devil for ever, where he saith: "What availeth it a man if he won all the whole world and lost his soul?"[15] . . .

VINCENT: This is, good uncle, in good faith very true. And what other thing any of them (that would not for this be content)[16] have for to allege in reason for the defense of their folly, that can I not imagine. Nor list [I] not in this matter to play their part no longer. But I pray God give me the grace to play the contrary part indeed, and that I never for any goods or substance of this wretched world forsake my faith toward God, neither in heart nor tongue—as I trust in His great goodness I never shall.

1 See Part III, Chap. 2, n. 8.
2 pretend that you are a rich person and answer as he would. As a page at Cardinal Morton's, More had delighted in this kind of impromptu acting. See Roper, p. 5.
3 increased too, provided . . .
4 on better terms. I.e., he has made a deal with the Turk, whereby he can "buy" (that is, keep) his worldly goods at a cheaper price than wholly forsaking Christ.
5 no half-hearted adherent.
6 2 Cor. 6:14.
7 Matt. 6:24.
8 agreement—i.e., the secret deal previously referred to.
9 Matt. 6:24.
10 Ostensibly a reference to the Turkish sultans Suleiman I and Selim I, but actually a strike at Henry VII and Henry VIII. See Hallett, *Dialogue*, p. viii. More had attacked the policies of Henry VII in his Coronation Poem celebrating the accession of Henry VIII. See Bradner and Lynch, p. xxviii.
11 I want you to know, knave . . .
12 I.e., the lord or nobleman whom Vincent is temporarily impersonating.
13 to help you keep them—i.e., to protect your riches from God's wrath.
14 See St. Augustine, Sermo 171 (in *Patrologia latina* 38, col. 935): "Magnae misericordiae est, nequitiam impunitam non relinquere: et cogatur in extremo gehennae damnare, modo flagello dignatur castigare." I am indebted to Sister M. Thecla of Seton Hill College for tracking down this and several other sources.
15 Matt. 16:26.
16 who would not, on the basis of the foregoing arguments, be convinced (of the folly of seeking to retain possessions by making a deal with the Turk).

Chapter 15

[How To Hide a Treasure]

[The threat of persecution should inspire a man to learn how to hide his treasure (says Anthony), so that even the Turkish army cannot steal it away. For Christ himself has noted that it is useless to bury money in the ground, where thieves can find it. He has instead instructed us to place our treasure in heaven. This we can do by giving our money to the poor, which is the same as giving it to Christ. The fact that we do not take seriously Christ's words on this matter indicates that our faith is hampered by our worldly possessions. These possessions are like thorns and briars that strangle the word of God which has been sown in our hearts. We should therefore thank God that, through his agents the Turks, these thorns and weeds are pruned away, so that the warm sun of God's grace can reach our faith and make it grow. When that happens, we will be glad to lay up our treasure in heaven rather than on earth; in so doing, our hearts will be in heaven too. Then no persecutor can hurt us.]

Chapter 16

[The Case for Poverty]

[One of the greatest comforts in losing one's possessions through persecution is that Christ himself willingly suffered poverty for us. He could have had all the wealth and kingdoms in the world, but he renounced them all to save us from damnation. Thus it is difficult to imagine how any man could forsake Christ rather than give up material goods.]

Chapter 17

[The Horror of Bodily Pain]

VINCENT: Forsooth, uncle, as for these outward goods, ... methinketh now . . . that if the Turk should take all that I have unto my very shirt except I would forsake my faith, and offer it me all again with five times as much thereto to fall into his sect,

I would not once stick thereat. Rather [would I] forsake it every whit than of Christ's holy faith to forsake any point. But surely, good uncle, when I bethink me farther on the grief and the pain that may turn unto my flesh, here find I the fear that forceth mine heart to tremble.

ANTHONY: Neither have I cause thereof to marvel nor you, cousin, cause to be dismayed therefor. The great horror and fear that our Savior had in His own flesh against his painful Passion maketh me little to marvel. And I may well make you take that comfort too, so that for no such manner of grudging felt in your sensual parts (the flesh shrinking at the meditation of pain and death) your reason shall give over, but resist it and manly master it. And though you would fain fly from the painful death and be loath to come thereto, yet may the meditation of His great grievous agony move you.

And Himself shall (if you so desire Him) not fail to work with you therein, and get and give you the grace, [so] that you shall submit and conform your will therein unto His, as He did His unto His Father. And [you] shall thereupon be . . . comforted with the secret inward inspiration of His Holy Spirit, as He was with the personal presence of that angel that after His agony came and comforted Him.[1] Th[en] you shall as His true disciple follow Him, and with goodwill without grudge do as He did, and take your cross of pain and passion upon your back. And die for the truth with Him, and thereby reign with Him crowned in eternal glory.

And this I say to give you warning . . . that . . . when a man feeleth such an horror of death in his heart, he should not thereby stand in courageous fear that he were falling. For many a such man standeth for all that fear full fast, and finally better abideth the brunt . . . than doth some other that in the beginning feeleth no fear at all. And yet may it be, and most often so it is. For God having many mansions (and all wonderful wealthful) in His Father's house, exalteth not every good man up to the glory of a martyr. [He] foresee[s] their infirmity, that though they be of goodwill before and peradventure of right good courage too, would yet play Saint Peter[2] if they were brought to the point, and thereby bring their souls into the peril of eternal damnation.

[So] He provideth otherwise for them before they come thereat. [He] either findeth a way that men shall not have the mind to lay any hands upon them, as He found for His disciples when Himself was willingly taken.[3] Or that if they set hand on them they shall have no power to hold them, as He found for Saint John the Evangelist.[4] Which let his sheet fall from him, whereupon they caught hold, and so fled himself naked away and escaped from them. Or though they hold [them] and bring [them] to prison too, yet God sometime delivereth them thence, as He did Saint Peter.[5]

And sometime He taketh them to Him out of the prison into heaven, and suffereth them not to come to their torment at all—as He hath done by many a good holy man. And some He suffereth to be brought into the torments and yet suffereth them not to die therein, but live many years after and die their natural death—as He did by Saint John the Evangelist and by many another more, as we may well see both by sundry stories[6] and in the epistles of Saint Cyprian also.[7] . . . . . .

And therefore, cousin, to begin with, let us be of good comfort. For . . . we be by our faith very sure that Holy Scripture is the very word of God, and that the word of God cannot be but true. And . . . we see that by the mouth of His holy prophet and by the mouth of His blessed apostle also, God hath made us [a] faithful promise . . . that He will not suffer us to be tempted above our power.[8] [He] will both provide a way out for us, and . . . He will also round about so compass us with His pavis and defend us, that we shall have no cause to fear this midday devil with all his persecution.

[Thus] we cannot now but be very sure . . . that either God shall not suffer the Turks to invade this land or, if they do, God shall provide such resistance that they shall not prevail. Or, if they prevail, yet if we take the way that I have told you, we shall by their persecution take little harm, or rather none harm at all. But that that shall seem harm shall indeed be to us none harm at all, but good. For if God make us and keep us good men, as He hath promised to do if we pray well therefor, then saith Holy Scripture: "Unto good folk all things turn them to good."[9] . . . . . .

VINCENT: By my troth, uncle, I thank you. Methinketh that though you never said more in the matter, yet have you even with this, that you have of the fear of bodily pain in this persecution spoken here already, marvellously comforted mine heart. . . . . . .

1 Mark 16:5-6.
2 Mark 14:66-72.
3 John 18:8.
4 See Mark 14:51-52.
5 Acts 12:7.
6 One such story of surviving torture is found in Book III, Chap. 3 of *The Ecclesiastical History* of Theodoret, bishop of Cyrus in Syria (386-460).
7 See e.g., Epistle 33, "To the Clergy and People about the Ordination of Celerinus as Reader," by St. Cyprian, Christian martyr and bishop of Carthage (248-258). References to the *Epistles* are to *The Writings of Cyprian, Bishop of Carthage,* trans. Robert E. Wallis, Ante-Nicene Christian Lib., Vol. VIII (1868-9).
8 See Psalms 90:5-6, and St. Paul in 1 Cor. 10:13—"God . . . will not suffer you to be tempted above that which you are able."
9 Rom. 8:28. More here returns to the central thesis of Part I (esp. Chaps. 7, 8, 9, 10), that tribulations—even persecution—are medicinal; that is, they are initially distasteful but ultimately beneficial to those who receive them in the right spirit.

Chapter 18

[On Captivity and Forced Labor]

[ANTHONY:] Now being somewhat in comfort and courage before,[1] whereby we may the more quietly consider everything, . . . let us examine the weight and the substance of those bodily pains as the sorest part of this persecution which you rehearsed before. Which were (if I remember you right) thraldom, imprisonment, painful and shameful death. And first let us (as reason is) begin with the thraldom—for that was, as I remember, the first.

VINCENT: I pray you, good uncle, say then somewhat thereof.

For methinketh, uncle, that captivity is a marvellous heavy thing, namely[2] when they shall (as they most commonly do) carry us far from home into a strange uncouth[3] land.

ANTHONY: I cannot say nay but that some grief it is, cousin, indeed. But yet as unto me, not half so much as it would be if they could carry me out into any such unknown country, that God could not wit where nor find the mean to come at me. But in good faith, cousin, now if my transmigration[4] into a strange country should be any great grief unto me, the fault should be much in myself. For . . . whithersoever men convey me, God is no more verily here than He shall be there, if I get (as I may if I will) the grace to set mine whole heart upon Him and long for nothing but Him. It can then make no great matter to my mind whether they carry me hence or leave me here!

And then if I find my mind much offended therewith that I am not still here in mine own country, I must consider that the cause of my grief is mine own wrong imagination, whereby I beguile myself with an untrue persuasion, weening that this were mine own country, whereas of truth it is not so. For as Saint Paul saith: "We have here no city nor dwelling country at all, but we seek for one that we shall come to."[5] And in what country soever we walk in this world, we be but as pilgrims and wayfaring men. . . . . . .

Now, as for all the other griefs and pains that are in captivity, thraldom, and bondage, I cannot deny but many there are and great. Howbeit, they seem yet somewhat . . . the more because we took our former liberty for more a great deal than indeed it was.[6] Let us therefore consider the matter thus: Captivity, bondage, or thraldom, what is it but the violent restraint of a man being so subdued under the dominion, rule, and power of another, that he must do what the other list to command him, and may not do at his liberty such things as he list himself?

Now when we shall be carried away with a Turk and be fain[7] to be occupied about such things as he list to set us, here shall we lament the loss of our liberty and think we bear an heavy burden of our servile condition. . . . But yet should we (I suppose) set thereby somewhat the less if we would remember well what liberty that was that we lost, and take it for no larger than it was indeed. For we reckon as though we might before do what we would, but therein we deceive ourself. For what free man is there so free that can be suffered to do what him list? In many things God hath restrained us by His high commandment; so many, that of those things which else we would do, I ween it be more than the half. Howbeit, because (God forgive us) we let so little therefore but do what we list—as though we heard Him not—we reckon our liberty never the less for that.

But then is our liberty much restrained by the laws made by men for the quiet and politic governance of the people. And these would, I ween, let our liberty but a little neither, were it not for fear of the pains that fall thereupon. Look, then, whether other men that have authority over us command us never no business which we dare not but do, and therefore do it full oft sore against our wills. Of which things some service is sometime so painful and so perilous too, that no lord can lightly command his bondman worse, nor seldom doth command him half so sore. Let every free man that reckoneth his liberty to stand in doing what he list consider well these points, and I ween he shall then find his liberty much less than he took it for before.

And yet have I left untouched the bondage that almost every man is in, that boasteth himself for free: the bondage, I mean, of sin. Which to be a very bondage I shall have our Savior Himself to bear me good record. For He saith: "Every man that committeth sin is the thrall or the bondman of sin."[8] And then, if this be thus . . . , who is there then that may make so much boast of his liberty, that he should take it for so sore a thing and so strange to become, through chance of war, bond[9] unto a man? Wh[y], he is already through sin become willingly thrall and bond unto the devil!

Let us look well how many things and of what vile wretched sort the devil driveth us to do daily through the rash braids[10] of our blind affections, which we be for our faultful lack of grace fain to follow and are too feeble to refrain. And then shall we find in our natural freedom our bond service such, that never was there any man lord of any so vile a villain that ever would for very shame command him so shameful service. And let us, in the doing of our service to the man that we be slave unto, remember what we were wont to do about the same time of the day while we were at our free liberty before—and were well likely, if we were at liberty, to do the like again. And we shall peradventure perceive that it were better for us to do this business than that.

Now shall we have great occasion of comfort if we consider that our servitude (though in the compt[11] of the world it seem to come by chance of war), cometh yet in very deed unto us by the provident hand of God. And that for our great good, if we will take it well, both in remission of sins and also matter of our merit. The greatest grief that is in bondage or captivity is this (as I trow), that we be forced to do such labor as with our goodwill we would not. But then against that grief Seneca teacheth us a good remedy: "Endeavor thyself evermore that thou do nothing against they will. But the thing that we see we shall needs do, let us use always to put our goodwill thereto."[12]

VINCENT: That is, uncle, soon said. But it is hard to do.

ANTHONY: Our froward mind maketh every good thing hard, and that to our own more hurt and harm. But in this case, if we will be good Christian men, we shall have great cause gladly to be content for the great comfort that we may take thereby. [For] we remember that in the patient and glad doing of our service unto that man for God's sake, according to His high commandment by the mouth of Saint Paul,[13] we shall have our thank and our whole reward of God.

Finally, remember the great humble meekness of our Savior Christ Himself, that He being very Almighty God humbled Himself and took the form of a bondman or slave rather than His Father should forsake us.[14] We may think ourself very unkind caitiffs,[15] and very frantic fools too if, rather than to endure this worldly bondage for a while, we would forsake Him that hath by His own death delivered us out of everlasting bondage of the devil, and will for our short bondage give us everlasting liberty.

VINCENT: Well fare you, good uncle, this is very well said. Albeit that bondage is a condition that every man of any courage would be glad to eschew and very loath to fall in, yet have you well made it open that it is a thing neither so strange nor so sore as it before seemed unto me. And specially far from such as any man, that any wit hath, should for fear thereof shrink from the confession of his faith. And now, therefore, I pray you somewhat speak of imprisonment.

1 in advance, by way of preparation.
2 especially.
3 unknown.
4 removal, being carried away.
5 Heb. 13:14. See Part I, Chap. 13, n. 1.
6 More begins here a long discussion of "universal" captivity and imprisonment. The discussion extends through Chapter 21, and in its deterministic implications seems to represent a considerable modification of the advocacy of free will found in his controversial writings. See the essay "Thomas More: Disenchanted Saint" in *Literature and Society* (1964), pp. 72-75.
7 compelled.
8 John 8:34.
9 given over in bondage to.
10 notions, fancies.
11 reckoning.
12 This statement is a loose paraphrase of Epistle 107 ("On Obedience to the Universal Will"), sec. 7-9, by Seneca (4 B.C.?-65 A.D.), Roman playwright, statesman, and Stoic philosopher. See *Seneca: Ad Lucilium epistulae morales* (Loeb ed., 1925), trans. Richard M. Gummere, III, 227: "We cannot change this order of things; but what we can do is to acquire stout hearts, worthy of good men, thereby courageously enduring chance and placing ourselves in harmony with Nature. . . . Whatever happens, assume that it was bound to happen, and do not be willing to rail at Nature. That which you cannot reform, it is best to endure." See also *Epistulae morales,* 61:3.
13 Ephes. 6:5—"Servants, obey your carnal masters."
14 See Philip. 2:8.
15 wretches.

Chapter 19

[Beggars and Kings]

ANTHONY: That shall I, cousin, with goodwill. And first, if we could consider what thing imprisonment is of his own nature we should not, methinketh, have so great horror thereof. For of itself it is, pardie, but a restraint of liberty which letteth a man from going whither he would.

VINCENT: Yes, by Saint Mary, uncle, methinketh it is much more sorrow than so. For beside the let and restraint of liberty, it hath many more displeasures and very sore griefs knit and adjoined thereto.

ANTHONY: That is, cousin, very true indeed. . . . Howbeit, I purpose now to consider first imprisonment, but as imprisonment only, without any other incommodity beside; for a man may be, pardie, imprisoned and yet not set in the stocks nor collared fast by the neck. . . .   . . . Those other kinds of griefs that come with imprisonment are but accidents thereunto. . . . We will, I say, therefore begin with the considering what manner pain or incommodity we should reckon imprisonment to be of himself and of his own nature alone. And then in the course of our communication, you shall as you list increase and aggrieve the cause of your horror with the terror of those painful accidents.

VINCENT: I am sorry that I did interrupt your tale. For you were about (I see well) to take an orderly way therein. And as yourself have devised, so I beseech you proceed. For though I reckon imprisonment much the sorer thing by sore and hard handling therein, yet reckon I not the prisonment of itself any less than a thing very tedious—all[1] were it used in the most favorable manner that it possibly might. For, uncle, [suppose there] were a great prince that were taken prisoner upon the field, and in the hand of a Christian king, which use in such case . . . to shew much humanity to them and in very favorable wise entreat[2] them. . . . (These infidel emperors handle oftentimes the princes that they take more villainously than they do the poorest men. . . . The great Tamburlaine[3] kept the great Turk when he had taken him, to tread on his[4] back alway while he[5] leapt on horseback.)

But as I began to say by the sample of a prince taken prisoner, were the imprisonment never so favorable, yet were it in my mind no little grief in itself for a man to be pinned up,[6] though not in a narrow chamber. But although his walk were right large and right fair gardens too therein, it could not but grieve his heart to be restrained by another man within certain limits and bounds, and lose the liberty to be where him list.

ANTHONY: This is, cousin, well considered of you. For in this you perceive well that imprisonment is of himself and his own very nature alone nothing else but the retaining of a man's person within the circuit of a certain space narrower or larger (as shall be limited to him), restraining his liberty from the further going into any other place.

VINCENT: Very well said, as methinketh.

ANTHONY: Yet forgat I, cousin, to ask you one question.

VINCENT: What is that, uncle?

ANTHONY: This, lo. If there be two men kept in two several chambers of one great castle, of which two chambers the one is much more large than the other, whether be they prisoners both? Or but the one that hath the less room to walk in?

VINCENT: What question is it, uncle, but that they be prisoners both (as I said myself before), although the one lay fast locked in the stocks and the other had all the whole castle to walk in.

ANTHONY: Me thinketh verily, cousin, that you say the truth. And then if prisonment be such a thing as yourself here agree it is, that is to wit, but a lack of liberty to go whither we list, now would I fain wit[7] of you what any one man you know that is at this day out of prison?

VINCENT: What one man, uncle? Marry, I know almost none other. For surely prisoner am I none acquainted with that I remember.

ANTHONY: Then I see well you visit poor prisoners seld[om].

VINCENT: No, by troth, uncle, I cry God mercy. I send them sometime mine alms, but by my troth I love not to come myself where I should see such misery.

ANTHONY: In good faith, cousin Vincent, ... I assure you it is hard to tell how much good to a man's soul the personal visiting of poor prisoners doth. But now sith ye can name me none of them that are in prison, I pray you name me some one of all them that you be (as you say) better acquainted with: men (I mean) that are out of prison. For I know, methinketh, as few of them as you know of the other.

VINCENT: That were, uncle, a strange case. For every man is, uncle, out of prison that may go where he will, though he be the poorest beggar in the town. And in good faith, uncle, . . . the poor beggar that is at his liberty and may walk where he will is (as meseemeth) in better case than is a king kept in prison, that cannot go but where men give him leave.

ANTHONY: Well, cousin, whether every waywalking beggar be by this reason out of prison or no we shall consider further when you will. But in the meantime I can by this reason see no prince that seemeth to be out of prison. For if the lack of liberty to go where a man will be imprisonment (as yourself say it is), then is the great Turk by whom we so fear to be put in prison, in prison already himself. For he may not go where he will. For an he might, he would into Portugal, Italy, Spain, France, Almaine, and England, and as far one another quarter too, both Prester John's[8] land and the Grand Khan's[9] too.

Now the beggar that you speak of: If he be [able] . . . to go where he will . . . , then is the beggar in better case not only than a prince in prison, but also than many a prince out of prison too. . . . . . . But . . . neither the beggar nor the prince is at free liberty to walk where they will. . . . If they would walk in some place [where] neither of them both should be suffered, . . . men would withstand them and say them nay. Therefore if imprisonment be (as you grant it is) a lack of liberty to go where we list, I cannot see but (as I say) the beggar and the prince whom you reckon both at liberty be, by your own reason, restrained in prison both.

VINCENT: Yea, but (uncle) both the one and the other have way enough to walk: the one in his own ground, the other in other men's; or in the common highway where they may walk till they be both weary of walking ere any man say them nay.

ANTHONY: So may, cousin, that king that had, as yourself put

PLATE 7. The Execution of More. Detail of an engraving by G. B. Cavalieri in *Ecclesiae Anglicanae Trophaea* (1584) after a fresco (c. 1580) by Niccolò Circignani.

the case, all the whole castle to walk in. And yet you say not nay but that he is prisoner for all that—though not so straitly kept, yet as verily prisoner as he that lieth in the stocks.

VINCENT: But they may go at the least wise to every place that they need or that is commodious for them. And therefore they do not will to go but where they may go. And therefore be they at liberty to go where they will.

ANTHONY: Me needeth not, cousin, to spend the time about the impugning every part of this answer. For letting pass by that though a prisoner were with his keeper brought into every place where need required, yet sith he might not when he would go where he would for his only pleasure, he were, ye wot well, a prisoner still. . . . Then let us look on our other prisoners enclosed within a castle. And we shall find that the straitest kept of them both . . . get[s] the wisdom and the grace to quiet his own mind and hold himself content with that place, and long not (like a woman with child for her lusts)[10] to be gadding out anywhere else. [Then he] is, by the same reason of yours, . . . at his free liberty to be where he will, and so is out of prison too.

And on the other side, if though his will be not longing to be anywhere else, yet because that if his will so were he should not so be suffered, he is therefore not at his free liberty, but a prisoner still. So [suppose] your free beggar that you speak of and the prince that you call out of prison too, . . . be (which I ween very few be) by some special wisdom so temperately disposed that they have not the will to be but where they see they may be suffered to be. Yet sith that if they would have that will, they could not then be where they would, they lack the effect of free liberty, and be both twain in prison too.

VINCENT: Well, uncle, if every man universally be by this reason in prison already, . . . yet to be imprisoned in this special manner (which manner is only commonly called imprisonment)[11] is a thing of great horror and fear, both for the straitness of the keeping and the hard handling that many men have therein. Of all which griefs and pains and displeasures in this other general imprisonment that you speak of, we feel nothing at all. And therefore every man abhorreth the one and would be loath to come into it, and no man abhorreth the other. For they feel none harm nor find no fault therein.

Wherefore, uncle, in good faith, though I cannot find answers convenient wherewith to avoid[12] your arguments, yet to be plain with you and tell you the very truth, my mind findeth not itself satisfied in this point. But . . . ever methinketh that these things, wherewith you rather convince and conclude me[13] than induce a credence and persuade me that every man is in prison already, be but sophistical fantasies.[14] Except those that are commonly called prisoners, other men are not in any prison at all.

1 even.

2 treat.

3 I.e., "Timur the Lame" (1336-1405), Oriental despot who conquered Persia in 1382-94. Whole cities were destroyed, their populations massacred, and towers built on their skulls. Invading India, Timur left Delhi in ruins, then attacked the Ottoman sultan Bayezid I. In 1401 he leveled Bagdad, massacred 20,000 citizens, destroyed Bayezid's army, and (according to legend) sentenced Bayezid to perpetual imprisonment in an iron cage. For a hostile account, see Ibn Arabshad, *Tamerlane; or Timur the Great Amir* (1936). Consult also Harold Lamb, *Tamerlane, The Earthshaker* (1932). The most famous treatment of Timur in English literature is Christopher Marlowe's play (1586). See the significant study by Roy Battenhouse, *Marlowe's "Tamburlaine"* (1964).

4 the Turk's.

5 Tamburlaine's—i.e., Tamburlaine when mounting his horse used the captured Turk as a platform. The Turk was presumably forced to crouch on the ground.

6 confined.

7 like to know.

8 Prester John was a semi-legendary medieval Christian monarch, at first identified (in the 12th c.) with a certain "John, archbishop of India." Later (13th c.) the name came to designate a mysterious Christian conqueror and priest-king who allegedly ruled over vast dominions in the Far East. From the 14th c. on, Prester John was identified with the king of Ethiopia, and it is in this latter sense that More is apparently using the name. One of the most authoritative early studies of this subject was *Der Priester Johannes,* by Freidrich Zarncke (Leipzig, 1876-9). The problem of Prester John has aroused considerable interest among modern scholars. See Boies Penrose, *Travel and Discovery in the Renaissance* (1952), pp. 12-13, 46-50, 138-41, and *passim;* and Francis M. Rogers, *The Quest for Eastern Christians: Travel and Rumor in the Age of Discovery* (1962).

9 The medieval ruler of China, including the Tatar and Mongol tribes.

10 desires; here in the sense of a restlessness to move about.

11 I.e., in this narrower sense of the term, which is the only sense in which "imprisonment" is ordinarily used.

12 turn aside, refute.

13 overwhelm me, box me in.

14 specious illusions.

Chapter 20

[All the World Is a Prison]

ANTHONY: Well fare thine heart, good cousin Vincent. There was, in good faith, no word that you spake since we first talked of these matters that half so well liked me as these that you speak now. For if you had assented in words and in your mind departed unpersuaded, then if the thing be true that I say, yet had you lost the fruit. And if it be peradventure false and myself deceived therein, then while I should ween that it like you too, you should have confirmed me in my folly. For in good faith, cousin, such an old fool am I that this thing, in the persuading [t]hereof unto you, I had weened I had quit me well. And when I have all done, [it] appeareth to your mind but a trifle and a sophistical fantasy. Myself have so many years taken [it] for so very substantial truth, that as yet my mind cannot give me to think it any other.

[Perhaps] I play as the French priest played, that had so long used to say *dominus* with the second syllable long, that at last he thought it must needs be so, and was ashamed to say it short. To the intent that you may the better perceive me or I the better myself, we shall here between us a little more consider the thing. And hardly[1] spit well on your hands and take good hold, and give it not over against your own mind.[2] For then were we never the nearer.[3]

VINCENT: Nay by my troth, uncle, that intend I not, nor nothing did yet since we began. And that may you well perceive by some things which without any great cause, save for the further satisfaction of mine own mind, I repeated and debated again.

ANTHONY: That guise, cousin, hold on hardly still. For in this matter I purpose to give over my part,[4] except I make yourself perceive [first] that every man universally is a very prisoner in very prison plainly without any sophistication at all. And that there is also no prince living upon earth but he is in worse case prisoner by this general imprisonment that I speak of, than is many a lewd simple wretch by the special imprisonment that you speak of. And over this, that in this general imprisonment that I speak of, men are for the time that they be therein so sore handled . . . that men's hearts have with reason great cause as sore to abhor this hard handling that is in this imprisonment, as the other that is in that.

VINCENT: By my troth, uncle, these things would I fain see well proved.

ANTHONY: Tell me then, cousin, first (by your troth), [suppose] there were a man attainted[5] of treason or of felony, and after judgment given of his death . . . , only the time of his execution delayed till the king's further pleasure known. And he [was] thereupon delivered to certain keepers and put up in a sure place out of which he could not scape. Were this man a prisoner or no?

VINCENT: This man, quoth he? Yea, marry, that he were in very deed if ever any man were!

ANTHONY: But now, what if for the time that were mean[6] between his attainder and his execution, he were so favorably handled that he were suffered to do what he would, as he was while he was abroad? To have the use of his lands and his goods, and his wife and his children licence to be with him, and his friends leave at liberty to resort unto him, and his servants not forboden to abide about him. And add yet thereunto that the place were a great castle royal with parks and other pleasures therein, a very great circuit about.

Yea, add yet (an ye will) that he were suffered to go and ride also, both when he would and whither he would, only this one point alway provided and foreseen, that he should ever be surely seen to and safely kept from scaping. So that took he never so much of his own mind in the meanwhile all other ways save scaping, yet he well knew that scape he could not. And that when he were called for, to execution and to death he should [come]. Now, cousin Vincent, what would you call this man? A prisoner because he is kept for execution, or no prisoner because he is in the meanwhile so favorably handled, and suffered to do all that he would save scape? And I bid you not here be hasty in your answer, but advise it well, that you grant no such thing in haste as you would after mislike by leisure and think yourself deceived.

VINCENT: Nay, by my troth, uncle, this thing needeth no study at all in my mind. But that for all this favor shewed him and all this liberty lent him, yet being condemned to death and being kept therefor, . . . he is all that while a very plain prisoner still.

ANTHONY: In good faith, cousin, methinketh you say very true. But then one thing must I yet desire you, cousin, to tell me a little further. [Suppose] there were another laid in prison for a fray, and through the jailer's displeasure were bolted and fettered and laid in a low dungeon in the stocks. [T]here he might hap to lie peradventure for a while, and abide in the mean season some pain but no danger of death at all but that out again he should come well enough. Which of these two prisoners stood in worse case? He that hath all this favor or he that is thus hardly handled?

VINCENT: By our Lady, uncle, I ween that most part of men, if they should needs choose, had liefer[7] be such prisoners in every point as he that so sorely lieth in the stocks, than in every point such as he that at such liberty walketh about the park.

ANTHONY: Consider then, cousin, whether this thing seem any sophistry to you that I shall shew you now. For it shall be such as seemeth in good faith substantial true to me. And if it so happen that you think otherwise, I will be very glad to perceive which of us both is beguiled. For it seemeth to me, cousin, first, that every man coming into this world here upon earth, as he is created by God, so cometh he hither by the providence of God. Is this any sophistry first or not?

VINCENT: Nay verily, this is very substantial truth.

ANTHONY: Now take I think this also for very truth in my mind: that there cometh no man nor woman hither into the earth but that ere ever they come quick[8] into the world out of the mother's womb, God condemneth them unto death by His own sentence and judgment for the original sin that they bring with them, contracted in the corrupted stock of our forefather Adam. Is this, think you, verily thus or not?

VINCENT: This is, uncle, very true indeed.

ANTHONY: Then seemeth this true further unto me: that God hath put every man here upon the earth under so sure and under so safe keeping, that of all the whole people living in this wide world there is neither man, woman, nor child . . . that possibly can find any way whereby they may scape from death. Is this, cousin, a fond imagined fantasy or is it very truth indeed?

VINCENT: Nay, this is none imagination, uncle, but a thing so clearly proved true that no man is so mad to say nay.

ANTHONY: Then need I no more, cousin. For then is all the matter plain and open evident truth which I said I took for truth. Which is yet more a little now than I told you before when you took my proof yet but for a sophistical fantasy. [You] said that, for all my reasoning that every man is a prisoner, yet you thought that except these whom the common people call prisoners, there is else no man a very prisoner indeed. And now you grant yourself again for very substantial open truth that every man is here (though he be the greatest king upon earth), set here by the ordinance of God in a place (be it never so large) . . . out of which no man can escape. But that therein is every man put under sure and safe keeping to be readily set forth when God calleth for him. And that then he shall surely die.

And is not then, cousin, by your own granting before, every man a very prisoner when he is put in a place to be kept to be brought forth when he would not, and himself not wot wither?

VINCENT: Yes, in good faith, uncle. I cannot but well perceive this to be so.

ANTHONY: This were (you wot well) true, although a man should be but taken by the arm and in fair manner led out of this world unto his judgment. But now . . . we well know that there is no king so great but that all the while he walketh here, walk he never so loose, ride he with never so strong an army for his deense, yet himself is very sure . . . that escape can he not. And very vell he knoweth that he hath already sentence given upon him to lie, and that verily die he shall. And that himself, though he hope ıpon long respite of his execution, yet can he not tell how soon.

And therefore (but if he be a fool) he can never be without fear, . . either on the morrow or on the selfsame day, [of] the grisly ruel hangman Death. . . . From his first coming in hath [Death] ver hoved aloof[9] and looked toward him and ever lien in a wait n him. [Death] shall amid among[10] all his royalty and all his nain strength neither kneel before him nor make him any rev-rence nor with any good manner desire him to come forth. But igorously and fiercely [shall he] grip him by the very breast and nake all his bones rattle, and so by long and divers sore torments trike him stark dead in this prison. And then cause his body to be ast into the ground in a foul pit within some corner of the same, here to rot and be eaten with the wretched worms of the arth.[11] . . .

Methinketh therefore, cousin, that (as I told you) this keeping f every man in this wretched world for execution of death is a ery plain imprisonment indeed. And that (as I say) such that the reatest king in this prison is in much worse case in all his wealth han many a man is by the other imprisonment,[12] that is therein ore and hardly handled. For where some of those lie not there ttainted nor condemned to death, the greatest man of this world nd the most wealthy in this universal prison is laid to be kept ndoubtedly for death.

VINCENT: But yet, uncle, in that case is the other prisoner too, or he is as sure that he shall die, pardie!

ANTHONY: This is very true, cousin, indeed, and well objected oo. But then you must consider that he is not in danger of death y reason of the prison into which he is put peradventure but for a ght fray. But his danger of death is by the other imprisonment, y which he is prisoner in the great prison of this whole earth—in vhich prison all the princes thereof be prisoners as well as he. . . . . .

Now may you, methinketh, very plainly perceive that this whole earth is . . . for all the whole kind of man a very plain prison indeed.[13] . . . They that ween they stand in great wealth, do stand for all that indeed, by the reason of their imprisonment in this large prison of the whole earth, in the selfsame condition that other do stand which in the narrow prisons . . . [are] condemned already to death. And now, cousin, if this thing that I tell you seem but a sophistical fantasy to your mind, I would be glad to know what moveth you so to think. For in good faith, as I have told you twice, I am no wiser but that I verily ween that the thing is thus of very plain truth in very deed.

1 with energy.
2 I.e., brace yourself for my verbal assault, and refuse to agree unless you are really convinced.
3 I.e., nearer to the truth.
4 concede defeat.
5 condemned, found guilty of. More specifically, extinction of civil rights of a condemned person, including forfeiture of property.
6 I.e., the interval.
7 rather.
8 alive.
9 from his (the king's) birth, Death has constantly hovered in the distance.
10 in the midst of.
11 This passage shows the considerable impact which the "Dance of Death" tradition had on More's mind. In *The Four Last Things* (Campbell, I, 468), More confessed himself "greatly moved by the beholding of the Dance of Death pictured in [the north cloister of St.] Paul's [Cathedral]. . . . These pictures express . . . the loathly figure of our dead bony bodies, bitten away the flesh, which . . . be ugly to behold."
12 by imprisonment in the narrower sense.
13 This provocative conclusion, that the world is a prison, was anticipated in 1522 in *The Four Last Things* (Campbell I, 479-80): "Mark this well, . . . all the while we live in this world we be but prisoners, and be within a sure prison, out of which there can be no escape. . . ." Much of the imagery and phraseology of the foregoing passage is carried over almost verbatim into Chapters 20 and especially 21 of the *Dialogue of Comfort*. An even earlier Epigram 101, "On the Futility of Life," begins: "We are all shut up in the prison of this world under sentence of death." See Bradner and Lynch, *More's Epigrams*, pp xxix, 174.

Chapter 21

[God as Chief Jailer]

VINCENT: In good faith, uncle, as for thus farforth, I not only can make with any reason no resistance thereagainst; but also [I] see very clearly proved that it can be none otherwise but that every man is in this world a very prisoner—sith we be all put here into a sure hold to be kept till we be put unto execution, as folk already condemned all to death. But yet, uncle, the strait keeping, collaring, bolting, and stocking, with lying in straw or on the cold ground . . . must needs make the imprisonment which only beareth among the people that name, much more odious and dreadful than the general imprisonment. Wherewith[1] we be every man universally prisoned at large, walking where we will round about the wide world. To [that] broad prison out[side] of those narrow prisons, there is with the prisoners no such hard handling used.

ANTHONY: I said (I trow) cousin, that I purposed to prove you further yet that in this general prison—the large prison I mean of this whole world—folk be for the time that they be therein [so] sore handled, . . . that our hearts (save that we consider it not) have with reason . . . as much horror to conceive against the hard handling that is in this [universal] prison, as the other that is in that [narrower prison.]

VINCENT: Indeed, uncle, truth it is that this you said you would prove.

ANTHONY: Nay, so much said I not, cousin. But I said I would if I could, and if I could not then would I therein give over my part.[2] But that, trust I cousin, I shall not need to do, the thing seemeth me so plain. For, cousin, not only [over] the prince and king, but also (although he have both angels and devils that are jailers under him) yet the chief jailer over this whole broad prison the world is (as I take it) God; and that I suppose ye will grant me too.

VINCENT: That will I not, uncle, deny.

ANTHONY: [Now suppose] a man be, cousin, committed unto prison for no cause but to be kept. Though there be never so great charge upon him, yet his keeper (if he be good and honest) is neither so cruel that would pain the man of malice, nor so covetous that would put him to pain to make him seek his friends and to pay for a pennyworth of ease.[3] . . . But, marry, if the place be such as the keeper cannot otherwise be sure, then is he compelled to keep him after the rate the straiter.[4] And also, if the prisoner be unruly and fall to fighting with his fellows or do some other manner of shrewd turns,[5] then useth the keeper to punish him sundry wise in some of such fashions as yourself have spoken of.

So is it now, cousin, that God, the chief jailer, as I say, of this broad prison the world, is neither cruel nor covetous. And this prison is also so sure and so subtly builded that albeit that it lieth open on every side without any wall in the world, yet wander we never so far about therein, the way to get out at shall we never find. So that He neither needeth to collar us nor to stock[6] us for any fear of scaping away. And therefore, except He see some other cause than our only keeping for death, He letteth us in the mean-while (for as long as He list to respite us) walk about in the prison and do therein what we will, using ourself in such wise as He hath by reason and revelation from time to time told us His pleasure.

And hereof it cometh, lo, that by reason of this favor for a time we wax, as I said, so wanton that we forget where we be, weening that we were lords at large. Whereas we be indeed (if we would consider it) even silly poor wretches in prison. For, of very truth, our very prison this earth is. And yet thereof we cant us out,[7] part by covenants that we make among us and part by fraud and part by violence too, divers parts diversely to ourself,[8] and change the name thereof from the odious name of prison and call it our own land and and our livelihood.

Upon our prison we build. Our prison we garnish with gold and make it glorious; in this prison they buy and sell; in this prison they brawl and chide; in this they run together and fight; in this they dice; in this they card;[9] in this they pipe and revel; in this they sing and dance. And in this prison many a man reputed right honest letteth not for his pleasure in the dark privily to play the knave. And thus while God, our king and our chief jailer too, suffereth us and letteth us alone, we ween ourself at liberty, and we abhor the state of those whom we call prisoners, taking ourself for no prisoners at all. . . .

We forget with our folly both ourself and our jail and our underjailers, angels and devils both, and our chief jailer God too. [But] God . . . forgetteth not us, but seeth us all the while well enough. And being sore discontent to see so shrewd rule[10] kept in the jail (beside that He sendeth the hangman Death to put to execution here and there sometime by the thousand at once), He handleth many of the remnant, whose execution He forbeareth yet unto a farther time, even as hardly, and punisheth them as sore in this common prison of the world as there are any handled in those special prisons. . . .

VINCENT: The remnant will I not gainsay, for methinketh I see it so indeed. But that God, our chief jailer in this world, useth any such prisonly fashion of punishment, that point must I needs deny. For I neither see Him lay any man in the stocks, or strike fetters on his legs, or so much as shut him up in a chamber either.

ANTHONY: Is he no minstrel, cousin, that playeth not on an harp? Maketh no man melody but he that playeth on a lute? He may be a minstrel and make melody, you wot well, with some other instruments—some strange fashioned [instrument] peradventure that never was seen before. God our chief jailer, as Himself is invisible, so useth He in His punishments invisible instruments, and therefore not of like fashion as the other jailers do, but yet of like effect and as painful in feeling as those.

For He layeth[11] one of His prisoners with an hot fever as evil at his ease in a warm bed, as the other jailer layeth his [prisoner] on the cold ground. He wringeth them by the brows with a megrim.[12] He collareth them by the neck with a quinsy.[13] He bolteth them by the arm with a palsy that they cannot lift their hands to their head. He manacleth their hands with the gout in their fingers. He wringeth them by the legs with the cramp in their shins. He bindeth them to the bed board with the crick in the back, and layeth one there along and as unable to rise as though he lay fast by the feet in the stocks.

Some prisoner of another jail singeth, danceth in his two fetters, and feareth not his feet for stumbling at a stone; while God's prisoner that hath his one foot fettered with the gout lieth groaning on a couch and quaketh, and crieth out if he fear there would fall on his foot no more but a cushion. And therefore, cousin, as I said, if we consider it well, we shall find this general prison of this whole earth a place in which the prisoners be as sore handled as they be in the other. . . . . . .

[Finally, suppose] there were some folk born and brought up in a prison that never came on the wall, nor looked out at the door, nor never heard of other world abroad. But [they] saw some, for shrewd turns done among themself, locked up in straiter room, and heard them only called prisoners that were so served, and themself ever called free folk at large. The like opinion would they have there of themself then, that we have here of ourself now. And when we take ourself for other than prisoners now, as verily be we now deceived as those prisoners should there be then.

VINCENT: I cannot, uncle, in good faith say nay but that you have performed all that you have promised. But . . . we wot well for all this that when we come to those [narrower] prisons, we shall not fail to be in a straiter prison than we be now, and to have a door shut upon us where we have none shut on us now. This shall we be sure of at the least wise, if there come no worse. And then may there come worse, ye wot well, it cometh there so commonly. Wherefore, for all this, it is yet little marvel though men's hearts grudge much thereagainst. . . . . . .

[ANTHONY:] The incommodities proper to the imprisonment, of their own nature, [are] to have less room to walk in and to have the door shut upon us. These are (methinketh) so very slender and slight, that in so great a cause as to suffer for God's sake, we might be sore ashamed so much as once to think upon them. Many a good man there is, ye wot well, which without any force at all or any necessity wherefore he should so do, suffereth these two things willingly of his own choice with much other hardness more.

Holy monks, I mean, of the Charterhouse[14] order such as never pass[15] their cells but only to the church set fast by their cells, and thence to their cells again. And Saint Bridget's[16] order, and Saint Clare's[17] much like, and in a manner all close[18] religious houses.

And anchors[19] and anchoresses most especially, all those whose room is less than a meetly large chamber. And yet are they there as well content many long years together as are other men, and better too, that walk about the world.

And therefore you may see that the loathness of less room and the door shut upon us, while so many folk are so well content therewith, and will for God's love choose so to live,[20] is but an horror enhanced of our own fantasy. And indeed I wist a woman once that came into a prison to visit of her charity a poor prisoner there. Whom she found in a chamber to say the truth, meetly fair[21]—and at the least wise it was strong enough! But with mats of straw the prisoner had made it so warm both under the foot and round about the walls, that in these things for the keeping of his health she was on his behalf glad and very well comforted.

But among many other displeasures that for his sake she was sorry for, one she lamented much in her mind, that he should have the chamber door upon him by night made fast by the jailer that should shut him in. "For, by my troth," quoth she, "if the door should be shut upon me I would ween it would stop up my breath." At that word of hers the prisoner laughed in his mind, but he durst not laugh aloud nor say nothing to her, for somewhat indeed he stood in awe of her, and had his finding[22] there much part of her charity for alms. But he could not but laugh inwardly, why he wist well enough, that she used on the inside to shut every night full surely her own chamber to her, both door and windows too, and used not to open them of all the long night. And what difference, then, as to the stopping of the breath, whether they were shut up [from] within or without?[23]

And so surely, cousin, these two things that you speak of are neither other[24] of so great weight that in Christ's cause ought to move a Christian man. And the one[25] of the twain is so very a childish fantasy that in a matter almost of three chips[26] (but if it were in chance of fire[27]), [it] never should move any man. As for those other accidents of hard handling therein, so mad am I not to say they be no grief; but I say that our fear may imagine them much greater grief than they be. And I say that such as they be, many a man endureth them, yea and many a woman too, that after fare full well. . . . . . . In prison was Joseph while his brethren were at large; and yet after were his brethren fain to seek upon him for bread.[28] In prison was Daniel, and the wild lions about him; and yet even there God kept him harmless and brought him safe out again.[29]

If we think that He will not do the like wise for us, let us not doubt but He will do for us either the like or better. For better may He do for us if He suffer us there to die. Saint John the Baptist was, you wot well, in prison while Herod and Herodias sat full merry at the feast, and the daughter of Herodias delighted them with her dancing, till with her dancing she danced off Saint John's head.[30] And now sitteth he with great feast in heaven at God's board, while Herod and Herodias full heavily sit in hell burning both twain. And to make them sport withal, the devil with the damsel dance in the fire afore them!

Finally, cousin, to finish this piece with, our Savior was Himself take[n] prisoner for our sake. And prisoner was He carried, and prisoner was He kept, and prisoner was He brought forth before Annas, and prisoner from Annas carried unto Caiaphas. Then prisoner was He carried from Caiaphas unto Pilate, and prisoner was He sent from Pilate to King Herod, prisoner from Herod unto Pilate again, and so kept as prisoner to the end of His Passion. The time of His imprisonment, I grant well, was not long; but as for hard handling which our hearts most abhor, He had as much in that short while as many men among them all in much longer time.

And surely then, if we consider of what estate He was and therewith that He was prisoner in such wise for our sake, we shall I trow (but if we be worse than wretched beasts) never so shamefully play the unkind cowards as for fear of imprisonment sinfully to forsake Him. Nor [shall we be] so foolish neither as by forsaking of Him to give Him the occasion again to forsake us, and with the avoiding of an easier prison fall into a worse. Instead of prison that cannot keep us long, [we would then] fall into that prison out of which we can never come.[31] Where[as] the short prisonment would win us everlasting liberty.

1 I.e., in the "general imprisoning."
2 concede defeat.
3 The implication is that some jailers deliberately mistreat prisoners in order to elicit bribes to "go easy" from the prisoner's friends.
4 I.e., the jailer must guard the prisoner with a strictness proportionate to the physical flaws of the prison.
5 malicious behavior.
6 place us in the stocks.
7 apportion, divide up (the land).
8 I.e., each man to his own method.
9 play cards.
10 undisciplined behavior.
11 lays low.
12 migraine (headache).
13 severe sore throat.
14 The Carthusians, or Charterhouse order, were founded by St. Bruno of Cologne in 1086, at Chartreuse, near Grenoble. The rule was strict, prescribing silence and solitude. By piecing together comments by Roper, Harpsfield, and Erasmus, we deduce that More spent about four years (1501-5) in informal religious living at the London Charterhouse, while simultaneously continuing his legal studies. He ultimately decided he was more suited for an active life. See Reynolds, *St. Thomas More,* pp. 23-24.
15 leave, pass beyond.
16 Founded at Wadstena, in Sweden, by Princess Brigitta, c. 1346. The only house of the order was at Syon near Isleworth, where More used to visit his friend Richard Reynolds. See E. E. Reynolds, *St. Thomas More,* pp. 233, 259, and Hallett, *Dialogue,* p. vii.
17 St. Clare was the friend of St. Francis, and adapted the Franciscan rule for women, around 1212. For details on these organizations, see Dom David Knowles, *The Religious Orders in England* (1948).
18 strict.
19 anchorites—i.e., religious hermits.
20 More's word order "live so to choose" has here been reversed to clarify the meaning.
21 good enough.
22 expenses. I.e., the prisoner was dependent for his expenses on the charity of the woman who was visiting him.
23 The "woman" and the "prisoner" of this anecdote are probably Dame Alice and More himself, since we know that Alice visited More in the Tower—see Harpsfield, p. 97. The reference to "expenses" might well allude to the fact that Dame Alice had to pay fifteen shillings a week for board and lodging for support of her husband and his servant in prison —see Reynolds, pp. 243-4.
24 neither one nor the other.
25 I.e., the horror of having the door shut.
26 I.e., in a matter of so little consequence.
27 More is suggesting that a door locked from the outside is a problem only in the rare case of fire.
28 Gen. 37-45.
29 Daniel 6:16-24.
30 Matt. 14:1-2; cf. Mark 6:20-29.
31 I.e., hell.

Chapter 22

[Reason and the Body]

[Vincent thanks Anthony for his counsel up to this point. He is now convinced that, if necessary, he would forego outward goods and endure imprisonment rather than desert Christ. But he is terrified at the thought of painful and shameful death through torture. Anthony agrees that such death is the most dreadful of all tribulations. Yet our attitude toward such death is conditioned by our scale of values. Some men would rather be tortured to death than tell where their money is hidden. Our scale of values is in turn determined by whether our reason or bodily senses dominate our personalities. The devil, working through our bodily senses, tempts us to dread painful death. But God, working through the reason, seeks to strengthen us to endure it for his sake. Hence we are brave in this matter to the extent that reason, bolstered by prayer, is in command of our bodies. With this strategy in mind, says Anthony, let us turn now to the ultimate dread: shameful and painful death.]

Chapter 23

[What the Snail's Shell Signifies]

[ANTHONY:] And first I perceive well by these two things that you join unto Death, that is to wit "shameful and painful," [that] you would esteem Death so much the less if she should come alone without either shame or pain.

VINCENT: Without doubt, uncle, a great deal the less. But yet though he should come without them both by himself, whatsoever I would,[1] I wot well many a man would be for all that very loath to die.

ANTHONY: That I believe well, cousin, and the more pity it is. For that affection happeth in very few but that either the cause is lack of faith, lack of hope, or finally lack of wit. They that believe not the life to come after this (and ween themself here in wealth) are loath to leave this, for then they think they lose all. And thereof cometh the manifold foolish unfaithful words which are so rife in our many mouths: "This world we know and the other we know not."[2] And that [other remark] some say in sport and think in earnest: "The devil is not so black as he is painted; and let him be as black as he will, he is no blacker than a crow." With many such other foolish fantasies of the same sort.

Some that believe well enough, yet through the lewdness of living fall out of good hope of salvation. And then though they be loath to die I very little marvel. . . . . . . Some are there, I say also, that are loath to die for lack of wit. . . . They believe the world that is to come and hope also to come thither. Yet they love so much the wealth of this world and such things as delight them therein, that they would fain keep them as long as ever they might —even with tooth and nail. And when they may be suffered in no wise to keep it no longer, but that death taketh them therefrom, then if it may be no better they will agree to be (as soon as they be hence) hanced up[3] in heaven, and be with God by and by.[4] These folk are as very idiot fools as he that had kept from his childhood a bag full of cherry stones, and cast such a fantasy thereto[5] that he would not go from it for a bigger bag filled full of gold.

These folk fare, cousin, as Aesop telleth in a fable that the snail did.[6] For when Jupiter (whom the poets feign for[7] the great God) invited all the poor worms of the earth unto a great solemn feast that it pleased him . . . upon a time to prepare for them, the snail kept her at home and would not come thereat. And [t]hen Jupiter asked her after, wherefore she came not at his feast, where he said she should have been welcome and have faren well and should have seen a goodly palace and been delighted with many goodly pleasures. She answered him that she loved no place as well as her own house. With which answer Jupiter waxed so angry that he said, sith she loved her house so well, she should never after go from home, but should always after bear her house upon her back wheresoever she went. And so hath she done ever since, as they say; and at the least wise I wot well she doth so now, and hath done as long time as I can remember.

VINCENT: Forsooth, uncle, I would ween the tale were not all feigned. For I think verily that so much of your tale is true.

ANTHONY: Aesop meant by that feigned fable to touch the folly of such folk as so set their fantasy[8] upon some small simple pleasure, that they cannot find in their hearts to forbear it, neither for the pleasure of a better man nor for the gaining of a better thing. By which their fond froward fashion they sometime fall in a great indignation[9] and take thereby no little harm.

And surely such Christian folk . . . by their foolish affection . . . have set, like the snail, upon their own house here, this earth. [They] cannot, for the loathness of leaving that house, find in their heart with their goodwill to go to the great feast that God prepareth in heaven, and of His goodness so gently calleth them to belike.[10] I fear me (but if they mend that mind in time), [they will] be served as the snail was, and yet much worse too. For they be like to have their house here, the earth, bound fast upon their backs for ever—and not walk therewith where they will, as the snail creepeth about with hers, but lie fast bound in the midst with the foul fire of hell about them. For into this folly they bring themself by their own fault, as the drunken man bringeth himself into drunkenness. Whereby the evil that he doth in his drunkenness is not forgiven him for his folly, but to his pain imputed to his fault.

VINCENT: Surely, uncle, this seemeth not unlikely; and by their fault they fall in such folly indeed. And yet if this be folly indeed, there are then some folk fools that ween themself right wise.

ANTHONY: That ween themself wise? Marry, I never saw fool yet that thought himself other than wise! For as it is one spark of soberness left in a drunken head when he perceiveth himself drunk and getteth him fair[11] to bed, so if a fool perceive himself a fool, that point is no folly but a little spark of wit. But now, cousin, as for these kind of fools, . . . they be loath to die for the love that they bear to their worldly fantasies[12] which they should by their death leave behind them and forsake. They that would for that cause rather forsake the faith than die, would rather forsake it than lose their worldly goods—though there were offered them no peril of death at all. And then as touching those that are of that mind, we have, you wot well, said as much as yourself thought sufficient this afternoon herebefore.[13]

VINCENT: Verily, uncle, that is very true. And now have you rehearsed, as far as I can remember, all the other kinds of them that would be loath to die for any other respect than the grievous qualities of shame and pain joined unto death. And of all these kinds, except the kind of infidelity when no comfort can help but counsel only to the attaining of faith . . . , there is none of the remnant of those that were before untouched which were likely to forsake their faith in this persecution for the fear and dread of death, save for those grievous qualities—pain, I mean, and shame —that they see well would come therewith.[14]

And therefore, uncle, I pray you give us some comfort against those twain.[15] For in good faith, if death should come without them in such a case as this is, wherein by the losing of this life we should find a far better, mine own reason giveth me that (save for the other griefs going before the change) there would no man, that wit hath, anything stick at all.

ANTHONY: . . . They, cousin, that will consider the matter well, reason grounded upon the foundation of faith shall shew them very great substantial causes for which the dread of those grievous qualities that they see shall come with death—shame, I mean, and pain also—shall not so sore abash them as sinfully to drive them therefrom. For the proof whereof let us first begin at the consideration of the shame.

1 in whatsoever form I wanted.

2 A striking anticipation of Hamlet's soliloquy (III, i, lines 78-82):

> . . . who would fardels [burdens] bear,
> To grunt and sweat under a weary life,
> But that the dread of something after death,
> The undiscovered country from whose bourn [boundary]
> No traveller returns, puzzles the will
> And makes us rather bear those ills we have
> Than fly to others that we know not of?

3 exalted.

4 I.e., be placed right next to (side by side with) God.

5 attributed such magic to it.

6 See Fable 185, "Jupiter's Wedding," in L'Estrange's *Aesop* (1708), pp. 198-9. In this version, the turtle is the victim: "Jupiter took it very ill . . . that [the tortoise] should think himself better in a ditch than in a palace, and so he passed this judgment upon him: that . . . he should never stir abroad again from that day forward, without his house upon his head."

7 use to represent.

8 fancy.

9 agitation, emotional turmoil.

10 most likely, probably.

11 properly.

12 goods (which are illusory).

13 As e.g., in Part III, Chaps. 6, 8, 11, 12, 15, 16.

14 Vincent has apparently forgotten that, according to Anthony's categories, some men fear death through "lack of hope of salvation." Certainly men in this category would have a "dread of death," even if no pain or shame were attached thereto.

15 I.e., shame and pain.

Chapter 24

[The Shame of Death]

[ANTHONY:] How can any faithful wise man dread the death so sore for any respect of shame, when his reason and his faith together may shortly make him perceive that there is therein no piece of very shame at all? For how can that death be shameful that is glorious? Or how can it be but glorious to die for the faith of Christ, if we die both for the faith and in the faith, joined with hope and charity? [For] the Scripture so plainly saith: "Precious is in the sight of God the death of His saints."[1]

Now if the death of His saints be glorious in the sight of God, it can never be shameful in very deed, how shameful soever it seem here in the sight of men. For here we may see and be sure that not at the death of Saint Stephen[2] only (to whom it liked Him to shew Himself with the heaven open over His head), but at the death also of every man that so dieth for the faith, God with His heavenly company beholdeth his whole passion and verily looketh on.

Now, [suppose] it were so, cousin, that ye should be brought through the broad high street of a great long city.[3] And that all along the way that ye were going, there were on the one side of the way a rabble of ragged beggars and madmen that would despite and dispraise you with all the shameful names that they could call you, and all the villainous words that they could say to you. And [suppose] that there were then all along the other side of the same street where you should come by, a goodly company standing in a fair range,[4] a row of wise and worshipful folk allowing[5] and commending you—more than fifteen times as many as that rabble of ragged beggars and railing madmen are. Would you let your way by your will,[6] weening that ye went unto your shame for the shameful jesting and railing of those mad foolish wretches? Or hold on your way with a good cheer and a glad heart, thinking yourself much honored by the laud and approbation of that other honorable sort?

VINCENT: Nay, by my troth, uncle, there is no doubt but I would much regard the commendation of those commendable folk, and not regard a rush[7] the railing of all those ribalds.

ANTHONY: Then, cousin, can there no man that hath faith account himself shamed here by any manner death that he suffereth for the faith of Christ. While how vile and how shameful soever it seem in the sight here of a few worldly wretches, it is allowed and approved for very precious and honorable in the sight of God and all the glorious company of heaven. [They] as perfectly stand and behold it as those peevish people do, and are in number more than an hundred to one. And of that hundred, every one an hundred times more to be regarded and esteemed than of the other an hundred such whole rabbles.

And now if a man would be so mad as, for fear of the rebuke that he should have of such rebukeful beasts, he would be ashamed to confess the faith of Christ, [t]hen with fleeing from a shadow of shame he should fall into a very shame and a deadly painful shame indeed. For then hath our Savior made a sure promise that He will shew himself ashamed of that man before the Father of heaven and all His holy angels, saying in the ninth chapter of Saint Luke: "He that is ashamed of me and my words, of him shall the Son of Man be ashamed when He shall come in the majesty of himself and of his Father and of His holy angels."[8] And what manner of shameful shame shall that be then? If a man's cheeks glow sometime for shame in this world, they will fall on fire for shame when Christ shall shew himself ashamed of them there.

To suffer the thing for Christ's faith that we worldly wretched fools ween were villainy and shame, the blessed apostles reckoned for great glory. For they, when they were with despite and shame scourged and thereupon commanded to speak no more of the name of Christ, went their way from the council joyful and glad that God had vouchsafed to do them the worship[9] to suffer shameful despite for the name of Jesu. And so proud were they of the same and villainous pain put unto them, that for all the forbidding of that great council assembled, they ceased not every day to preach out the name of Jesu still. Not in the temple only (out of which they were set and whipped for the same before) but also, to double it with, [they went] preaching the name about from house to house too.

I would,[10] sith we regard so greatly the estimation of worldly folk, we would among many naughty things that they use, regard also some such as are good. For it is a manner among them in many places that some by handicraft, some by merchandise, some by other kind of living, arise and come forward in the world. And commonly folk are in youth set forth to convenient masters under whom they be brought up and grow. But now whensoever they find a servant such as he disdaineth to do such things as he that is his master did while he was servant himself, that servant every man accounteth for a proud unthrift,[11] never like to come to good proof.

Let us, lo, mark and consider this, and weigh well therewithal, that our Master Christ (not the Master only, but the Maker, too, of all this whole world) was not so proud to disdain for our sakes the most villainous and most shameful death after the worldly count[12] that then was used in the world. And [He disdained neither] the most despiteful mocking therewith joined to most grievous pain—as crowning Him with sharp thorn that the blood ran down about His face. Then they gave Him a reed in His hand for a sceptre, and kneeled down to Him and saluted Him like a king in scorn, and beat then the reed upon the sharp thorns about His holy head.

Now saith our Savior that the disciple or servant is not above his master.[13] And therefore, sith our Master endured so many kinds of painful shame, very proud beasts may we well think ourself if we disdain to do as our Master did. And whereas He through shame ascended into glory, would we[14] be so mad that we rather will fall into everlasting shame both before heaven and hell, than for fear of a short worldly shame to follow Him into everlasting glory?

1 Psalms 115:15.
2 Acts 7:57-59.
3 More might have been seeking here to imagine his own impending death procession. See the vivid account in Chambers, *Thomas More,* pp. 348-9, wherein More is reviled by a woman who felt he had judged her case unfairly.
4 smartly drawn up, in neat and orderly array.
5 praising.
6 would you voluntarily stop.
7 See Part I, Intro., n. 24.
8 Luke 9:26.
9 honor.
10 wish.
11 spendthrift, "no-good."
12 reckoning—i.e., in the world's eyes.
13 Luke 6:40.
14 The words "would" and "we" have been transposed, so as more closely to approximate More's apparent meaning.

Chapter 25

[Two Harts and a Bitch]

VINCENT: In good faith, uncle, as for the shame ye shall need to take no more pain.[1] For I suppose surely that any man that hath reason in his head shall hold himself satisfied with this. But of truth, uncle, all the pinch is in the pain. For as for shame, I perceive well now, a man may with wisdom so master it that it shall nothing move him at all. So farforth that it is almost in every country becomen a common proverb that shame is as it is taken. But, by God, uncle, all the wisdom in this world can never so master pain but that pain will be painful, spite of all the wit in this world.

ANTHONY: Truth it is, cousin, that no man can with all the reason he hath in such wise change the nature of pain, that in the having of pain he feel it not. For but if it be felt, it is pardie no pain. And that is the natural cause, cousin, for which a man may have his leg stricken off by the knee and grieve him not—if his head be off but half an hour afore! But reason may make a reasonable man . . . not to shrink therefrom and refuse it to his more hurt and harm, but for his far greater advantage and commodity content and glad to sustain it. And this doth reason alone in many cases where it hath much less help to take hold of than it hath in this matter of faith.

For well you wot, to take a sour and a bitter potion is great grief and displeasure. And to be lanced and have the flesh cut is no little pain. Now, [consider] when such things shall be ministered unto a child or to some childish man either. They will by their own wills rather let their sickness or their sore grow unto their more grief till it become incurable, than abide the pain of the curing in time—and that for faint heart joined with lack of discretion. But [take] a man that hath more wisdom, though he would without cause no more abide the pain willingly than would the other. Yet sith reason sheweth him what good he shall have by the suffering and what harm by the refusing, this maketh him well content and glad also for to take it.

Now then, if reason alone be sufficient to move a man to take pain for the gaining of worldly rest or pleasure . . . , why should not reason, grounded upon the sure foundation of faith, . . . be much more able first to engender in us . . . an habitual fast and deep rooted purpose of patient[ly] suffering the painful death of this body here in earth, for the gaining of everlasting wealthy life in heaven and avoiding of everlasting painful death in hell?

VINCENT: By my troth, uncle, words can I none find . . . wherewith I might reasonably counterplead this that you have said here already. But yet I remember the fable that Aesop telleth of a great old hart that had fled from a little bitch, which had made suit after[2] him and chased him so long that she had lost him.[3] And, as he hoped, more than half given him over. By occasion whereof having then some time to talk, and meeting with another of his fellows, he fell in deliberation with him what were best for him to do; whether to run on still and fly farther from her, or turn again and fight with her.

Whereunto the other hart advised him to fly no farther, lest the bitch might happen to find him again at such time as he should with the labor of farther fleeing be fallen out of breath, and thereby all out of strength too. [Then] should he be killed lying, where he could not stir him; whereas if he would turn and fight he were in no peril at all. "For the man with whom she hunteth be more than a mile behind her," [said the fellow-hart]. "She is but a little body scant half so much as thou. And thy horns may thrust her through before she can touch thy flesh, by more than ten times her tooth length." "By my troth," quoth the other hart, "I like your counsel well, and methinketh that the thing is even soothly such as you say. But I fear me when I hear once that urchin bitch bark I shall fall to my feet and forget all together. But yet an you will go back with me, then methink we shall be strong enough against that one bitch between us both." Whereunto the other hart agreed, and so they both appointed[4] them thereupon. But even as they were about to busk them forward to it,[5] the bitch had found the foot[6] again, and on she came yearning[7] toward the place. Whom as soon as the harts heard, they to go both twain apace![8]

And in good faith, uncle, even so I fear it would fare by myself and many other too, which though we think it reason that you say and in our minds agree that we should do as ye say, . . . yet as soon as we should once hear those hell-hounds, these Turks, come yelping and bawling upon us, our hearts should soon fall as clean from us as those other harts flee from the hounds.

ANTHONY: Cousin, in those days that Aesop speaketh of, though those harts and other brute beasts more had (if he say sooth) the power to speak and talk, and in their talking power to talk reason too, yet to follow reason and rule themself thereby —thereto had they never given them the power. And in good faith, cousin, as for such things as pertain toward the conducting of reasonable men to salvation, I think without help of grace, men's reasoning shall do little more. But then are we sure, as I said before, that as for grace, if we desire it God is at such reasoning alway present and very ready to give it. And but if that men will afterward willingly cast it away, He is ever still as ready to keep it and from time to time glad to increase it.

And therefore biddeth us our Lord by the mouth of the prophet, that we should not be like such brutish and unreasonable beasts as were those harts, and as are horses and mules: "Be not you like an horse and a mule that hath none understanding."[9] And therefore, cousin, let us . . . apply our minds to the gathering of comfort and courage against such persecutions, and hear reason, and let it sink into our heart, and cast it not out again, [nor] vomit it not up, nor even there choke it up and stifle it with pampering and stuffing up our stomachs with a surfeit of worldly vanities. God shall so well work therewith that we shall feel strength therein, and not in such wise have all such shameful cowardous hearts as to forsake our Savior and thereby lose our own salvation, and run into eternal fire for fear of death joined therewith.[10] Though bitter and sharp, yet [it is] short for all that, and in a manner a momentary pain.

VINCENT: Every man, uncle, naturally grudgeth at pain and is very loath to come to it.

ANTHONY: That is very truth. Nor no man biddeth any man to go run into it, but that if he be taken and may not flee. Then we say that reason plainly telleth us that we should rather suffer and endure the less and the shorter [pain] here than in hell the sorer—and so far the longer too.

1 pains (in the sense of "concern"). Vincent might be punning here on the previous linking of shame and pain.
2 pursued.
3 Aesop tells a number of tales about harts (stags) fleeing from hunters or dogs—e.g., Bk. III, Fables 7 and 19, and Bk. IV, Fable 9 in Caxton's 1484 ed.; and Fables 43, 53, 57, 147, and 148 in the 5th (1708) L'Estrange ed. However, neither of these two editions, which span the Renaissance and 17th century use of Aesop, contains the particular story related by Vincent.
4 fixed or settled (on the plan) proposed by the other hart.
5 I.e., hurry forward into position to carry out the ambush of the bitch.
6 scent.
7 yelping, baying.
8 I.e., they both fled, panic-stricken! In the 1553 edition, this fable contains a passage on technical hunting terms. The passage is not found in Rastell, and is omitted from this edition.
9 Psalms 31:9.
10 I.e., with pain.

Chapter 26

[A Tottering Stool]

VINCENT: I heard, uncle, of late where such a reason was made as you make me now, which reason seemeth undoubted and inevitable unto me. Yet heard I late, as I say, a man answer it thus. He said that if a man in this persecution should stand still in the confession of his faith and thereby fall into painful tormentry,[1] he might peradventure hap for the sharpness and bitterness of the pain to forsake our Savior even in the midst, and die there with his sin and so be damned for ever. Whereas by the forsaking of the faith in the beginning betime,[2] and for the time (and yet not but in word neither, keeping it still nevertheless in his heart), a man may save himself from that painful death. And after [he may] ask mercy and have it, and live long, and do many good deeds, and be saved as Saint Peter was.

ANTHONY: That man's reason, cousin, is like a three-footed stool, so tottering on every side that whoso sit thereon may soon take a foul fall. For these are the three feet of this tottering stool: fantastical fear, false faith, false flattering hope.

First, it is a fantastical fear that the man conceiveth that it should be perilous to stand in the confession of the faith at the beginning, lest he might afterward through the bitterness of pain fall to the forsaking and so die there in the pain therewith out of hand, and thereby be utterly damned. As though that if a man by pain were overcome and so forsook his faith, God could not or would not as well give him grace to repent again and thereupon give him forgiveness. . . . As though the more pain that a man taketh for God's sake, the worse would God be to him. If this reason were not unreasonable, then should our Savior not have said as He did: "Fear not them that may kill the body, and after that have nothing that they can do farther."[3] For He should by this reason have said: "Dread and fear them that may slay the body, for they may by the torment of painful death . . . make thee peradventure forsake me too late, and so to be damned for ever!"

The second foot of this tottering stool is a false faith. For it is but a feigned faith for a man to say to God secretly that he believeth Him, trusteth Him, and loveth Him, and then openly, where he should to God's honor tell the same tale . . . , flatter God's enemies and do them pleasure and worldly worship, with the forsaking of God's faith before the world. [Such a person] is either faithless in his heart too, or else wotteth well that he doth God this despite even before His own face. For, except he lack faith, he cannot but know that our Lord is everywhere present, and while he so shamefully forsaketh Him, full angerly looketh on.

The third foot of this tottering stool is false flattering hope. For [surely] the thing that he doth when he forsaketh his faith for fear, is by the mouth of God upon the pain of eternal death forboden. Though the goodness of God forgiveth many folk the fault, yet to be bolder in offending for the hope of forgiving[4] is a very false pestilent hope, wherewith a man flattereth himself toward his own destruction. He that in a sudden braid[5] for fear or other affection unadvisedly falleth, and after in laboring to rise again comforteth himself with hope of God's gracious forgiveness, walketh in the ready way toward his salvation. But he that with the hope of God's mercy to follow doth encourage himself to sin and therewith offendeth God first—. . . I very sore fear that such a man may miss the grace to require it in such effectual wise as to have it granted.

. . . . . .

And where the man that you speak of took in his reason a sample of Saint Peter which forsook our Savior, and got forgiveness after: Let him consider again on the other side that he[6] forsook Him not upon the boldness of any such sinful trust, but was overcomen and vanquished upon a sudden fear. And yet by that forsaking Saint Peter won but little, for he did but delay his trouble for a little while, you wot well. For beside that he repented

Beatus: Thomas: Morus: Martyr.

PLATE 8. More as a Martyr. Depicted by an anonymous twentieth-century painter, hired by the French publisher Desclée to do paintings of all the saints in the *Calendar of Saints*. More is holding in his left arm the axe and the block with which he was beheaded.

forthwith very sore that he so had done, and wept therefor by and by full bitterly, he came forth at the Whitsuntide ensuing and confessed his Master again. And soon after that he was imprisoned therefore, and not ceasing so,[7] was thereupon sore scourged for the confession of his faith, and yet after that imprisoned again afresh. And being from thence delivered, [he] stinted not to preach on still until that after manifold labors, travels, and troubles, he was at Rome crucified and with cruel torment slain.[8]

And in like wise, I ween, I might in a manner well warrant that there shall no man which denieth our Savior once, and after attaineth remission,[9] escape through that denying one penny the better cheap.[10] But that he shall, ere he come in heaven, full surely pay therefor.

VINCENT: He shall peradventure, uncle, afterward work it out in the fruitful works of penance, prayer, and alms deed done in true faith and due charity, and attain in such wise forgiveness well enough.

ANTHONY: All his forgiveness goeth, cousin, you see well, but by "perhaps." But as it may be "perhaps yea," so may it be "perhaps nay." And where is he then? And yet, you wot well, by no manner hap[11] he shall never hap finally to scape from death for fear of which he forsook his faith.

VINCENT: No, but he may die his natural death and escape that violent death. And then he saveth himself from much pain, and so winneth therewith much ease. For evermore a violent death is painful.

ANTHONY: Peradventure he shall not avoid a violent death thereby. For God is without doubt displeased, and can bring him shortly to a death as violent by some other way. Howbeit, I see well that you reckon that whoso dieth a natural death dieth like a wanton even at his ease. You make me remember a man that was once in a galley-suttle[12] with us on the sea. . . . The sea was sore wrought and the waves rose very high, and he came never on the sea afore, and lay tossed hither and thither. The poor soul groaned sore and for pain he thought he would very fain be dead, and ever he wished: "Would God I were on land that I might die in rest!" The waves so troubled him there with tossing him up and down, to and fro, that he thought that trouble letted him to die because the waves would not let him rest. But if he might get once to land he thought he should then die there even at his ease.

VINCENT: Nay, uncle, this is no doubt but that death is to every man painful. But yet is not the natural death so painful as is the violent.

ANTHONY: By my troth, cousin, methinketh that the death which men call commonly natural is a violent death to every man whom it fetcheth hence by force against his will. And that is every man which when he dieth is loath to die and fain would yet live longer if he might.

Howbeit, how small the pain is in the natural death, cousin, fain would I wit who hath told you. As far as I can perceive, those folk that commonly depart of their natural death have ever one disease and sickness or other. Whereof if the pain of the whole week or twain in which they lie pining in their bed were gathered together into so short a time as a man hath his pain that dieth a violent death, it would, I ween, make double the pain that it is. So that he that naturally dieth ofter suffereth more pain than less, though he suffer it in a longer time.

And then would many a man be more loath to suffer so long, lingering in pain, than with a sharper [pain] to be sooner rid. And yet lieth many a man more days than one in well near as great pain continually as is the pain that with the violent death riddeth the man in less than half an hour.[13] Except a man would ween that whereas the pain is great to have a knife to cut his flesh on the outside from the skin inward, the pain would be much less if the knife might begin on the inside and cut from the midst outward. [For] some we hear in their deathbed complain that they think they feel sharp knives cut a-two their heart-strings.[14] Some cry out and think they feel within the brain-pan their head pricked even full of pins. And they that lie in a pleurisy think that every time they cough they feel a sharp sword swap them to the heart.

1 torture.
2 speedily, without delay.
3 Luke 12:5.
4 being forgiven.
5 startled movement, emotional impulse.
6 St. Peter.
7 I.e., not ceasing to preach the Word.
8 Tertullian states that Peter was crucified under Nero, and Origen adds that at his own request he was crucified head downwards. Recent scholarship has tended to limit Peter's sufferings to old age and restraint on his liberty. See under "Peter" in Hastings' *Dictionary of the Bible.*
9 forgiveness.
10 I.e., escape with any less suffering.
11 by no kind of luck.
12 a skiff, a small sailing ship.
13 A significant remark, confirming that More's "violent or painful death" refers not only to quick execution but to the kind of torture that keeps a man alive for almost "half an hour."
14 This sentence echoes a similar passage from More's *The Four Last Things* (Campbell, I, 468): "Think what it will be then, when thou shalt feel so many pains in every part of thy body, breaking thy veins and thy life-strings, . . . as though as many knives as thy body might receive should everywhere enter and meet in the midst." More specialized in detailed descriptions of the disintegration of the body on the deathbed and after. See Campbell, I, 468-9, and E. E. Reynolds, *St. Thomas More,* pp. 130-131.

Chapter 27

[The Pains of Hell]

ANTHONY (continuing):] Howbeit, what should we need to make any such comparison between the natural death and the violent, for the matter that we be in hand with here? We may put it out of doubt that he which for fear of the violent death forsaketh the faith of Christ, putteth himself in the peril to find his natural death more painful a thousand times. For his natural death hath his everlasting pain so suddenly knit unto it, that there is not one moment of an hour between. But the end of the one is the beginning of the other, that after never shall have end.[1]

And therefore was it not without great cause that Christ gave us so good warning before, when He said as Saint Luke in the twelfth chapter rehearseth: "I say to you that are my friends, be not afeard of them that kill the body, and which when that is done are able to do no more. But . . . fear Him which when He hath killed, hath in His power farther to cast him whom He killeth into everlasting fire. . . ."[2]

God meaneth not here that we should nothing dread at all any man that can but kill the body. But he meaneth that we should not . . . for dread of them, displease Him that can everlastingly kill both body and soul with a death ever dying, and that shall yet never die. And therefore He addeth and repeateth in the end again the fear that we should have of Him, and saith: "So I say to you, fear Him."[3]

Oh, good God, cousin, if a man would well weigh those words and let them sink (as they should do) down deep into his heart and often bethink himself thereon, it would, I doubt not, be able enough to make us set at nought all the great Turk's threats, and esteem him not at a straw. [We would then be] well content to endure all the pain that all the world could put upon us, for so short while as all they were able to make us dwell therein, rather than by the shrinking from those pains (though never so sharp, yet but short) to cast ourself into the pain of hell, an hundred thousand times more intolerable and whereof there shall never come an end.

A woeful death is that death in which folk shall evermore be dying and never can once be dead. Whereof the Scripture saith: "They shall call and cry for death and death shall fly from them."[4] Oh, good Lord, if one of them[5] were now put in choice of the both, they would rather suffer the whole year together the most terrible death that all the Turks in Turkey could devise, than the [natural] death that they lie in for the space of half an hour.[6] In how wretched folly fall then those faithless or feeble-faithed folk that, to avoid the pain so far the less and so short, fall in the stead thereof into pain a thousand thousand times more horrible, and of which terrible torment they be sure they shall never have end.

This matter, cousin, lacketh (as I believe) but either full faith or sufficient minding.[7] For I think, on my faith, if we have the grace verily to believe it and often to think well thereon, the fear of all the Turk's persecution (with all this midday devil were able to make them do in the forcing us to forsake our faith) should never be able to turn us.

VINCENT: By my troth, uncle, I think it is as you say. For

urely if we would as often think on these pains of hell as we be 'ery loath to do (. . . seek[ing] us peevish pastimes of purpose[8] o put such heavy things out of our thought), this one point alone vere able enough to make, I think, many a martyr.

1 A reference to the Christian teaching that one possesses eternal life or death now, depending on whether one is in a state of grace. See Paul's Col. 3:4.
2 Luke 12:5.
3 *Ibid.*
4 Rev. 9:6.
5 I.e., one of those in the previous Scriptural quotation, who are now suffering the eternal pains of hell.
6 The reference here is to the eventual natural death of the man who has earlier saved himself by forsaking Christ. Such a natural death, though it takes only half an hour, will bring eternal death in hell.
7 understanding.
8 for the purpose of (putting).

Chapter 28

[The Joys of Heaven]

NTHONY: Forsooth, cousin, if we were such as we should be, I 'ould scant for very shame (in exhortation to the keeping of 'hrist's faith) speak of the pains of hell. I would rather put us in iind of the joys of heaven, the pleasure whereof we should be iore glad to get than we should be to flee and escape all the pains hell. But surely God, in the thing wherein He may seem most gorous, is marvellous merciful to us. And that is (which many ien would little ween in that He provided hell. For I suppose very irely, cousin, that many a man and woman too, of whom there ow sit some (and more shall hereafter sit) full gloriously crowned heaven, had they not first been afraid of hell, would toward eaven never have set foot forward.

But yet undoubtedly, were it so that we could as well conceive our hearts the marvellous joys of heaven as we conceive the earful pains of hell . . . , we would not fail to be far more moved nd stirred to the suffering (for Christ's sake) in this world for the winning of these heavenly joys, than for the eschewing of all those infernal pains. But forasmuch as the fleshly pleasures be far less pleasant than the fleshly pains are painful, therefore we fleshly folk . . . are so drowned in these fleshly pleasures and in the desire thereof, that we can almost have no manner savor or taste in any pleasure spiritual. [Thus we] have no cause to marvel that our fleshly affections be more abated and refrained by the dread and terror of hell, than affections spiritual imprinted in us and pricked forward with the desire and joyful hope of heaven.

Howbeit, [let us] somewhat set less by the filthy voluptuous appetites of the flesh, and by withdrawing from them with help of prayer through the grace of God, draw nearer to the secret inward pleasure of the spirit. We shall [then] by the little sipping that our hearts should have here now, and that sudden taste thereof, have . . . an estimation of the incomparable and uncogitable joy that we shall have (if we will) in heaven by the very draught thereof whereof it is written: "I shall be satiate, satisfied, or fulfilled, when Thy glory, good Lord, shall appear."[1] [This refers to] the fruition of the sight of God's glorious Majesty face to face. . . . The desire, expectation, and heavenly hope thereof shall more encourage us, and make us strong[er] to suffer and sustain [pain] for the love of God and salvation of our soul, than ever we could be made to suffer here worldly pain by the terrible dread of all the horrible pains that damned wretches have in hell.

Wherefore, in the meantime, for lack of such experimental[2] taste as God giveth here sometime to some of His special servants, [let us] draw toward the spiritual exercise[3] too. For[4] which spiritual exercise God with that gift,[5] as with an earnest[6] penny of their whole reward after in heaven, comforteth them here in earth. Let us not so much with looking to have described what manner of joys they shall be, as with hearing what our Lord telleth us in Holy Scripture how marvellous great they shall be, labor by prayer to conceive in our hearts . . . a fervent longing for them. Th[en] we may for attaining to them utterly set at nought all fleshly delight, all worldly pleasures, all earthly losses, all bodily torment and pain. Howbeit, some things are there in Scripture expressed of the manner of the pleasures and joys that we shall have in heaven, as: "Righteous men shall shine as the sun, and shall run about like sparkles of fire among reed."[7]

Now tell some carnal-minded man of this manner pleasure, and he shall take little pleasure therein and say he careth not to have his flesh shine, he, nor like a spark of fire to skip about in the sky. Tell him that his body shall be impassible and never feel harm. Yet . . . he think then therewith, that he shall never be an-hungered nor athirst, and shall thereby forbear all his pleasure of eating and drinking. And that he shall never have list to sleep, and thereby lose the pleasure that he was wont to take in slugging.[8] And that men and women shall there live together as angels without any manner mind or motion unto the carnal act of generation. And that he shall thereby not use there his old filthy voluptuous fashion. [Then] he will say he is better at ease already, and would not give this world for that. For, as Saint Paul saith: "A carnal man feeleth not the things that be of the spirit of God, for it is foolishness to him."[9]

But the time shall come that these foul filthy pleasures shall be so taken from him that it shall abhor his heart once to think on them. Whereof every man hath among a certain shadow of experience in a fervent grief of a sore painful sickness, while the stomach can scant abide to look upon any meat. And as for the acts of other foul filthy lust, [he] is ready to vomit if it hap him to think thereon . . . .[He] shall, I say, after this life feel that horrible abomination in heart at the remembrance of these voluptuous pleasures, of which abomination sickness hath here a shadow —for which voluptuous pleasures he would here be loath to [ex]change with the joys of heaven. [T]hen he shall, I say, after this life have his fleshly pleasures in abomination, and shall of those heavenly joys which he set here so little by, have there a glimmering (though far from a perfect sight). O good God, how . . . glad will he then give this whole world (if it were his), to have the feeling of some little part of those [heavenly] joys.

And therefore let us all, that cannot now conceive such delight in the consideration of them as we should, have often in our eyes by reading, often in our ears by hearing, often in our mouths by rehearsing, often in our hearts by meditation and thinking, those joyful words of Holy Scripture by which we learn how wonderful huge and great those spiritual heavenly joys are, of which our carnal hearts hath so feeble and so faint a feeling. And our dull worldly wits [be] little able to conceive so much as a shadow[10] of the right imagination.

A shadow, I say. For as for the thing as it is, that cannot only no fleshly carnal fantasy[11] conceive, but over that no spiritual ghostly[12] person peradventure neither, that here is living still in this world. For sith the very substance essential of all the celestial joy standeth in blessed beholding of the glorious Godhead face to face, there may no man presume or look to attain it in this life. For God hath so said Himself: "There shall no man here living behold Me."[13] And therefore we may well know that for the state of this life we be not only shut from the fruition of the bliss of heaven, but also that the very best man living here upon earth . . . cannot, I ween, attain the right imagination thereof. But those that are very virtuous are yet in a manner as far therefrom as the born blind man from the right imagination of colors.

The words that Saint Paul rehearseth of the prophet Isaias, prophesying of Christ's incarnation, may properly be verified of the joys of heaven.[14] For surely, for this state of this world, the joys of heaven are by man's mouth unspeakable, to man's ears not audible, to men's hearts uncogitable. So far forth excel they all that ever men have heard of, all that ever men can speak of, and all that ever any man can by natural possibility think on. And yet where the joys of heaven be such prepared for every saved soul, our Lord saith yet by the mouth of Saint John that He will give His holy martyrs that suffer for His sake many a special kind of joy.

For he saith: "To him that overcometh I shall give him to eat of the tree of life. And also he that overcometh shall be clothed in white clothes. And I shall confess his name before My Father and before His Angels."[15] And also He saith: "Fear none of those things that thou shalt suffer, but be faithful unto the death, and I shall give thee the crown of life. He that overcometh shall not be hurt of the second death."[16] He saith also: "To him that overcometh will I give manna secret and hid, and I will give him a white suffrage, and in his suffrage a new name written which no man knoweth but he that receiveth it."[17]

They used of old in Greece (where Saint John did write) to elect and choose men unto honorable rooms, and every man's assent[18] was called his suffrage, which in some place was by the voices, in some place by hands. And one kind of those suffrages was by certain things that are in Latin called *calculi* because that in some places they used thereto round stones. Now saith our Lord that unto him which overcometh, He will give a white suffrage. For those that were white signified approving, as the black signified reproving.[19] And in those [white] suffrages did they use to write the name of him to whom they gave their voice.[20] And now saith our Lord that to him that overcometh, He will in the suffrage give him a new name which no man knoweth but he that receiveth it. . . .   . . .

The blessed apostle Saint Paul . . . suffered so many perils and so many passions. He . . . saith of himself that he hath been in many labors; in prisons ofter than other; in stripes[21] above measure; at point of death oftentimes. "Of the Jews had I five times forty stripes save one. Thrice have I been beaten with rods; once was I stoned; thrice have I been in shipwreck; a day and a night was I in the depth of the sea. In my journeys oft have I been in peril of flood, in peril of thieves, in peril by the Jews, in peril by the paynims,[22] in perils in the city, in perils in desert, in perils in the sea, perils by false brethren. [I have been] in labor and misery, in many nights' watch, in hunger and thirst, in many fastings, in cold and nakedness—beside those things that are outward: my daily instant labor, I mean my care and solicitude about all the churches."[23] And yet saith he more of his tribulations which for the length I let pass.

This blessed apostle, I say, for all these tribulations that himself suffered in the continuance of so many years, calleth . . . all the tribulations of this world but light and as short as a moment, in respect of the weighty glory that it after this world winneth us: "This same short and momentary tribulation of ours that is in this present time, worketh within us the weight of glory above measure, on high. We behold . . . not these things that we see, but those things that we see not. For those things that we see be but temporal things, but those things that are not seen are eternal."[24]

Now to this great glory can there no man come headless. Our head is Christ. And therefore to Him must we be joined, and as members of His must we follow Him if we will come thither. He is our guide to guide us thither and is entered in before us. And he, therefore, that will enter in after—the same way that Christ walked, the same way must he walk.[25] And what was the way by which he walked into heaven? Himself sheweth what way it was that His Father had provided for him, where he said unto the two disciples going toward the castle of Emmaus: "Knew you not that Christ must suffer passion and by that way enter into His kingdom?"[26] Who can for very shame desire to enter into the kingdom of Christ with ease, when Himself entered not into His own without pain?

1 Psalms 16:15.
2 experienced.
3 meditation or prayer in solitude. The phrase is possibly an allusion to St. Ignatius Loyola's *Spiritual Exercises,* an early version of which was in circulation around 1524; or to the work of the same title (on which Loyola based his own treatise) by Garcia de Cisneros (d. 1510). Loyola (1491-1556), founder of the Society of Jesus, specialized in prayer and fasting.
4 in return for which.
5 I.e., the "sudden taste" or brief "sip" of heavenly joy mentioned in the previous paragraph.
6 a penny on deposit toward (their heavenly reward). In More's day, an "earnest" was something of value given by a buyer to a seller, as a pledge to honor the bargain and as symbol of the full payment to come.
7 Wisdom 3:7.
8 lying late abed.
9 1 Cor. 2:14.
10 The prominence of shadow imagery in these paragraphs probably stems from Plato's "Allegory of the Cave" (*Republic* VII, 514-16), where earthly phenomena are described as cave-wall shadows of the reality which exists outside (i.e., in heaven). One gets the impression that More is here falling back on the Platonic doctrine implied in the cave allegory and expressed in *Phaedo* 66, that higher knowledge (in Plato's case, of Ideas; in More's case, of God) is impossible until after death.
11 I.e., no person whose imagination is cluttered with fleshly and material thoughts.
12 religious.

13 Exod. 33:20.
14 Isaias 64:4—"From the beginning of the world they have not heard nor perceived with the ears; the eye hath not seen, O God, besides thee, what things thou hast prepared for them that wait for thee."
15 See Rev. 2-7.
16 Ibid., 10:11.
17 Ibid., 2:17.
18 More must mean "vote" here, because later in the same paragraph, some "suffrages" are said to be "black" or negative votes.
19 a negative vote; a "blackball"
20 approval.
21 welts (on the back, caused by whipping).
22 pagans.
23 2 Cor. 11:23.
24 Ibid., 4:17.
25 1 John 2:6.
26 Luke 24:26.

Chapter 29

[Romantic and Divine Lovers]

[ANTHONY (continuing):] Surely, cousin, as I said before, in bearing the loss of worldly goods, in suffering of captivity, thraldom, and imprisonment, and in the glad sustaining of worldly shame—if we would in all those points deeply ponder the sample of our Savior Himself, it were of itself alone sufficient to encourage every kind [of] Christian man and woman to refuse none of all those calamities for His sake. So say I now for painful death also, that . . . we could and [sh]ould with due compassion conceive in our minds a right imagination and remembrance of Christ's bitter painful Passion.

[Consider] the many sore bloody strokes that the cruel tormentors with rods and whips gave Him upon every part of His holy tender body; the scornful crown of sharp thorns beaten down upon His holy head so strait and so deep, that on every part His blessed blood issued out and streamed down; His lovely limbs drawn and stretched out upon the cross, to the intolerable pain of his forebeaten[1] and sore beaten veins and sinews—new feeling with the cruel stretching and straining, [and with] pain far passing any cramp in every part of His blessed body at once. Then [consider] the great long nails cruelly driven with hammers through His holy hands and feet; and in this horrible pain lift[ed] up and let hang with the peise[2] of all His body bearing down upon the painful wounded places so greviously pierced with nails; and in such torment . . . suffered to be pinned and pained the space of more than three long hours, till Himself willingly gave up unto His Father His holy soul. After which, yet to shew the mightiness of their malice after His holy soul departed, they pierced His holy heart with a sharp spear, at which issued out the holy blood and water whereof His holy sacraments have inestimable secret strength.

If we would, I say, remember these things in such wise as would God we would, I verily suppose that the consideration of His incomparable kindness could not fail in such wise to inflame our key-cold hearts and set them on fire in His love. Th[en] we should find ourself not only content but also glad and desirous to suffer death for His sake, that so marvellous lovingly letted not to sustain so far passing painful death for ours.

Would God we would . . . consider what hot affection many of these fleshly[3] lovers have borne and daily do to those upon whom they dote. How many of them have not letted to jeopard their lives. And how many have willingly lost their lives indeed without either great kindness shewed them before—[or] afterward, you wot well, they could nothing win. But . . . it contented and satisfied their mind, that by their death their lover should clearly see how faithfully they loved. The delight whereof imprinted in their fantasy not assuaged only but counterpoised[4] also, they thought, all their pain. Of these affections, with the wonderful dolorous affects following thereon, not only old written stories,[5] but over that I think in every country, Christian and heathen both, experience giveth us proof enough. . . .

Oh, if he that is content to die for his love, of whom he looketh after for no reward and yet by his death goeth from her, might by his death be sure to come to her and ever after in delight and pleasure to dwell with her—such a lover would not let there to die for her twice! And how cold lovers be we then unto God if rather than die for Him once, we will refuse Him and forsake Him for ever. [For he] both died for us before and hath also provided that if we die here for Him, we shall in heaven everlastingly both live and also reign with Him. For, as Saint Paul saith: "If we suffer with Him we shall reign with Him.[6]

How many Romans, how many noble courages[7] of other sundry countries, have willingly given their own lives and suffered great deadly pains and very painful deaths for their countries and the respect of winning by their deaths the only reward of worldly renown and fame? And should we then shrink to suffer as much for eternal honor in heaven and everlasting glory? The devil hath also some so obstinate heretics that endure wittingly painful death for vainglory. And is it not then more than shame that Christ shall see His Catholics forsake His faith, rather than suffer the same for heaven and very glory?

Would God (as I many times have said) that the remembrance of Christ's kindness in suffering His Passion for us, the consideration of hell that we should fall in by forsaking of Him, the joyful meditation of eternal life in heaven that we shall win with this short temporal death patiently taken for Him, had so deep a place in our breast as reason would they should. . . . For then should they take up our mind and ravish it all another way, that [we would be like] a man hurt in a fray [who] feeleth not sometime his wound, nor yet is not ware thereof till his mind fall more thereon. So farforth that sometime another man sheweth him that he hath lost an hand before he perceive it himself.

So the mind ravished in the thinking deeply of those other things—Christ's death, hell, and heaven—were likely to minish and put away of our painful death four parts of the feeling either of the fear or the pain. For of this am I very sure, if we had the fifteenth part of the love to Christ that He both had and hath unto us, all the pain of this Turk's persecution could not keep us from Him, but that there would be at this day as many martyrs here in Hungary as have been afore in other countries of old.

And of this point put[8] I nothing doubt: [Suppose] the Turk stood even here with all his whole army about him, and every of them all were ready at our hand with all the terrible torments that they could imagine, and (but if we would forsake the faith) were setting their torments to us. And to the increase of our terror [they] fell at once in a shout with trumpets, tabrets,[9] and timbrels[10] all blowen up at once, and all their guns let go therewith to make us a fearful noise. [Suppose also] there should suddenly then on the other side the ground quake and rive atwain, and the devils rise out of hell and shew themself in such ugly shape as damned wretches shall see them. And with that hideous howling that those hell-hounds should shriek, lay hell open on every side round about our feet. Th[en] as we stood we should look down into that pestilent pit and see the swarm of silly souls in the terrible torments there. We would wax so feard of the sight, that as for the Turk's host we should scantly remember we saw them![11]

And in good faith, for all that, yet think I farther this: [Suppose] there might then appear the great glory of God, the Trinity in His high marvellous majesty, our Savior in His glorious manhood sitting on His throne with His immaculate Mother and all that glorious company calling us there unto them. And that yet our way should lie through marvellous painful death before we could come at them. Upon the sight (I say) of that glory, there would, I ween, be no man that once would shrink thereat. But every man would run on toward them in all that ever he might, though there lay for malice to kill us by the way both all the Turk's tormentors and all the devils.

And therefore, cousin, let us well consider these things, and let us have sure hope in the help of God. And then I doubt not but that we shall be sure that (as the prophet saith) the truth of His promise shall so compass us with a pavis, that of this incursion of this midday devil[12]—this Turk's persecution—we shall never need to fear. For either if we trust in God well and prepare us therefor the Turk shall never meddle with us; or else, if he do, harm shall he none do us but instead of harm inestimable good.

Of whose gracious help wherefore should [w]e so sore now despair . . . , when we see [that] so many a thousand holy martyrs by His holy help suffered as much before as any man shall be put to now?[13] Or what excuse can we have by the tenderness of our flesh when we can be no more tender than were many of them, among whom were not only men of strength but also weak women and children?[14] And sith the strength of them all stood in the help of God, . . . the very strongest of them all was never able of them-self. And with God's help the feeblest of them all was strong enough to stand against all the world. [Therefore] let us prepare ourself with prayer, with our whole trust in His help without any trust in our own strength. . . .   . . .

If [Satan] put in our minds the terror of the Turks, let us consider his false sleight therein, for this tale he telleth us to make us forget him. But let us remember well that in respect of himself the Turk is but a shadow. Nor all that they can do can be but a flea biting in comparison of the mischief[15] that he goeth about. The Turks are but his tormentors, for himself doeth the deed. Our Lord saith in the Apocalypse: "The devil shall send some of you to prison to tempt you. . . ."[16] . . . He saith not that men shall, but that the devil shall himself. . . .   . . .

Thus may we see that in such persecutions it is the midday devil himself that maketh such incursion upon us, by the men that are his ministers,[17] to make us fall for fear. For till we fall he can never hurt us. And therefore saith Saint James: "Stand against the devil and he shall flee from you."[18] For he never runneth upon a man to seize him with his claws till he see him down on the ground willingly fallen himself. For his fashion is to set his servants against us, and by them to make us for fear or for impatience[19] to fall. And himself in the meanwhile compasseth us, running and roaring like a ramping[20] lion about us, looking who will fall that he then may devour him. Saith Saint Peter: "Your adversary the devil like a roaring lion runneth about in circuit, seeking whom he may devour."[21]

The devil it is, therefore, that if we for fear of men will fall, is ready to run upon us and devour us. And is it wisdom, then, so much to think upon the Turks that we forget the devil? What madman is he that when a lion were about to devour him, would vouchsafe to regard the biting of a little fisting cur?[22] Therefore when he roareth out upon us by the threats of mortal men, let us tell him that with our inward eye we see him well enough, and intend to stand and fight with him even hand to hand. If he threaten us that we be too weak, let us tell him that our captain Christ is with us, and that we shall fight with His strength, that hath vanquished him already.

And let us fence us with faith and comfort us with hope, and smite the devil in the face with a firebrand of charity. For surely . . . we [should] be of the tender loving mind that our Master was, and not hate them that kill us, but pity them and pray for them with sorrow for the peril that they work unto themself.[23] That fire of charity thrown in his face striketh the devil suddenly so blind that he cannot see where to fasten a stroke on us. . . . . . .

The apostle saith: "The passions of this time be not worthy to the glory that is to come which shall be shewed in us."[24] We should not, I ween, cousin, need much more in all this whole matter than that one text of Saint Paul, if we would consider it well. For surely, mine own good cousin, remember that if it were possible for me and you alone to suffer as much trouble as the whole world doth together, all that were not worthy of itself to bring us to the joy which we hope to have everlastingly. And therefore, I pray you, let the consideration of that joy put out all worldly trouble out of your heart; and also pray that it may do the same in me.

And even thus will I, good cousin, with these words make a sudden end of mine whole tale and bid you farewell. For now begin I to feel myself somewhat weary.

VINCENT: Forsooth, good uncle, this is a good end. And it is no marvel though you be waxen weary, for I have this day put you to so much labor. . . . Saving for the comfort that yourself may take of your time so well bestowed, and for the comfort that I have myself taken (and more shall, I trust) of your good counsel given, I would else[25] be very sorry to have put you to so much pain.

But now shall our Lord reward and recompense you therefor and many shall, I trust, pray for you. For to the intent that the more may take profit by you I purpose, uncle, as my poor wit and learning will serve me, to put your good counsel in remembrance.[26] Not in our own language only, but in the Almaine[27] tongue too. And thus praying God to give me and all other that shall read it the grace to follow your good counsel therein, I shall commit you to God.

ANTHONY: Sith you be minded, cousin, to bestow so much labor thereon, I would it had happed you to fetch the counsel at some wiser man that could have given you better. But better men may set more things and better also thereto. And in the meantime I beseech our Lord breathe of His Holy Spirit into the reader's breast, which inwardly may teach him in heart. Without [Him] little availeth all that all the mouths of the world were able to teach in men's ears. And thus, good cousin, farewell till God bring us together again, either here or in heaven. Amen.

1 beaten (unto death).
2 weight.
3 Here used to designate earthly or romantic lovers, as distinguished from "divine lovers" whose object of veneration is God. Analogies between these two types of lovers were prominent in Florentine Platonism.
4 outweighed.
5 The reference here is to Arthurian romances, especially to those featuring Courtly Love—e.g., works like Chretien de Troyes' Lancelot (12th c.). According to the courtly love ideal, the woman was haughty, the lover was abject, and he underwent trials of adventure to prove his allegiance to her. The concept was codified by Andreas Capellanus in *De arte honeste amandi* (early 13th c.). See "Courtly Literature" in Cassell's *Encyclopedia of Literature* (1953), I, 122; and C. S. Lewis, *Allegory of Love* (1936), pp. 2, 23, 32. Note also Robert P. Adams' "Bold Bawdry and Open Manslaughter: The English New Humanist Attack on Medieval Romance," *Huntington Library Quarterly,* XXII (May 1959), 33-48.
6 Rom. 8:17.
7 spirits, hearts.
8 have (I no doubt).
9 drums.
10 tambourines.
11 the antecedent of "them" is "Turk's host."
12 An artistic repetition of the theme, drawn from Psalms 90:5-6, which More has been expounding since Part II, Chapter 11.
13 See Part III, Chap. 3, n. 6. Theodoret, in his *Ecclesiastical History,* Book V, Chap. 38, tells how some Christians were flayed alive and similarly tortured.
14 More must have had in mind here, among others, the inspiring St. Blandina, who persevered in the face of incredible tortures (177 A.D.). See Book V, Chap. 1, sec. 41-56 in the *Ecclesiastical History* of Eusebius. Theodoret, in his own *History,* Book IV, Chap. 15, tells an equally inspiring but happier story of a woman carrying a baby who successfully defied potential executors.
15 evil schemes.
16 Rev. 2:10.

17 agents, intermediaries.
18 James 4:7; cf. Eph. 6:11.
19 restlessness—i.e., unwillingness to endure persecution.
20 rampaging.
21 1 Peter 5:8.
22 pet dog.
23 More followed this precept in one of his final prayers. See "Pro inimicis" ("For Enemies"), Rastell ed., p. 1418—"Almighty God, have mercy on . . . all that bear me evil will, and would me harm. And their faults and mine together . . . vouchsafe to amend and redress. And make us saved souls in heaven together, where we may ever live and love together with Thee."
24 Rom. 8:18.
25 The "else would I" has here been transposed from More's word order, to improve the reading.
26 Cf. Part I, Chap. 21, n. 5.
27 German.

Appendices

Appendix A

Synopsis: The Chief Line of Argument in the *Dialogue of Comfort*

Note: Chapter numbers are indicated in parentheses. Not every chapter is included.

PART I

(1) The pagans ignored the chief source of comfort, namely the Spirit of Christ within us. Therefore, we must regard the old philosophers as merely druggists helping the great physician God, rather than as physicians in their own right. (2) No man can be given adequate comfort unless he already possesses a foundation of faith. (3) Those faithful ones who desire comfort from God are already comforted by the mere desire itself. For they know they are beseeching the one source that will not fail them. Also, they realize that their desire to be comforted emanates from God, and He is therefore on their side.

(4) Actually, God sends tribulation to prompt men to pray to Him for help. (6) In praying, we should never ask for removal of the tribulation without implying this condition: that if God think suffering better for us, we gladly yield to His will, and ask only that He send us strength to endure. (7) Tribulation is really like medicine, ill tasting but beneficial provided men accept and use it in the right spirit. (8) Thus tribulation is sent to make us repent of past sin, or (9) to discourage us from some potential sin, or (10) to test our patience and thereby increase our merit.

(11) Even the lowest type of tribulation, that sent to punish and

prompt repentance, remits purgatorial punishment and counts toward heavenly merit, if the tribulation is accepted humbly. (12) To be sure, Protestants deny the existence of purgatory and the value of works. Yet there are many areas of Protestant-Catholic agreement, including the agreement to close ranks against the Turk. The only major issue is the Protestant contention that salvation is granted for faith alone. This doctrine might be true, but the church fathers have testified to the contrary.

(13) Purgatory aside, hell is certainly the destination of those who suffer no tribulation in this life. This world is designed for weeping, so that through tribulation one earns the right to heaven, the place of laughing. (14) Those chaplains are wrong who tell rich men that continual merriment and prosperity are compatible with heaven. (15) It is true that many apparently prosperous men have been loved by God. (16) But they underwent numerous invisible spiritual tribulations. The perpetually wealthy Abraham, for example, endured sorrow at leaving his land, and grief at the thought of killing Isaac.

Tribulation, then, can be spiritual as well as physical. Prosperity, especially wealth, would certainly seem to be preferable to any kind of tribulation. Yet (19) tribulation has many subtle advantages over wealth. For example, God rewards the patient sufferer proportionately to his pain; but He does not reward the appreciative wealthy man proportionately to his money. Again (20), the man in tribulation can wish to do the good deeds of the rich man, and thus gain merit simply for his wish. But the rich man will not so easily wish for tribulation. Finally, any wicked man can thank God for riches, but it takes a good man to thank Him for trouble. Hence more merit is attached to thanking God for tribulation than to thanking Him for good fortune.

To sum up (21), tribulation is a gift which God sends to His friends. Through His Spirit He strengthens us as we suffer, and welcomes us to heaven if we die.

PART II

(1) There is no great harm in worldly pleasures like merry tales or pleasant conversations. Such innocent recreation dims sorrow, refreshes the mind, and settles the stomach. But far transcending such

comfort is contemplation of the joys of heaven. Such contemplation stands us in good stead if we must undergo any of the three chief kinds of tribulation: (3) those sought willingly; those suffered willingly though not sought; and those which cannot be avoided. (4) An example of the first kind is the man who voluntarily inflicts pain on himself for penance. Such a man needs no comfort. He can stop when he wants, and will not exceed his own endurance for pain. Even in the pain of penance he will be joyful at the thought of salvation—as was the thief who was crucified with Christ.

It is true that the thief was a deathbed-repenter. But (5) such last-minute converts usually get less favorable accommodations in heaven than do those who have been in grace all along. Also, those who make merry and delay repentance run the risk of dying suddenly without conversion. It is best then for men to repent of their sins, sorrowfully, as they commit them, and to take willingly upon themselves the tribulation of penance. (6) Lutherans, of course, say that sorrow for past sin is needless. They argue further that affliction of the body, fasting, and other penance is superstitious folly. Such men speak falsely. If fasting is folly, why did Christ fast? If men should not be sorrowful for past sins, why did the prophet David say otherwise? To be sure (7), some men find it impossible to weep over their sins. But at least they can be sorry that they cannot be sorry! Moreover, if men who laugh at their sins will compensate by afflicting their bodies, they will cry soon enough.

Of all the tribulations, temptation is the most difficult. (8) Persecution is really a kind of temptation because through it the devil tempts us to desert Christ. As this implies (9), the devil is behind all temptation; and no man gets to heaven unless he successfully resists Satan. (10) In this match, man's greatest comfort is the knowledge that God, like a mother hen, will shelter and strengthen him against the devil's countless tricks. (11) Such divine protection is promised in Psalms 90, where we are told that God's shield will protect us from the four major temptations: fear of the night; the arrow flying in the day; the business walking about in the darkness; and the invasion of the devil in the midday.

(12) The first of these devil-inspired temptations is fear of danger—just as men sometimes fear the night. However, we should remember that no outside agency can do more than kill our bodies. Our real fear should therefore be of God, who can destroy the soul. There is

consolation in the fact that our fears are often foolishly exaggerated. (14) Closely akin to fear is the over-scrupulous conscience, which produces the worry-wart: i.e., the sort of person who always worries lest he is not doing the right thing. At the other extreme is the person who has such a flexible conscience that he never worries about anything. (15) To achieve a happy mean between these two dangerous extremes, one needs the objective counsel of a friend or priest.

(16) Cowardice and fear cause most suicides. However (17), the temptation to kill one's self is not a tribulation if prompted by a spirit of revenge or by devilish delusions. In such cases, the persons tempted are overjoyed at the prospect of suicide.

The first step, therefore, in trying to prevent suicide is to determine in what category a man falls. If he is sad, he is planning suicide out of fear; if joyous, he is a victim of devilish delusion. (18) The best approach in dealing with men in the second category is to stress that in His Ten Commandments God opposes the very killing which the allegedly angelic vision has ordered. If such arguments do not work, the only resource left is to tie the man to his bed. (19) The more common type of potential suicide, however, is the man who falls into terrible sin, or who has some secret sin exposed. He despairs of salvation, or is ashamed of his loss of reputation. In such a case, the man's friends should attempt to bolster his morale. They should tell him that his close brush with the devil has made him a wiser man and a valued counselor for others in trouble.

The two factors contributing the most to suicide are (a) the devil, and (b) the bodily humours or fluids, which the devil seeks to manipulate. Hence, a man needs both bodily and spiritual physicians: a sick soul can hurt the body, and vice versa. The most effective methods of fighting the temptation toward suicide are laughing at the devil, who cannot stand scorn, and praying to God through His saints.

(20) Turning to the second of the four major temptations, namely "the arrow flying in the day," we may interpret the arrow as pride and the day as prosperity, which inspires pride. Temptation toward pride is not a tribulation for wicked men, who foolishly think that their prosperity is perpetual. But, just as an arrow which flies high soon returns to the ground, so are our fortunes suddenly reversed, and all our pride turned suddenly to shame. For the good man, however, prosperity causes a troublesome fear of becoming proud. Because of this fear, some men resign their offices or retire from their businesses.

They should instead remain with their jobs, no matter how elevated or successful, because that is where they can make the best contribution. If they are worried about pride, let them pray to God for the compassion to recognize every beggar as a brother.

(21) The third temptation mentioned by the Psalmist is "the business walking about in the darkness." "Business" can be interpreted as that sub-devil who tempts people to covet fleshly pleasure or worldly goods. The "darkness" is that state in which this devil likes to operate—i.e., where conditions are such that grace has either not yet arrived in, or is about to depart from, the soul. This devil inspires men to such frantic pursuit of wealth that they resemble confused players in a maze, getting nowhere, and then suddenly finding themselves in the maze's center, namely hell. Many men take a fiendish delight in acquiring material possessions. For them, the temptation of covetousness is no tribulation. But many good men are deeply troubled when they become rich, because of the apparently harsh words spoken against the rich by Christ.

(22) Here we must remember that, though God invited men to follow him in poverty, He did not command them to do so on peril of damnation. In fact, Christ simply said that to be saved, men must be willing to lose all their possessions rather than displease God. Actually, the world could not function if there were no rich men to provide a living for others. Granted (23) that the rich man should give money to those who might perish without his help. But apart from such emergencies, he has no obligation to every beggar who comes along. Philanthropy properly begins at home, with the care of our own children, parents, and servants.

PART III

(2) The fourth major temptation is "the invasion of the devil in the midday" (Psalms 90:6)—i.e., open persecution. "Midday" symbolizes the light of faith shining in Christian hearts. Thus persecution is directed toward those who are professed Christians. Persecution is the most difficult of all tribulations to resist, because the devil uses a two-pronged attack: infliction of pain, and the promise of pleasurable release from pain for those who forsake Christ. Thus (3) men should bolster themselves for persecution well in advance.

No harm can come to the soul unless it slide from the faith. (4) As for the outward goods of fortune, which the Turk can take away, their importance is exaggerated. (5) When even kingships and empires are so easily lost, why should men value trivialities like gold and silver? (6) Men worship land because presumably it cannot be stolen. But the owners can easily be dragged away; *they* are movable, even if the land is not! As for the alleged conveniences of being rich (8), plain cloth is as warm as expensive apparel, and plain fare is healthier than gourmet food. We must consider the exhausting labor of getting the riches, the fear in attempting to retain them, and the pain when they are stolen.

(9) Neither is fame necessarily an asset. A famous man might be harmed as a result of jealousy. Fame is nothing more than hot air emanating from men's mouths. The man who praises us to our face will denounce us behind our backs. (10) We should not be like a certain great man of the church, who encouraged flattery to the point where he saw himself falsely. This man became so arrogant that, even when he professed to ask frank advice, he denounced those who gave it if it differed from his own preconceptions. As for high office (11), men usually want this so they can rule others. Yet except for the king, all men, no matter how high their stations, are more ruled by their superiors than they themselves rule their underlings. Even a king cannot have his own way; his ambitions are constantly frustrated by rivals. Then, too, a nobleman is often called out of bed to fulfill his responsibilities, while the peasant may sleep on. Nor is there any guarantee that, having spent most of his life reaching the top, the nobleman will be permitted to stay there. After all, high office is held at the caprice of princes.

(12) Worldly goods are not only of little value to the body; they can also be harmful to the soul. A man who desires high office for selfish reasons will abuse his authority once he gets there. Of course (13), every man claims that he seeks the goods of fortune in order to further God's purpose on earth. Persecution will provide the touchstone for determining how sincerely such men speak. If they desire worldly goods only to glorify God, they will not hesitate to give up these goods rather than forsake the faith. (14) Some men will argue, to be sure, that it is possible to make a secret arrangement with the Turk, under which one can keep his goods and still remain a Christian. All one needs to do is forswear a few minor points of Christian-

ity which are incompatible with Mohammedanism. But Christ will not tolerate this kind of juggling. Even if the Turk would honor such an agreement (which he won't), God would not permit a man to retain and enjoy goods purchased by apostasy.

(15) The threat of persecution should inspire men to store their treasures in heaven, where even the Turkish army cannot steal them. This we can do by giving our money to the poor. The fact that we do not take seriously Christ's instructions on this score suggests that our faith is hampered by worldly possessions. We should, therefore, thank God that, through His agents the Turks, these materialistic thorns and weeds are pruned away from our soul, so that our faith can better grow. (16) One of the greatest comforts in losing one's possessions is that Christ Himself willingly suffered poverty for us. How, then, could we forsake Him in order to retain material goods?

(17) Far more difficult to withstand, of course, is direct bodily persecution. God appreciates this; He does not expect every man to be a martyr. He therefore acts to save men from bodily persecution by helping them to escape if seized, or by delivering them from prison, or by not permitting a man to be tortured beyond his endurance. (18) The least severe degree of bodily persecution is, of course, captivity and forced labor. God is with us, no matter what country we are carried into. Captivity seems hard only because we have overestimated our previous liberty. Actually, we are already restricted by laws, by the bondage of sin, and by the domination of oppressive noblemen who force us to do much labor against our wills.

(19) Our fear of imprisonment is also the result of exaggerating our present liberty. Actually (20), the whole world is a prison, because men are set here in one place (earth) from which they cannot escape. Here they await execution (death) for their crime (original sin). (21) God Himself is the Chief Jailer and universal hangman. Like any competent jailer, God punishes unruly prisoners. This He does, not by putting them in stocks and chains, but by afflicting them with fever, palsy, and gout. It is true that in the narrower prison the door is always shut and we have little room in which to walk. But men like Joseph and Daniel happily survived the ordeal. Monks and nuns voluntarily cloister themselves in even smaller places, and it does not bother them.

Even the most rigorous imprisonment (in the narrower sense) pales by comparison with death through torture. (22) Our attitude toward such a death is determined by our individual personalities. Do reason or the bodily senses dominate us? God works through the former, and the devil through the latter. (23) Most men fear death from lack of faith, lack of hope, or lack of intelligence. That is, they are loath to die because they no longer believe in an afterlife, or because they despair of salvation, or because they are in love with this world. However, quite a few men would probably face death gladly if no shame or pain were involved. Yet (24) how can anything be shameful which is glorious in God's eyes? The Turkish rabble might rebuke us as they kill us, but the angelic host will be singing our praises. (25) As for the pain of violent death, reason, with the aid of grace, can master it. Any sensible man will gladly take an unpleasant medicine if it will bring him health. So should a reasonable Christian accept painful death, which brings salvation.

(26) Some men argue, of course, that, in the face of torture, it is best to forsake Christ and repent later. Otherwise a man, unable to stand the pain, might forsake Christ and die damned in the middle of the torture. But it is absurd to think that God would not forgive one who forsook him under such conditions. Other men argue that a natural death is preferable to a violent one. Yet men on their deathbeds often cry that knives are cutting their heart strings. What difference does it make whether knives cut the flesh from the inside out or vice versa? In any event (27), natural death purchased with apostasy will turn out to be more painful than violent death, because it will then become the eternal death of hell.

Actually (28), God is merciful in providing a hell—without it many now in heaven might never have been prompted to repentance. Yet the joys of heaven are a far more powerful argument for defying the Turk. If we could catch but the barest glimpse of such joys, we would be overwhelmed by the marvels thereof. Unfortunately, only a glimpse is possible, because the essence of celestial joy is in beholding God face to face, and that no man can do in this life. But Christ assures us that those who overcome persecution will enjoy such a vision.

(29) Consider the case of romantic lovers. A man often dies for his lady-love, even though she shows him no kindness before his death, and even though after death he can earn no reward from her. What cold lovers of Christ are we, then, if we fail to die gladly for One who has already shown us much kindness, and who will reward

us handsomely if we die courageously! If we could meditate sufficiently on Christ's Passion, we would become so enraptured as to feel no pain—much as the soldier, in the excitement of battle, is not even aware that he has lost a hand. Never forget that the tortures a man might endure from the whole Turkish army are not so painful as hell-fire. Remember, too, that if a man had to suffer all the trouble that the whole world now suffers, his pain would still be as nothing considering the incomparable reward of heavenly joys.

Appendix B

A Thomas More Chronology

Note: More's literary activities are placed in brackets. Historical events in which he did not participate, but which influenced his career, are in small capitals.

EARLY LIFE

1478 Born in London. Father, Sir John, became judge (1517).

1485? Attends St. Anthony's School. Chief subject: Latin.

1490? Page at Archbishop (later Cardinal) Morton's household. "Steps in among the players" at dramatic productions.

1492-4 At Canterbury College, Oxford. Chief subjects: trivium (grammar, rhetoric, logic), Latin, elementary Greek.

1494-1500 Law student at New Inn and Lincoln's Inn, London. Meets Erasmus (1499) on latter's first visit to England.

1501 Called to bar.
Begins three-year lectureship at Furnivall's Inn (law school), while living informally at Charterhouse (Carthusian Order).
[Produces Latin *Epigrams* (pub. 1518)]

c. 1502 Gives lectures on Augustine's *City of God* at St. Lawrence's Church.

1503 [Composes "Lamentation on Death of Queen Elizabeth" and other juvenile poems: "A Merry Jest" (first pub. 1516), "Nine Pageants," "Meters for Book of Fortune"—all pub. by Rastell, 1557.]

POLITICIAN AND CIVIC SERVANT

1504 Decides on active life.
Elected Member of Parliament.
Writes letter to John Colet, calling him "the director of my life."
1504-5 [Translates Latin biography of Pico della Mirandola (1463-94), and appends thereto verse-paraphrases of Pico's "Rules for Christian Life," "Weapons of Spiritual Warfare," and "Properties of a Lover" (pub. 1510).]
1505 Marries Jane Colt.
Children Margaret, Elizabeth, Cecily, and John born 1505-9.
1506 [With guest Erasmus, translates various dialogues of Lucian from Greek into Latin (pub. Paris, 1506).]
1509 [Writes joyful poem celebrating ascension of Henry VIII.]
1510 Appointed Under-Sheriff of London.
1511 Death of Jane (Colt) More.
More marries Alice Middleton ("Dame Alice").
1513 [At work on *History of Richard III*—first authentic text pub. by Rastell, 1557.]
1514 Appointed Commissioner of Sewers for River Thames.
1515 Chosen for commercial embassy to Flanders on behalf of London merchants.
[Writes Book II of *Utopia.*]
1516 Returns to England.
[Writes Book I of *Utopia.* Whole work pub. in Latin.]
1517 *Aug.*: Commercial embassy to Calais on behalf of London merchants. Henry VIII and Wolsey impressed with More's proficiency.

RISE TO POWER

1517 *Christmas*: Persuaded to enter King's Service.
Made Privy Counselor.
1518 Appointed Master of Requests (i.e., a judge on the court hearing complaints of poor people).

1521 Knighted.
Made Under-Treasurer.
Embassy to Calais with Wolsey to arrange alliance between Henry and Emperor Charles.

1522 [Begins but never finishes *The Four Last Things*—pub. by Rastell, 1557.]

1523 Elected Speaker of House of Commons.
Resists Wolsey's attempt to close debate on subsidy for war against France.

1524 Buys land at Chelsea, builds home on site straddling present Beaufort Street; moves family there (1526); later builds "The New Building" with chapel for private prayer.
Becomes High Steward, Oxford University.

1525 Becomes Chancellor of Duchy of Lancaster.
Becomes High Steward, Cambridge University.

1526 Holbein visits More at Chelsea, paints (1527) famous More family portrait (see Plate 4).

1527 HENRY VIII DECIDES TO DIVORCE CATHERINE OF ARAGON.
WOLSEY SENDS DIVORCE PETITION TO POPE CLEMENT VII.
Henry asks More's counsel on the divorce issue; More declines opinion, instead refers king to patristic writings.

1528 *Mar.*: Receives license from Bishop Tunstal to read and refute heretical books.
[Begins literary war against heresy with *Dialogue concerning Tyndale* (pub. 1529), continued in such works as *Supplication of Souls* (1529), *Apology* (1532), *Reply to Frith* (1533), *Answer to Book on Lord's Supper* (1534).]

1529 *May*: PAPAL COURT OF INQUIRY (AT BLACKFRIARS) BEGINS HEARING TESTIMONY ON DIVORCE.
Aug.: POPE ADVOKES CASE TO ROME.
Oct.: WOLSEY DISMISSED FOR FAILURE WITH DIVORCE NEGOTIATIONS.
Sir Thomas More appointed Lord Chancellor.
More serves on committee to study divorce issue, privately gives Henry negative verdict.
Nov.: More opens "Reformation Parliament."

1530 Refuses to sign new divorce appeal to Pope.

1531 *Feb.*: HENRY FORCES CLERGY TO PROCLAIM HIM SUPREME HEAD OF CHURCH, "SO FAR AS THE LAW OF CHRIST ALLOWS."

Mar.: More announces to Parliament the results of divorce research conducted by European universities.

1532 *May*: Resigns Lord Chancellorship, releases retinue, falls into increasing sickness. Succeeded by Thomas Audley.

Falsely charged with taking bribes.

IMPRISONMENT AND EXECUTION

1533 *Jan.*: HENRY MARRIES PREGNANT ANNE BOLEYN.

HENRY ASSIGNS DIVORCE ISSUE TO ARCHBISHOP CRANMER.

May: CRANMER NULLIFIES CATHERINE MARRIAGE AND VALIDATES HENRY'S MARRIAGE TO ANNE.

June: More refuses to attend Anne Boleyn's coronation at Westminster Abbey.

Sept.: POPE EXCOMMUNICATES HENRY.

Dec.: More falsely accused of writing an attack on the "Book of Nine Articles," issued by King's Council to justify Boleyn marriage.

1534 *Feb.*: More charged by Cromwell with misprision (concealment) of treason for failing to report revelations of Nun of Kent. More's name dropped from Bill of Attainder.

Mar.: PARLIAMENT PASSES ACT OF SUCCESSION. ALL SUBJECTS REQUIRED TO TAKE OATH OF ALLEGIANCE TO ACT. REFUSING OATH DECLARED MISPRISION OF TREASON, PUNISHABLE BY IMPRISONMENT AND CONFISCATION OF PROPERTY.

Apr. 12: More summoned before Commissioners at Lambeth and asked to take Oath. Refuses (Apr. 13) because Oath contains repudiation of papal supremacy.

Apr. 17: Committed to Tower of London. Begins 15-month imprisonment, probably in Beauchamp tower.

May-Oct.: [*Writes Dialogue of Comfort against Tribulation* (pub. 1553), Eucharist treatise, *History of the Passion,* Meditations, most of Tower Letters to Margaret Roper—all pub. by Rastell, 1557.]

Nov.: PARLIAMENT PASSES ACT OF SUPREMACY (THE OFFICIAL "BREAK WITH ROME") DECLARING KING "THE ONLY SUPREME HEAD IN EARTH OF THE CHURCH OF ENGLAND"

PARLIAMENT PASSES ACT OF TREASONS, WHEREBY VOCAL DENIAL OF KING'S SUPREMACY IS HIGH TREASON, PUNISHABLE BY DEATH.

Act of Attainder passed against More, confiscating his property for Crown.

1535 *Apr.-Jun.*: Four interrogations of More, in vain effort to make him take Oath or vocally deny King's supremacy.

May: [Writes poem on "flattering Fortune."]

June: More's friend, Bishop John Fisher, tried and executed for refusal to swear Oath.

July 1: More's trial at Westminster. More found guilty of treason on probably perjured evidence by Solicitor-General Rich. More sentenced to be drawn and quartered (later commuted to beheading).

July 2-4: [Writes final "Devout Prayer"—Rastell, pp. 1417-18.]

July 5: [More's farewell letter to daughter Margaret—Rogers, pp. 563-5.]

July 6: Execution. Head exhibited on London Bridge, recovered by Margaret, now in Roper vault at St. Dunstan's, Canterbury. Body buried in St. Peter's Chapel, Tower. News of execution spread through Europe by *Paris News Letter*.

AFTERMATH

1551 Publication of Ralph Robinson's English trans. of *Utopia*.

1553 *Dialogue of Comfort* first published.

1555-7 William Roper writes *Life of More* (pub. 1626, ed. Hitchcock, 1935).

Nicholas Harpsfield writes his *Life of More* (ed. Hitchcock, 1932).

1557 William Rastell edits and publishes More's *English Works*.

1565 More's Latin works published (Louvain).

1588 Thomas Stapleton's account of More (ed. Hallett, 1928) in *Tres Thomae*.

1599 Biography of More by Ro. Ba. (ed. Hitchcock, 1950).

1627 More's great-grandson Cresacre writes his *Life of More*.

1886 Beatification: More becomes "Blessed."

May 19, 1935 Canonization: "Saint Thomas More."

Appendix C

Corresponding Chapter Divisions in This and Earlier Editions

	Rastell	Tottell, Fowler and the Brit. Mus. MS.	This Edition
Part I	Chap. 19	19	19, 20
	20	20	21
Part II	Chap. 14	14	14, 15
	15	15	16
	16	16, 17	17, 18, 19, 20
	17	18, 19*	21, 22, 23
Part III	Chap. 19	19	19, 20
	20-23	20-23	21-24
	24	24	25, 26
	25-27	25-27	27-29

*Not in 1573 (Fowler) edition.

A SELECTED

Dialogue of Comfort

BIBLIOGRAPHY

SELECTED BIBLIOGRAPHY

I
Historical and Biographical Background

Burford, Eleanor [Jean Plaidy, pseud.]. *Meg Roper, Daughter of Sir Thomas More.* London: Constable, 1961.

Calendar of Letters and Papers, Foreign and Domestic, of the Reign of Henry VIII. Ed. J. S. Brewer and J. Gairdner. 21 vols. London: Longmans & others, 1862-1910.

Chambers, R. W., ed. *The Fame of Blessed Thomas More, Being Addresses Delivered in His Honor.* London: Sheed and Ward, 1929.

———. *Thomas More.* Ann Arbor: University of Michigan Press, 1958 [orig. 1935].

Dart, J. L. C. "Thomas Beckett and Thomas More: Were They Both Martyrs?" *Church Quarterly Review,* CLVII (1956), 35-46.

Davies, E. T. *Episcopacy and the Royal Supremacy in the Church of England.* Oxford: Basil Blackwell, 1950.

Davies, Randall. *The Greatest House at Chelsey.* London and New York: Lane, 1914.

Derrett, J. Duncan. "Neglected Versions of the Contemporary Account of The Trial of Sir Thomas More." *Bulletin Institute for Historical Research,* XXXIII (1960), 202-23.

Elton, Geoffrey R. *The Reformation, 1520-1559.* Vol. II of *The New Cambridge Modern History.* Cambridge: University Press, 1962.

Gelder, H. A. Enno Van. *The Two Reformations in the 16th Century. A Study of the Religious Aspects and Consequences of Renaissance and Humanism.* The Hague: Martinus Nijhoff, 1961.

Harpsfield, Nicholas. *The Life and Death of Sr Thomas Moore, knight, sometymes Lord high Chancellor of England*. Ed. Elsie V. Hitchcock. Intro. R. W. Chambers on "The Continuity of English Prose." Early English Text Society, No. 186. London: Oxford University Press, 1932. [New ed.-1963].

Manning, Anne. *The Household of Sir Thomas More*. Intro. Richard Garnett. London: Chatto and Windus, 1909.

Ministry of Public Building and Works. *The Tower of London*. London: Her Majesty's Stationery Office, 1957.

Morison, Stanley. *The Likeness of Thomas More. An Iconographical Survey of Three Centuries*. London: Burns & Oates, 1963 .

Parmiter, Geoffrey de C. "Tudor Indictments, Illustrated by the Indictment of St. Thomas More." *Recusant History*, VI (1961), 141-56.

Reynolds, E. E. *St. Thomas More*. Image Book D-66. Garden City, N.Y.: Doubleday, 1958.

———. *The Trial of Saint Thomas More*. London: Burns & Oates, 1964.

Roper, William. *The Lyfe of Sir Thomas Moore, knighte*. Ed. Elsie V. Hitchcock. Early English Text Society, No. 197. London: Oxford University Press, 1935.

State Papers during the Reign of Henry the Eighth. 11 vols. London: Published under the Authority of His Majesty's Commission, 1830-52.

Smith, H. Maynard. *Henry VIII and the Reformation*. London: Macmillan, 1948.

Vocht, Henri de. *Acta Thomas More: History of the Reports of His Trial and Death, with an Unedited Contemporary Narrative*. Louvain: Institute for Economics of the University, 1947.

II
Works of More Relevant to the *Dialogue*

Bullough, Geoffrey. "More in Valencia. A Holograph MS of More's Latin *Passion*." *The Tablet*, CCXVII (Dec. 21, 1963), 1379-80.

Bradner, Leicester, and Charles Arthur Lynch, trans. *The Latin Epigrams of Thomas More*. Chicago: University Press, 1953.

Campbell, W. E., ed. *The English Works of Sir Thomas More, Re-*

produced in Facsimile from William Rastell's Edition of 1557. . . . with a Modern Version of the Same. 2 vols. London and New York: Eyre & Spottiswoode and Lincoln MacVeagh, 1931.

Hallett, Philip E., ed. *English Prayers and Treatise on The Holy Eucharist.* Paternoster Series, No. 17. Springfield, Ill.: Templegate, 1959.

———, ed. Mary Bassett's English Trans. of the Second or Latin Part of Thomas More's *History of the Passion.* London: Burns, Oates & Washbourne, 1941.

Hutton, William H. "Religious Writings of Sir Thomas More," *English Historical Review,* IV (1889), 667-83.

Rogers, Elizabeth. *The Correspondence of Sir Thomas More.* Princeton: University Press, 1947.

Surtz, Rev. Edward and J. H. Hexter, eds. *Utopia.* Yale Ed. of Complete Works of St. Thomas More, Vol. IV. New Haven: Yale University Press, 1965.

Sylvester, Richard S. *The History of King Richard III.* Yale Ed. of Complete Works of St. Thomas More, Vol. II. New Haven: Yale University Press, 1963.

Thompson, Craig R., ed. *The Translations of Lucian by Erasmus and St. Thomas More.* Ithaca, N.Y.: The Vail-Ballou Press, 1940.

III
The *Dialogue of Comfort*

Chambers, R. W. *The Place of St. Thomas More in English Literature and History.* London: Longmans, Green, 1937.

Creasy, Edward S. *History of the Ottoman Turks.* Beirut: Khayats, 1961.

Crosset, J. "More and Lucian." *Modern Language Notes,* LXXII (Mar. 1957), 169-70.

Daly, J. J. "Neglected Classic: A Dialogue of Comfort against Tribulation." *Catholic World,* CXIII (July 1921), 514-23.

Davis, Norman. "Styles in English Prose of the Late Middle and Early Modern Period." *Langue et littérature,* VI (1962), 165-84.

Delcourt, J. "Some Aspects of Sir Thomas More's English." In: *Essays and Studies,* Vol. XXI. London: English Association, 1936.

Gordon, Walter M., S.J. *Dramatic Elements in the Writings of St. Thomas More.* University of London Ph.D. Thesis, c. 1965.

Hills, Arnold C. *Some Early Tudor Dialogues, Referred to by Sir Thomas More in His Controversial Works.* University of London M.A. Thesis, 1938.

Lewis, C. S. *English Literature in the Sixteenth Century.* London: Oxford University Press, 1958.

More's Utopia and A Dialogue of Comfort. Intro. John Warrington. Everyman's Library, No. 461. Revised Edition, with Spelling Modernized. London: Dent; New York: Dutton, 1951.

Patrides, C. A. " 'The Bloody and Cruell Turke': The Background of a Renaissance Commonplace." *Studies in the Renaissance,* X (1963), 126-35.

Pineas, Rainer. "Thomas More's Use of The Dialogue Form as a Weapon of Religious Controversy." *Studies in the Renaissance,* VII (1960), 193-206.

———. "Thomas More's Use of Humor as a Weapon of Religious Controversy." *Studies in Philology,* LXVIII (1961), 97-114.

Reed, A. W. *Early Tudor Drama. Medwall, The Rastells, Heywood, and the More Circle.* London: Methuen, 1926.

Tilley, Morris P. *A Dictionary of The Proverbs in England in the 16th and 17th Centuries.* Ann Arbor: University of Michigan Press, 1950.

Williamson, C. "Sir Thomas More's View of Drama." *Modern Language Notes,* XLIII (May 1928), 294-96.

Zall, P. M., ed. *A Hundred Merry Tales and Other English Jestbooks of the Fifteenth and Sixteenth Centuries.* Lincoln: University of Nebraska Press, 1963.

IV
More's Philosophy and Theology

Anciaux, Paul. *The Sacrament of Penance.* New York: Sheed and Ward, 1962.

Bewkes, Eugene G., and others. *The Western Tradition of Faith and Reason.* New York: Harper and Row, 1963.

Gilson, Étienne. *History of Christian Philosophy in the Middle Ages.* London: Sheed and Ward, 1956.

Guy, Harold A. *The New Testament Doctrine of Last Things.* London: Oxford University Press, 1948.

Hardman, Oscar. *The Christian Doctrine of Grace*. New York: Macmillan, 1947.

Hexter, J. H. "Thomas More: On the Margins of Modernity." *Journal of British Studies*, I (1961), 20-37.

Holdsworth, C. J. "Visions and Visionaries in the Middle Ages." *History*, XLVIII (June 1963), 141-53.

Hoopes, Robert. *Right Reason in the English Renaissance*. Cambridge: Harvard University Press, 1962.

Lehmberg, Stanford E. "English Humanists, the Reformation, and the Problem of Counsel." *Archiv fur Reformationsgeschichte*, LII (1962), 74-91.

Marc'hadour, M. l'ábbe G. *L'Univers de Thomas More. Chronologie critique de More, Erasme et leur epoque* (1477-1536). Paris: J. Vrin, 1963.

Miles, Leland. "Thomas More: Disenchanted Saint." In: *Literature and Society*, by Germaine Breé and others, pp. 65-84. Lincoln: University of Nebraska Press, 1964.

Pineas, Rainer. "Erasmus and More: Some Contrasting Theological Opinions." *Renaissance News*, XIII (1960), 298-300.

Torrance, T. F. *Kingdom and Church: A Study of the Theology of the Reformation*. London and Edinburgh: Oliver and Boyd, 1956.

V

Themes and Traditions in the Comfort Treatise

Arbesmann, Rudolph. "The Concept of 'Christus medicus' in St. Augustine." *Traditio*, X (1954), 1-28.

Beyenka, Mary M. *Consolation in Saint Augustine*. Washington, D.C.: Catholic University Press, 1950.

Bloomfield, M. W. *The Seven Deadly Sins*. East Lansing: Michigan State College Press, 1952.

Butler, Cuthbert. *Western Mysticism: The Teaching of Saints Augustine, Gregory, and Bernard*. 2nd ed. London: Constable, 1927.

Collmer, Robert G. "The Meditation on Death and Its Appearance in Metaphysical Poetry." *Neophilologus*, XLV (1961), 323-33.

Dechert, Charles. *Thomas More and Society: A Study in Renaissance Thought*. Washington, D.C.: Catholic University of America, 1952.

Fern, Sister Mary E. *The Latin Consolatio as a Literary Type*. St. Louis: University Press, 1941.

Howard, Donald R. "Thirty New Manuscripts of Pope Innocent III's *De miseria humanae conditionis* [or] *De contemptu mundi.*" *Manuscripta,* Feb. 1963, pp. 31-35.

Innocentii III. *De miseria humanae conditionis*. Ed. Michele Maccarrone. Luciani: Thesaurus Mundi, 1955.

Knowles, Dom David. *The English Mystical Tradition*. New York: Harpers, 1961.

Martz, Louis L. *The Poetry of Meditation*. New Haven: Yale University Press, 1962.

O'Connell, J. R. "Saint Thomas More as Citizen." *Dublin Review,* CXCVII (July 1935), 37-52.

O'Connor, Sister Mary. *The Art of Dying Well. The Development of the Ars moriendi*. New York: Columbia University Press, 1942.

Patch, Howard. *The Goddess Fortuna in Medieval Literature*. Cambridge: Harvard University Press, 1927.

———. *The Tradition of Boethius. A Study of His Importance in Medieval Culture*. London: Oxford University Press, 1935.

Scarlett, Earle P. "The Dance of Death." *Dalhousie Review,* XXXVIII (1958), 378-97.

Stewart, William. *The Fortuna Concept in the English Writings of Sir Thomas More*. Unpublished Dissertation, University of Mainz, 1953.

Sutherland, Raymond Carter, Jr. *Medieval English Conceptions of Hell as Developed from Biblical, Patristic, and Native German Influence*. University of Kentucky Ph.D. Thesis, 1960. *Dissertation Abstracts,* XX, 4115-116.

VI
Christian Sources: "The Physicians"

Augustine. *The City of God*. Trans. by John Healey, with a Selection from Vives' Commentaries. Ed. R. B. Tasker. Intro. Ernest Barker. 2 vols. Everyman's Library, No. 982-3. London and New York: Dent and Dutton, 1945.

———. *Later Works*. Ed. John Burnaby. Library of Christian Classics, Vol. VIII. Philadelphia: Westminster Press, 1955.

Barrett, Helen M. *Boethius. Some Aspects of His Times and Work.* Cambridge: University Press, 1940.

Battenhouse, Roy, ed. *Companion to the Study of St. Augustine.* New York: Oxford University Press, 1955.

Bernard. *The Steps of Humility.* Trans. George B. Burch. Notre Dame Paperbacks, No. 30. South Bend, Ind.: University of Notre Dame Press, 1963.

Boethius. *The Consolation of Philosophy.* Ed. Irwin Edman. Modern Library. New York: Random, 1943.

Boland, Paschal. *The Concept of "discretio spirituum" in John Gerson's "De probatione spirituum" and "De distinctione verarum visionum a falsis."* Washington, D.C.: Catholic University Press, 1959.

Burleigh, John H. *The City of God. A Study of St. Augustine's Philosophy.* London: Nisbet, 1949.

Cassianus, John. "The Conferences and the Institutes of John Cassianus." In: *A Select Library of Nicene and Post-Nicene Fathers of the Christian Church.* Second Series. Trans. Philip Schaff and Henry Wace. Vol. XI, 201-546. Grand Rapids: Eerdmans, 1955.

Chadwick, Owen. *John Cassian. A Study in Primitive Monasticism.* Cambridge: University Press, 1950.

Cyprian. *The Writings of Cyprian, Bishop of Carthage.* Trans. Robert E. Wallis. Ante-Nicene Christian Library, Vols. VIII, XIII. Edinburgh: T. & T. Clark, 1868-69.

Dodd, Charles H. *The Epistle of Paul of the Romans.* London: Hodder and Stoughton, 1932.

Fichter, Joseph H. *Saint Cecil Cyprian, Early Defender of the Faith.* St. Louis: Herder, 1942.

Gilson, Étienne. *The Christian Philosophy of Saint Augustine.* New York: Random, 1960.

———. *The Mystical Theology of St. Bernard.* London: Sheed and Ward, 1955.

Hamilton, Neill Q. *The Holy Spirit and Eschatology in Paul.* Edinburgh: Oliver and Boyd, 1957.

Merton, Thomas, trans. *The Wisdom of the Desert: Sayings from the Desert Fathers of the Fourth Century.* Norfolk, Conn.: New Directions, 1960.

Morrall, John B. *Gerson and the Great Schism.* New York: Barnes and Noble, 1961.

Newman, John H. "Trials of Theodoret." In: *Historical Sketches,* Vol. II. 5th ed. London: B. M. Pickering, 1882.

Payne, Robert. *The Holy Fire. The Story of the Fathers of the Eastern Church.* New York: Harpers, 1957.

Prat, Fernand. *The Theology of St. Paul.* Trans. John L. Stoddard from eleventh French edition. 2 vols. London: Burns, Oates & Washbourne, 1926.

Sevenster, Jan N. *Paul and Seneca.* Leiden: Brill, 1961.

Stevenson, J., ed. *A New Eusebius.* London: Society for Promotion of Christian Knowledge, 1964.

Thecla, Sister M. "St. Thomas More and the *Catena aurea.*" *Modern Language Notes,* LXI (1946), 523-29.

Theodoret, Bishop of Cyrus. "The Ecclesiastical History, Dialogues, and Letters of Theodoret." Trans. Blomfield Jackson. In: *A Select Library of Nicene and Post-Nicene Fathers of the Christian Church,* Vol. III. Ed. Henry Wace and Philip Schaff. Oxford: James Parker; New York: Christian Literature Co., 1892.

Wallace-Hadrill, David. *Eusebius of Caesarea.* London: Mowbray, 1960.

Wand, J. W. C. *Doctors and Councils.* London: Faith, 1963.

Wiles, M. F. "The Theological Legacy of St. Cyprian." *Journal of Ecclesiastical History* XIV (Oct. 1963), 139-49.

VII
Pagan Sources: "The Apothecaries"

Bush, Douglas. *The Renaissance and English Humanism.* Toronto: University of Toronto Press, 1956. [Orig. 1939.]

Cicero, *Basic Works.* Ed. Moses Hadas. Modern Library. New York: Random, 1951.

Grossett, John. "More and Seneca." *Philological Quarterly,* XL (1961), 577-80.

Highet, Gilbert. *Juvenal the Satirist.* Oxford: Clarendon, 1954.

Jacobs, Joseph, ed. *The Fables of Aesop as First Printed by William Caxton in 1484, with Those of Avian, Alfonso, and Poggio.* 2 Vols. London: David Nutt, 1889.

Juvenal. *Satires.* Trans. Rolfe Humphries. Bloomington: Indiana University Press, 1958.

Kennedy, William H. *The Influence of Cicero in England during the Sixteenth Century.* Harvard University Press Ph.D. Thesis, 1957.

Kristeller, Paul Oskar. *Renaissance Thought: The Classic, Scholastic, and Humanist Strains.* New York: Harper Torchbooks, 1961.

Martial. *Epigrams.* Trans. W. C. Ker. Loeb Classical Library. Cambridge: Harvard University Press, 1947.

Palmer, Ralph G. *Seneca's "De remediï fortuitorum" and the Elizabethans* [plus Latin text and the 1547 English trans.] Chicago: Institute of Elizabethan Studies, 1953.

Plato. [*The Complete Dialogues in Greek,*] *with an English Translation.* Ed. H. N. Flower, W. R. M. Lamb, and R. G. Bury. 9 vols. Loeb Classical Library. Cambridge: Harvard University Press, 1953-55.

Pliny. *The Letters of the Younger Pliny.* Trans. Betty Radice. Baltimore and Harmondson, England: Penguin, 1963.

Rand, Edward K. "The Art of Terence's *Eunuchus.*" *Transactions of the American Philological Association,* LXIII (1932), 54-72.

Runciman, Walter G. *Plato's Later Epistemology.* Cambridge: University Press, 1962.

Sage, Evan Taylor. *The Pseudo-Ciceronian Consolatio.* Chicago: University Press, 1910.

Seneca. *The Stoic Philosophy of Seneca: Essays and Letters.* Trans. M. Hadas. Garden City, N.Y.: Doubleday, 1958.

Terence. *The Comedies.* Ed. Robert Graves. Garden City, N.Y.: Anchor Books, 1962.

Thomson, James A. *The Classical Background of English Literature.* London: Allen and Unwin, 1948.

Twigg-Porter, George. "Cicero, Classic Gerontologist." *Classical Bulletin,* XXXIX (Nov. 1962), 1-4.

Wethered, Herbert N. *The Mind of the Ancient World. A Consideration of Pliny's Natural History.* London: Longmans, Green, 1937.

Whipple, Thomas King. *Martial and the English Epigram from Sir Thomas Wyatt to Ben Jonson.* Berkeley: University of California Press, 1925.